THE BRITISH SOLDIER IN AMERICA

THE BRITISH SOLDIER
IN AMERICA *A Social History*
of Military Life in the Revolutionary Period

BY SYLVIA R. FREY

 UNIVERSITY OF TEXAS PRESS, AUSTIN

Publication of this book was assisted by the Maher Contingency Fund.

An earlier version of part of Chapter 1 appeared in *Societas* V (Spring 1975). Reprinted with permission.

Parts of Chapter 4 reprinted from MILITARY AFFAIRS, February 1979, pp. 5–11, with permission. Copyright 1979 by the American Military Institute. No additional copies may be made without the express permission of the author and of the editor of MILITARY AFFAIRS.

Requests for permission to reproduce material from this work should be sent to Permissions, University of Texas Press, Box 7819, Austin, Texas 78712.

Library of Congress Cataloging in Publication Data
Frey, Sylvia R   1935–
   The British soldier in America.

   A revision of the author's thesis, Tulane University, 1969.
   Bibliography: p.
   Includes index.
   1. Great Britain. Army—Military life—History. 2. United States—History—Revolution 1775–1783. I. Title.
U767.F73   1981   973.3'41   80-29213

ISBN 978-0-292-74092-1

To the memory of Gary and Kim Myers

Contents

TABLES

Acknowledgments

This book is the product of several years' work in Britain and the United States. During those years I have contracted more debts than I can acknowledge here. Some of them are, however, outstanding. I am indebted to Professor Hugh F. Rankin, who suggested the topic to me and under whose direction it was first produced as a doctoral dissertation. From its inception through the final product, Professor Rankin has remained a friend and counselor. I gratefully acknowledge his thoughtful comments and criticisms, and the useful criticism of Professor Charles Davis, which helped to improve the work, but I discharge both of them of all responsibility for its shortcomings.

I am also indebted to the staffs of the libraries and archives where the research was carried out, particularly the Public Record Office, which generously granted me permission to quote extensively from official documents. The manuscript holdings of the P.R.O. relating to the British side of the American Revolution are unmatched anywhere in the world; without access to them the project would have been impossible. The British Museum, the National Army Museum, the National Maritime Museum, the Scottish Record Office, the National Library of Scotland, the Bodleian Library, the Rhodes House Library, and the Institute of Historical Research in Britain, and the Library of Congress, the William L. Clements Library, the National Archives, and Colonial Williamsburg, Inc., in the United States gave me not only access to their collections but invaluable assistance in locating sources as well.

Research on two continents would not have been possible without the generous support of the American Philosophical Society, the Tulane University Council on Research, and Colonial Williamsburg, Inc. Special thanks are also due to my family and to special friends in and out of the Department of History of Tulane University, who gave me moral support when I needed it. To all of the above I owe, and gladly give, deep thanks.

Introduction

The historiography of the British army is extensive, but it is by no means complete. Historians on both sides of the Atlantic have written about the organization, structure, and administration of the army; they have analyzed its campaigns and tactics, criticized its logistics, and studied its leaders.[1] What is conspicuously missing is a scholarly treatment of the common soldier. Because the War Office maintained no records on the rank and file in the eighteenth century and regimental records are very fragmentary, what we know about the common soldier is insignificant and probably incorrect. Occasional references in contemporary records have produced a stereotype which depicts ordinary soldiers as the dregs of society: beggars, vagrants, criminals, untrustworthy men held together only by a savage system of discipline. Lacking significant collections of records, such as are available to French and German scholars, most historians have been understandably reluctant to challenge that model.[2] The result is a crude and misleading portrait of the rank and file.

The most fundamental questions remain unanswered. Who were the common soldiers? What was their social background? Were they social misfits forced into the army by a press? Were they volunteers who joined the army for a cause or simply to make a living? Were they markedly different as a group from the general character of the English population? Were they young boys or older men? Were they healthy or diseased? Did most of them remain in the army as career soldiers, or did they, perhaps, abandon soldiering for a less hazardous occupation at the first opportunity? What made them fight? Was it fear or savage discipline? Were they inspired by a common ideal or was there something else?

To be sure, the disparity is great between what needs to be done and what can be done. Without comprehensive collections of documents only the bare bones of the soldier can be reconstructed. The fleshing out of his character must be left largely to inference and to the imagination. There is, however, something that can be learned about the soldier by studying him in an organizational setting. The army, particularly in the eighteenth century, possessed institutional characteristics which contrasted sharply with civilian life around it. It was an isolated, closed, authoritarian, paternalistic system of the type sociologists now call a "total institution." Its primary task in training its members was to make them disciplined and obedient privates. In order to accomplish this, elaborate rules regulated every aspect of the soldier's highly routinized life: his daily existence, his patterns of friendship, his social relations, ultimately his self-image. Repeated punishment or the fear of punishment influenced the soldier to conform to authority and to the rules of proper behavior as defined by the institution—or at least to caricature obedience and conformity. Although not all soldiers adapted as completely as some did, over time the military regimen produced certain common attitudinal tendencies. By studying the characteristics of the military and the adjustment of soldiers to it, it is thus possible to abstract the basic personality patterns of the group, and to provide at least flashes of insight into the life and mind of the eighteenth-century soldier.

THE BRITISH SOLDIER IN AMERICA

1 VOLUNTEERS AND CONSCRIPTS

THE BRITISH ARMY in the eighteenth century, like all armies then and now, was an aggregate of heterogeneous individuals with widely different civilian backgrounds and experiences. Unlike volunteers of more recent wars, the men who enlisted in it were probably not spurred on by identification with ideals of patriotism or, so far as we know, by conventional stereotypes of masculine behavior. English culture and tradition revered bravery and glory in military heroes, but feared and hated the military institution. The clear popular preference was for an emergency army raised in periods of crisis and demobilized as quickly as possible after victory was achieved. Despite the relatively low prestige that the military profession had for civilians, many men were driven to volunteer for a variety of reasons, the most common of which was economic. In addition to native volunteers, Britian, like every power in Europe, employed large numbers of foreign mercenaries to fill the ranks.

The social origins of eighteenth-century European armies were by no means uniform.[1] Britain's army was no exception. The rank and file came from towns, villages, and shires, from fields and broad moors, from farms, forges, and mills. Although mercenaries and social misfits comprised a sizable percentage, most soldiers were men of respectable origins, decent by birth and character. The majority were obliged to enter the service, some by state coercion, many by economic constraints. Finding relative security in the employ of the state, those who did not desert to other armies or to seek new opportunities in foreign lands became career soldiers.

Although a variety of methods were used by European armies, the chief means of raising troops in Britain was the recruitment of genuine volunteers. In regular recruiting, men were enlisted through a process known as "beating up for volunteers," in which recruiting parties induced volunteers to sign enlistment papers by offering a bounty of one and a half guineas. Out of this sum each recruit was provided with a shirt and shoes.[2] A system known as "raising men for rank" was used with particular success

in Scotland. There peers or wealthy men of local reputation and
influence assumed the obligation of raising an established quota
of men. Each individual agreeing to raise recruits had to deposit
with an agent or banker an amount of money adequate to cover
recruiting expenses and bounty payments for enlistees.[3]

During the American Revolution the War Office allowed a
number of towns to raise regiments. Manchester, Liverpool,
London, Coventry, Edinburgh, and Glasgow each contributed by
voluntary subscription to underwrite the cost of recruiting. The
citizens of Bristol subscribed over £30,000.[4] In some cases the
subscription money was used to augment the bounty offered by
the government to attract new recruits to fill old corps. Most
towns, however, preferred to embody their recruits in separate
corps. Although there were precedents for raising regiments by
private subscription in the Scottish rebellion of 1745 and in the
Seven Years War, the practice created great controversy in Parliament in 1778. Members of both houses condemned the raising of
troops without the consent of Parliament as illegal, unconstitu-
tional, and a breach of the fundamental privileges of Parliament.
They objected as well to the fact that many of the large subscrib-
ers were "Jacobites, Tories and Highlanders," whose loyalty to
parliamentary authority was suspect, and contractors or would-be
contractors, "who were under the immediate influence of the
Crown." In order to prevent future encroachments on parliamentary authority, the Commons adopted a resolution requiring all
private subscriptions for the purpose of raising troops to state
explicitly that any such corps raised would be employed "for such
uses as the Parliament should think fit."[5]

Through regular recruiting methods such as these, over
2,000 men were signed annually from 1765 through 1769. With
the outbreak of hostilities in the American colonies, the recruiting drive intensified, and some 15,000 men were enlisted in 1778
alone. Two-thirds of them were of Scottish origin. In the first
three years of the war almost 7,000 Irish were signed. The new
recruits were either brought into existing regiments or assigned
to new regiments. Because of battle casualties, desertions, and the
completion of enlistment terms, regiments were rarely at full
strength, and it was common practice to draft men from one
regiment to another. Whenever possible, soldiers were permitted
to choose among the regiments having vacancies.[6]

During national emergencies, Britain, like other great military powers, resorted to strong-arm methods to fill newly raised
regiments or regiments depleted by death, desertion, or the completion of enlistment terms. The press system, known in France
as *la presse* and in Germany as *Zwangswerbung*,[7] was employed
twice by Britain during the period of the American Revolution.

Directed specifically at the nonprivileged elements of society, the press acts of 1778 and 1779 were based on the premise that the state had the right to conscript into the army those who had received its benevolence under the poor laws and were a burden to society, as well as those misfits who disturbed the civil order—in short, the least productive citizens. The act of 1778 required every clergyman to secure from the overseers and churchwardens of his parish an exact account of poor rates collected during the three preceding years. Each parish was instructed to conscript one man to serve in the army, the marines, or the navy for every £100 of poor rates collected in each parish. Justices of the peace, commissioners of the land, and tax justices were charged with the execution of the act.[8] They were empowered to press "all able bodied loose idle and disorderly persons, vagrants," and the like who were unable to prove lawful employment and who had not substance enough to support themselves without working. The act embraced all persons "pretending to be journeymen, artificers, workmen or labourers not having been apprenticed to, or exercised in any trade," as well as "all persons convicted by due course of law of cheating deceiving and imposing upon their employers" and others who similarly violated the law. The only persons exempted from seizure were freeholders eligible to vote for members of Parliament under the property qualification law. Later, qualifying letters from the War Office to county sheriffs instructed that the press not be enforced during the hay and corn harvests, except in London, Westminster, and those parts of Middlesex that lay within the area of the Bills of Mortality.[9]

While this approach had obvious detrimental consequences not only for the civilian population but for the morale and reputation of the army itself, it also had certain immediate advantages which both civil and military officials were quick to note. It was economical: it slowed the drain on the public money by eliminating the bounty; it spared the financial resources of the parish by reducing the number of its indigents. Secretary at War William Wildman, Lord Barrington, optimistically predicted more far-reaching social effects: a stint in the army would reform all but the most unregenerate by teaching the idle "honest and regular habits" and by protecting the weak from "dangerous connexions and perhaps a criminal Course of Life"; and "after it is over [the soldier] will probably be the better Citizen for the Discipline he has been under," Barrington sanguinely concluded.[10]

No matter which method was used, there was bound to be great diversity in the quality of recruits. Without doubt some of the scum of society was netted by the press. Convicted criminals, highway robbers, sheepstealers, smugglers, "desperate rogues" awaiting transportation to penal colonies, and the bottom of society wasting away in taverns, jails, and prisons were coerced into the army by press gangs. This is the source of the stereotype of the common soldier, but it is a misconstruction to suppose that such men were a majority in the British army. Strong-arm methods also brought into all armies a disproportionate number of paupers, derelicts, declassés, and deserters from other armies. In 1768, for example, when the Prussian army was 160,000 men strong, 90,000 had been more or less forced into military service.[11] However, owing to several factors peculiar to Britain, these categories were somewhat smaller in the British army. For one thing, the press had become politically infeasible. Intense opposition to it centered in the anti-Pitt element in Parliament, which at the height of the debate in the 1750s nearly succeeded in passing a bill to extend the right of habeas corpus to pressed men on the assumption that it was just as wrong to condemn a man to military service without recourse to legal action as it was to detain him in prison without a trial.[12]

Even when the nation was forced to resort to a press, the number of involuntary recruits was relatively small. The press act of 1779, for example, snared only 2,200 men. As a matter of fact, its chief importance was in the stimulus it gave to regular recruiting. In the eleven-week period preceding the operation of the act, 1,981 men were signed for the land service. During the eleven weeks it was in effect 3,008 volunteered, while in the following eleven-week period 1,925 enlisted. The final result was an overall increase of better than one-third in ordinary recruiting for the land service alone. The marines more than doubled the numbers recruited in the eleven weeks preceding the act and showed a small increase in the subsequent period. The militia filled up vacancies "on the first appearance of Land Impress."[13]

It is also significant that very few unwilling recruits saw conventional action. Because they were considered incorrigibles and almost certain to desert, they were seldom stationed in England, and only a small number saw service in America. Normally they were confined in the Savoy Prison and from there sent as expeditiously as possible to foreign posts in the West Indies or Minorca or Gibraltar, posts from which desertion was difficult.[14]

Special conditions in all countries guaranteed every army a share of ordinary respectable recruits. Younger sons of the declining French nobility often chose careers as common soldiers over service in the church or immigration; non-Prussian East-Elbian peasants sometimes joined the Prussian army as a way to gain freedom from serfdom.[15] In England, changing economic conditions produced a special kind of recruit: an urbanite either by birth or migration, of lower-class or lower-middle-class background, with a defined occupational skill, the victim neither of

crimps (civilians who forcibly recruited men for the army) nor of
a press gang but of incipient industrialization—of machines, of
technology, of demographic change.

Although economic historians continue to debate the question of precisely when the relatively static economy of Britain
began to grow at a more rapid and sustained rate, expansion of
the iron and coal industry, the development of the factory system,
innovations in such industries as textiles, and changes in agricultural methods, together with a burgeoning and increasingly
mobile population, produced a surplus of labor in some areas to
fill the ranks of the army with average citizens fallen on hard
times.

The use of coal and the rise of the factory system permanently altered English home industry, as working people, following the lead of new entrepreneurs, gradually abandoned the old
domestic "putting-out" system and part-time agriculture and began to engage full-time in manufacturing. New urban centers
opened up in areas where water, coal, iron, and roads and canals
were readily available for industrial development. The Midlands,
doubly blessed by the presence of the Severn River and the
Shropshire and Staffordshire coal fields, became an important
industrial region. But the Pennine Upland dominated northern
industrial growth. Industrial towns such as Manchester, Bolton,
Oldham, and Bury sprang up where sheep had once grazed.
Lancashire became a major center for the production of cotton,
Leeds the market center for woolen textiles, and Birmingham the
center of metallurgical trades.

By contrast with the booming north, some areas of England
were experiencing relative decline. The South West had a history
of riot associated with economic distress dating back to the early
part of the century. Together with the Midlands these were the
counties principally affected by the Bread Riots of 1766. Particularly significant was the apparent decline of the cloth industry
as it moved away from the South West and to the North, driven in
that direction by the decline of the Dutch trade, the increased
competition of Irish linens, and the rising demand for lighter-
weight textiles—all of which cut heavily into the market for the
heavy wool cloths produced in the South West.[16] Norfolk in the
South East was also in a period of downswing. Norwich had enjoyed a long reign as the center of the worsted trade, but after
1763 the Norwich trade began to lose ground to the West Riding
of Yorkshire. The loss of the American market in the years preceding and during the Revolution only added to the problems of
the failing industry and led to great depression in the Norwich
trade.[17]

Developments in agriculture caused similar changes in rural

growth patterns. England remained essentially an agricultural nation, but agriculture was being transformed under the impact of industrialization. Between 1760 and 1780 over four thousand acts passed the British Parliament providing for enclosure; farms spread out over the heaths and commons; two or perhaps three million acres of wasteland alone were brought under cultivation in the last forty years of the century. Large-scale consolidated farms gradually replaced the open fields once cultivated in continuous strips, and livestock husbandry expanded.

A generally rising level of prices beginning in 1760 encouraged efforts to increase production and led to experimentation with such new techniques as crop rotation with roots and legumes, as well as to improvements in breeds of livestock and innovations in farm implements. As a result, overall agricultural production jumped from 40 to 50 percent; new jobs were created because of the expansion of acreage under cultivation, the growing of root crops—which required more labor—and hedging and ditching operations.[18]

Prosperity was not, however, general. Such areas of progressive farming as Norfolk, with its four-course rotation system, and the Midlands and eastern counties enjoyed good yields and high prices. But the West Country, where conservative farmers were slow to adopt improved farming methods, suffered from chronic economic malaise.[19] Large numbers of marginal farmers were squeezed out of agriculture as higher prices affected the demand for land and prompted landowners to exact higher rents.[20]

Moreover, economic prosperity did not necessarily benefit the average English worker. A sharp reduction in the death rate dating from the 1740s and an increase in the birth rate after 1750 produced an upward surge in the English population from a modest 3 percent to nearly 10 percent annually by the end of the century.[21] There was a significant migration from Ireland, beginning in the 1770s, as unemployed handloom weavers flooded Glasgow and Lancashire in search of jobs. Scotland, already beset by a labor surplus, sent great numbers of skilled workers south to England.[22] The growth of population together with increased migration led to a scarcity of jobs in some areas, although recurring labor shortages continued in the developing North and West.[23] Seventeenth-century settlement laws, which established birth and residence requirements for poor relief, trapped thousands of unemployed workers in areas of economic decline. Their growing numbers constituted a drain on community resources and created serious social problems.

There were, moreover, wide regional variations in wages. Industrial workers tended to earn more than agricultural workers, but because their income was derived exclusively from factory earnings they were vulnerable to depression and economic dislocations resulting from war. When daily wage rates were balanced against inflated wartime prices, there was little evidence of great improvement in real income for most workers.[24] In short, although the expanding economy created progress, it also caused problems. It was in such distress that the British army discovered a source of military strength.

At the outbreak of the American Revolution the total land force of Britain, excluding militia, included 39,294 infantrymen, 6,869 cavalry, and 2,484 artillerymen, for a total of 48,647. These troops were divided between two separate military establishments, the English and the Irish—the Scottish establishment having been abolished in 1707.[25] Other than the method by which they were recruited into the military, very little is known about these men. Unfortunately, the War Office did not maintain comprehensive records on the rank and file in the eighteenth century, nor were there any significant collections relating to the army comparable to the *controle de troupes* kept for the French army under the *ancien régime*, which contain invaluable data on the regional origins and on the social and economic backgrounds of nearly two million soldiers.[26]

The principal sources about the common British soldier are recruiting returns and regimental records, both of which are extremely limited in quantity and quality. The fact that they are not continuous means that the information contained therein applies only to particular soldiers in a given regiment at a specific time. Moreover, since each regiment had its own history and developed distinguishing characteristics, it is hazardous to generalize about the whole army on the basis of data accumulated for individual regiments. Interpretation of the data also poses numerous problems. A presumption of general ignorance of geography in the eighteenth century raises questions about the accuracy of demographic data relative to birth and residence. As André Corvisier points out, the personal questions which contemporary citizens submit to without objection were received with hostility in the eighteenth century, that kind of interrogation being usually reserved for criminals and foreigners.[27] It is thus quite possible that recruits gave incorrect answers about age and size, or that recruiters themselves falsified the records in order to complete enlistment quotas by accepting recruits who failed to meet legal standards.

In spite of all these difficulties, surviving documents offer sufficient evidence to warrant the conclusion that beginning as early as the 1750s the economic plight of thousands of ordinary men drove them in desperation into the army, where most of them remained. The two most comprehensive extant collections of regimental records are the returns of one of the oldest elite regiments in the history of the army, the Coldstream Guards, which embrace most of the Revolutionary war years, and the enlistment records of an infantry regiment, the 58th Regiment of Foot, which span a half century.[28] These and other fragmented records,[29] taken together with local recruiting records, such as the Corporation of London Public Records for the years 1759 and 1797 and the Middlesex County Recruiting Records of 1796–1797, discovered and analyzed by Arthur N. Gilbert,[30] strike a mortal blow at the old stereotype.

Predictably, analysis of the geographic origins of recruits for both the Guards and the 58th Regiment shows a rough approximation of the population distribution of the British Isles. In 1760, the combined population of England and Wales was an estimated 6.5–6.75 million, of Scotland, 1.25 million, of Ireland 3.25 million.[31] Out of more than 1,500 recruits, better than 60 percent of the 58th Regiment were English, nearly 25 percent were Irish, roughly 10 percent Scottish, and the remainder Welsh. Almost 90 percent of the 412 recruits for the Guards listed an English county as their birthplace; slightly less than 7 percent claimed Scottish birth, under 3 percent Welsh and not quite 4 percent Irish. The comparatively high percentage of Irish in the infantry regiment is probably due to the custom of most regiments trying to avoid recruiting these hard-to discipline men; since the elite regiments had first choice in the selection of new recruits, marching regiments usually contained more of the less desirable candidates.

More important, the records reveal a clear correlation between demographic change and recruiting patterns. Regions experiencing economic decline contributed heavily in manpower to the service. Although both regiments recruited over all England, the South West and the North West furnished more soldiers than any other geographic area. A crescent beginning in Cornwall and extending through Devon, Somerset, Wilts, and Gloucester and continuing north through Hereford, Worcester, Shropshire, and Stafford forms a curving spine from which recruits were drawn in the West Country. The great population centers in the South East and in the developing North West were also major recruiting centers. With Middlesex as the focal point, the marketing-gardening counties of Surrey, Oxford, Berks, Hertford, and Cambridge formed the southeastern center for recruiting. The industrial county of Lancashire, where the textile and worsted or woolen industries were located, was another area where recruiting parties beat with particular success. (See Table 1.)

Probably a substantial percentage of those who migrated to

TABLE 1. Regional Origins of British Recruits in Two Regiments in the Late Eighteenth Century

Coldstream Guards (%) March 1776– December 1779		58th Regiment of Foot (%) 1756–1800	
Stafford	8.90	Somerset	8.17
Norfolk	8.64	Worcester	8.17
York	6.41	York	6.90
Somerset	6.13	Stafford	4.25
Warwick	4.46	Devon	4.35
Gloucester	4.18	Warwick	4.14
Devon	4.18	Gloucester	4.14
Middlesex	3.70	Lancashire	3.82
Wilts	3.62	Hereford	3.61
Hampshire	3.62	Oxford	2.97
Lancashire	3.34	Nottingham	2.87

Sources: See note 28.

London and other burgeoning urban centers in the late eighteenth century found jobs in newly developing industries. Many of the recent arrivals did not, however; some of these ended up in the army. The Middlesex recruiting records show that almost one-third of all recruits enlisted under the 1796 recruiting bill were first-generation Irish immigrants. By the time of the American Revolution, restrictions on Catholics serving in the army had been lifted, opening the way for recruiting parties to tap the predominantly Irish Catholic areas of St. Giles in the Field, Whitechapel, St. George in the East, Holborn, and Marylebone. The recent Irish arrivals, perhaps finding job opportunities limited, enlisted in numbers sufficient to fill entire regiments.[32]

It is the analysis of the social composition of the army that does most damage to the traditional view of the eighteenth-century soldier as the scum of society. Unfortunately it is also in this aspect of the records that the most difficult problems are encountered, primarily because the records are imprecise. Even if a trade was honestly claimed by a recruit and faithfully recorded by the officer, there is still a problem of accuracy. Only such general occupational categories as carpenter, brazier, and mason are listed. But different gradations existed within every trade and craft in the eighteenth century, each denoting a degree of skill and consequently a separate and distinct social and economic status.[33] The records provide no hint as to whether the soldier

was an apprentice, a journeyman, or, less likely, a master crafts-
man. Because eighteenth-century English society viewed itself in
terms of rank or station, such distinctions are important.

The recorded civilian occupations of the soldiers recruited by
the Guards and by the 58th Regiment establish one fact: as civilians the men had defined socioeconomic roles. The great majority
appear to have been either permanently or temporarily displaced
by changes in the English economy. The textile industry felt the
impact of industrialization first and it was that industry which
furnished most recruits to the service. Twenty percent of both the
Guards and the 58th Regiment were former textile workers. Volunteers enrolled by other regiments during the period of the
Revolution show similarly high proportions of textile workers:
fifteen out of thirty-four recruits signed by the Royal Welch
Fusiliers in 1772 were textile workers, as were three out of eight
recruits enlisted in 1780 by the 84th Regiment. A register of
British deserters kept by Americans shows that one-fifth of the
British war prisoners held in American prison camps were former textile workers. In fact, of the 2,500 soldiers for whom occupational information exists, approximately 20 percent had
some previous association with the textile industry.

The great majority came from the two areas where the industry was in decline, perhaps as a result of the loss of the American
market during the Revolution and increased competition from
the textile area developing in the north.[34] Most were from the
Midlands, especially Derby, Nottingham, Leicester, Northampton,
Warwick, and Stafford; from the southwest counties of Gloucester, Somerset, and Devon; and from Norfolk in the southeast.
These were essentially the same depressed areas that sent thousands of unemployed workers as emigrants to America. Most of
the stocking weavers in Germantown and Kensington outside of
Philadelphia were immigrants from Leicester and Nottingham or
the Rhineland. Nearly eleven thousand linen weavers left Dublin
as emigrants in 1784 alone, pointing up the hard times in the
industry, and in the weaving sector in particular.[35]

Better than 65 percent of all the former textile workers studied were weavers; over 46 percent of the weavers were English
and 38 percent were Irish. The chronic depression in weaving
was largely the result of overexpansion. The use of machine yarn
put out by cotton mills led to an almost explosive boom in weaving. Around 1770, migrant Irish, women and children, small
farmers, agricultural workers, immigrant artisans, and even in-
mates from the Liverpool workhouse entered weaving in such
numbers as to produce a surfeit of labor, with the predictable
result of wage-cutting. Soon weaving, even in the skilled

branches, was among the poorest paid of all trades; even the best workers seldom earned over fifteen shillings a week.[36]

Older workers appear to have been particularly vulnerable; the overwhelming majority of workers in the cotton and silk mills and in the flax and worsted industries were under eighteen, suggesting that older workers had been forced out into the ranks of the unemployed or, in some cases, into the military. The average age of the ex-weavers in Lord Robert Bertie's company of the 7th Regiment of Foot was twenty-nine (youngest twenty, oldest forty-one); that of the forty-five weavers in the Coldstream Guards nearly thirty-one (youngest twenty-three, oldest forty-five). Out of 170 weavers in the 58th Regiment the average age was almost twenty-seven (youngest fourteen, oldest fifty-four).[37]

Local recruiting records not only establish a similarly high incidence of weavers in the army, but point to the persistence of their presence. Corporation of London records for the year 1759, for example, show that the largest occupational group among enlistees was weavers, who made up almost 20 percent of the total. The Middlesex records for 1796 reveal a preponderance of artisans, with almost 80 percent listing definable trades, including substantial numbers of weavers and tailors.[38]

Indeed, the correlation between economic conditions and the social composition of the army is confirmed through an analysis of artisan recruits. Here again, however, there are problems of interpretation. Significant differences existed within artisan ranks and between rural and urban craftsmen, but extant data are neither definitive enough nor extensive enough to permit more than superficial distinctions to be made. Moreover, the artisan ranks included a wide variety of unrelated crafts. By definition artisans were the skilled or semiskilled workers who manufactured most products used by society and did so at home or in small shops. Such a broad definition makes for an extremely heterogeneous grouping, with great diversity in working conditions and attitudes and a great spread in wage differentials. As a result, generalizations about artisans as a group are open to question—with one possible exception: it seems reasonably certain that those crafts suffering the worst effects of economic change furnished the most soldiers to the army.

Mechanization and overcrowding were already beginning to displace workers in some crafts. Although artisan guilds still protected the economic status of many craftsmen by limiting the numbers in the trade, the guilds were losing their influence and various crafts were suffering a labor glut leading to increasing numbers of unemployed workers.[39] Shoemaking, for example, was one of the earliest trades hit by change. By mid-century, the self-employed master, working alone or with one or two helpers, was gradually being squeezed out of business by the competition of cheap ready-made shoes and by large shopkeeping masters using primitive assembly-line techniques of production. One alternative to unemployment was military service, and comparatively large numbers of cordwainers entered the army. One hundred and thirty volunteered for the Guards and the 58th Regiment—a number exceeded only by weavers among skilled workers. Shoemakers appeared in conspicuous numbers in the London and Middlesex rosters of recruits as well, underlining the chronic malaise in the trade.[40] By contrast, better-organized trades, such as cabinetmaking, were able to limit the numbers of craftsmen and so maintain high wages. Their relatively secure economic status is reflected in the social composition of the army—only thirteen cabinetmakers served in the two regiments studied.

Some crafts were hooked in a double snare of static wages and spiraling prices. Taxes on consumer commodities added to the slowly rising cost of such necessities as salt, soap, candles, bread, and meat.[41] But wages for many workers, such as bricklayers, plasterers, and masons, had remained static for over a century.[42] The seasonal nature of work also contributed to the straitened economic condition of many workers in the building trades. Winter brought a slowdown in construction, and jobs became scarce after October. During the slack season—which corresponded with the height of the recruiting season—unemployed workers were driven to the edge of beggary and were more vulnerable to the enticements of recruiting parties; 11 percent of all artisans in the sample had a previous association with the construction industry; most were carpenters, bricklayers, and masons.

One of the most exploited groups in European society consisted of the common laborers. Largely unskilled, these men represented the lowest level of urban social and economic life. Making up as much as 30 percent of the population of European cities, they did manual labor for subsistence wages.[43] In Britain, laborers' wages varied from place to place; in London the average rate was eighteen pence a day, but just outside of London the daily wage fell to fourteen pence. In Edinburgh, the average worker earned ten pence a day, but in most of the low country of Scotland the basic pay was only eight pence a day. Practically everywhere in Britain a distinction was made between summer and winter wages. Unfortunately, rates were lowest in the winter, when, because of the high cost of fuel, living expenses were highest. Moreover, wage levels bore no relationship to the cost of living. Prices fluctuated from year to year, even from month to month, and the decade preceding the American Revolution was marked by generally rising prices. But the wages of labor had remained more or less static for half a century.[44] To make matters worse, the burgeoning population combined with the heavy Irish migration had produced a surplus of labor everywhere except in the towns of the north and west, which continued to experience recurring labor shortages.[45] Contract laborers hired on a year-round basis enjoyed legal protection from the draft and were unlikely to enlist voluntarily, but the unemployed and the casual laborer, paid on a day-rate or piece-rate basis, found military service preferable to starvation.

The military—and particularly the infantry—traditionally drew from the laboring classes, capitalizing on their chronic distress. Almost 40 percent of the Guards and over 16 percent of the 58th Regiment were laborers. Only 10 percent of the two regiments came from the area north of the river Humber in the east and the Mersey in the west, where labor remained at a premium.

Although recruiting laws exempted agricultural workers from conscription during harvest time, during periods of seasonal unemployment they were eligible for the service. Cottagers, squatters, and countless marginal farmers driven from the land by their own inefficiency, by the enclosure movement, or by rack-renting, joined the army out of economic need. Although the Guards listed no agricultural workers, more than 15 percent of the 58th Regiment were former husbandmen. Almost 57 percent of them were English, and the great bulk of these came from the western counties, an area of persistent agricultural depression.[46] In striking contrast is the fact that Norfolk, an area noted for its progressive farming methods, furnished few agricultural workers to the 58th Regiment—although it contributed sizable numbers of recruits of other backgrounds to both regiments.

Generally speaking, socially and economically stable groups did not furnish high proportions of soldiers to the army. Only a small percentage (2.85 percent of the Guards and 2.39 percent of the 58th) were self-classified industrial workers—by definition workers who were probably not self-employed but were wage-earners in mines, iron-works, foundaries, distilleries, or small-scale industrial operations—workers such as colliers, forgemen, founders, nailers, miners, and quarriers.[47] The majority were English.

Industrialization depended to a large degree upon the availability of coal and iron. Innovations in the iron industry, together with Watt's steam engine, contributed to the termination of the migratory phase of the iron industry and led to its concentration in regions where coal and iron were present and water transportation convenient. The second half of the eighteenth century was a period of expansion and relative prosperity for the industry and consequently a good time for workers associated with it.[48] It is surely no coincidence that so few industrial workers volunteered for the army.

In reckoning the social makeup of the army it is impossible to ascertain the precise proportion represented by the victims of economic misfortune. If not in the majority, they were at least a distinct plurality. Once drawn into the army they merged with men of disparate backgrounds: paupers, fugitives from the law, deserters from other armies, social undesirables of every description. The only thing they shared in common with men from the latter categories was that they too were trying to escape—not the law but the frowns of fortune. Military life guaranteed them minimal security: bread, clothing, a little money.

Besides the respectable volunteers and the disgruntled involuntary soldiers, contemporary armies included large numbers of foreigners. Although combat casualties were comparatively low in the eighteenth century, military establishments were heavy consumers of manpower. Old age, disease, and desertion cost European armies an estimated one-fifth of their strength each year. Ordinarily replacements were made with foreign troops: for example, during the Seven Years War foreign regiments comprised about a fifth of the French regulars, and were mainly infantry.[49] In 1776, 50 percent of the Prussian troops were foreigners; later the percentage varied according to the branch of the service.[50] As the wealthiest power in Europe, Britain also hired a number of foreign troops. Usually, however, they served in their own units, commanded by their own officers. Only a small number of Germans served in British regiments, some of which had recruiting stations on the Rhine. Although the percentage varied from regiment to regiment, during the Revolutionary War years foreign recruits made up less than 2 percent of elite corps, such as the dragoons regiments, and only slightly more than 10 percent of most infantry regiments.[51]

After first negotiating with Catherine III for 20,000 Russian troops, the British government turned to the traditional source of foreign soldiers, Swift's "beggarly princes not able to make war by themselves." In April 1776, the agreements were signed with the rulers of Hesse-Cassel, Brunswick, Hesse-Hanau, and Waldeck for 18,000 mercenaries; 12,000 more were hired from Anspach-Bayreuth and 600 from Anhalt-Zerbst at the rate of 30 crowns banco, or £7 4s. 4½d. a head and an annual subsidy. By the end of the war a total of 29,166 German soldiers had seen service in America. From 1779 on to the signing of the peace, German troops outnumbered British troops in Canada.[52]

The social composition of the German mercenaries in British

service in America can only be guessed at. The German armies used a variety of methods of recruiting, ranging from voluntary recruiting to impressment by strong-arm methods to conscription under the law, which militated against social uniformity. Besides genuine volunteers of respectable origins, who were found in varying numbers in all armies, and decent peasant-soldiers brought into the army by conscription for limited service, the German armies apparently included a disproportionately large number of profligates of diverse types.[53] The haste with which regiments bound for America were raised argues strongly for such heterogeneity, and relevant documents suggest that a substantial number of ordinary men fell into the crude traps laid by recruiting agents in the employ of the German princes.

Although the documentation is thin, many of the mercenaries claimed definable trades. A good number had formerly been associated with the textile industry; most of them were weavers. Shoemaking was heavily represented, as were the building trades. Some mercenaries had previously worked in agriculture, a few were self-classified laborers.[54] The circumstances which brought them into the army cannot be ascertained, but that constraints of one type or another were at work is highly probable. Rumors were rife among the British troops that the German princes met their quotas by having churches surrounded during services.[55] Colonel Augustin Valentin Voit von Saltzburg was given command of a regiment and ordered to be prepared to take the field in three weeks. To meet the deadline he combed country villages, drafting all likely candidates. The Landgrave of Cassel forcibly enlisted an estimated 1,500 men, including a recent student from the University of Leipzig whose academic papers were destroyed to prevent his claiming exemption from military service, a bankrupt merchant from Vienna, a lace-maker from Hanau, a discharged mail-clerk from Muniger, a tailor from Gottinger, and a Prussian sergeant; a "true pell mell of human souls" were locked in the prison at Zeigenhain until arrangements for their passage to America were complete. In both of these cases guns and whips had to be used to control the rebellious recruits.[56]

Regardless of whether they came from the lower or upper strata of society, the fact that so many apparently began their military careers with bitter feelings had a negative, perhaps even a critical effect on morale, manifested in disciplinary problems, particularly plundering, in high desertion levels, and in a sometimes desultory performance in battle.

Although they were not regular combat troops, blacks and camp followers were part of the operational apparatus of the British army in America. In addition to the regular troops, the army contained perhaps five thousand women and tens of thousands of black troops called pioneers. The curtain had hardly been raised on the war before a number of British officers began urging the London government to make full military use of the 500,000 black slaves in the region below the Chesapeake. The adoption of an official policy designed to encourage black desertion to the British would rob the South of its labor force and ultimately wreck its economy, at the same time crippling the rebel war effort. Black runaways could be employed in the production of supplies, relieving the army of its dependence on European food shipments, or could be trained and armed for combat.[57]

Even though the devastating psychological shock of armed black troops had already been demonstrated by the Earl of Dunmore's abortive attempt to raise an Ethiopian corps composed of Maryland and Virginia slaves,[58] the British took a cautious approach to the idea of armed black regiments. No general campaign was undertaken to enlist black soldiers, although those who sought British protection were received. Several wary moves were made early in the war in northern colonies where blacks were in a distinct minority of the population and where slavery was later declared illegal: in the spring of 1776, a few black soldiers were taken prisoners by American forces in Rhode Island. In November, Rhode Island troops crossed the Sound and clashed with a party of British soldiers on Long Island; the Rhode Islanders took about twenty-three prisoners, about half of whom were blacks and Indians. Shortly after Newport fell to the British in December 1776, an overture was made to free blacks to join the British in return for pay and provisions. A few voluntarily enlisted and some others were sent to Boston by their owners to provincial regiments being raised there.[59]

But the British decision to lay aside caution with regard to blacks was not taken until 1778, and then reluctantly and principally as a war measure. The shifting of the seat of the war to the South made it impossible for either side to ignore the latent potential of the vast slave population. Beset by manpower shortages, the Continental Army began to incorporate blacks and a number of northern states began to quietly enroll free blacks in the militia. Then, and only then, did the British military command catch the flame; on 30 June 1779, General Henry Clinton issued a proclamation warning that all Negroes taken in arms would be "purchased for the public service and sold for the benefit of their captors," while those who joined the British would receive protection and freedom at the war's end.[60] Although it was not intended to be a general statement of emancipation, blacks read it as such and fled to the British in such numbers that a dismayed Clinton, concerned over the army's ability to maintain and control them, wrote to Lord Cornwallis to "make such arrangements as will discourage their joining us."[61]

Clinton's reluctance to take the yield was typical of the pattern of relations that existed between the British and the blacks. Although some officers continued to urge the full military use of blacks as "indispensably necessary" to the war effort in the South,[62] there is virtually no evidence that they ever saw combat. An intelligence report from Nathanael Greene to Francis Marion in 1781, warning that the British intended to take the field with seven hundred Negroes, was apparently without foundation. Probably the closest the former slaves came to regular military service was in South Carolina, where they were used to round up deserters.[63]

Britain's temporizing policy was predicated on two sets of factors: inherited racial attitudes and a pressing need for labor.[64] Although changes in cultural values had undermined the old justifications for slavery, theories of racial inferiority still enjoyed wide acceptance in England. Slavery was declared illegal in England in 1772, and in Scotland in 1778, but the British continued to engage in the slave trade, and the institution had legal sanction in the British West Indies. With the exception of a few Arab states, governments of slave societies throughout human history have resisted the idea of arming slaves,[65] both because of the danger of a revolt and because the tacit inference of equality would undermine the basic rationale for slavery—racial inferiority.

Prejudice predisposed the military to employ black soldiers in a capacity consistent with contemporary racial attitudes. Over five thousand were put to work producing supplies for the army on confiscated estates in South Carolina.[66] To prevent their "becoming a burden to government," they were hired out to the civil departments at the rate of six pence a day and rations. Three or four "pioneers" were assigned to every infantry regiment for heavy menial service. Skilled workers, including carpenters, collarmakers, wheelers, smiths, sawyers, and turnwheels, were usually given to the Royal Artillery where there was an urgent need for their talents.[67] Many worked as orderlies in military hospitals or as pilots on inland waterways; a few were used as recruiters to enlist other blacks, and some worked on the British privateering barges which were landed to plunder and abduct slaves from nearby plantations.[68] To spare the north-European troops from "toil and fatigue" in the intense southern heat, unskilled blacks dug the latrines and cleaned the streets and did most of the manual labor necessary to support the army.[69] Most officers and even some enlisted men had black servants.[70] The most notable military service performed by the black troops, however, was with the Corps of Engineering, where they worked in the construction of batteries, opened trenches, and repaired crumbling lines.[71]

Women have been identified with pacifism, at least since Aristophanes' *Lysistrata*, and have rarely been fighters. Nonetheless they played a key role in eighteenth-century wars. While no precise figures are available, perhaps as many as five thousand women attended the British army in America.[72] Some, including Baroness von Riedesel, Mrs. Thomas Gage, and Lady Harriet Ackland, were the wives of general and field officers; but the great majority were the wives of soldiers or the "trulls and doxies" who inevitably accompanied all European armies.

Although the majority of women and children remained in quarters when the army took the field, it was not unusual for a few women to accompany the army on campaigns. Whether they were armed cannot be ascertained, but there is considerable evidence that they were sometimes in the thick of the fighting. Several women were among the British prisoners taken at Princeton; a curious American inquired about their presence and was told that it was "sometimes allowed a Sergeant to have his wife with him who drew Rations the same as a Soldier were very Serviceable and supported virtuous characters." The wife of a grenadier was killed in the action leading to the occupation of Philadelphia. In the fighting at Fort Ann, a woman "who kept close by her husband's side during the engagement" was mortally wounded. The wife of a musketeer died a prisoner of war in the terrible barracks at New Frederick near Winchester, where the Convention Army was held prisoner.[73]

Women, disabled soldiers, and even children were sometimes left behind as camp watch when the regiments marched out. In the Virginia campaign John Graves Simcoe deployed the women and the baggage in the woods on the summit of a hill to deceive the enemy by giving the appearance of a "numerous corps."[74] Many women, whose husbands were sick or wounded, volunteered to work as nurses in military hospitals; hundreds worked under compulsion—those refusing to serve were struck from the provision list.[75] The "most industrious and best behaved" were, in some regiments, ordered to cook and clean the barracks "at the moderate allowance of six pence for each man per week." Those who declined lost provisions for themselves and for their children and also drew "on themselves and their Husbands in all shape the Disapprobation and Resentment of their Officers." A number of women hired out as domestics to earn income, working as housemaids, "chore" women or launderers for officers. Some worked for the various regiments handwashing shirts at the rate of three pence a piece.[76]

Aside from the women, the blacks, and the mercenaries, and taking into account only those troops considered as part of the regular establishment, by the end of the eighteenth century the British army had begun to take on a modern look. For one thing it drew heavily upon groups from economically distressed areas, ranging from those on the margins of society pressed into the service, to the bottom ranks of the working class, up through the ranks of the semiskilled and skilled workers temporarily or permanently unemployed.

The fact that men from varied social conditions answered the call of the recruiters' drums was not of course unique to the British army; André Corvisier's monumental study of the French army produced similar findings, indicating perhaps the general nature of the trend. Moreover, given the deficiency of extensive usable data for the eighteenth-century British army, the significance of this development should not be exaggerated. It is perhaps enough to say that the rank and file of the British army were not the scum of society but ordinary men of modest origins who joined the army for a variety of reasons, including the need to earn a living.

2 DISEASES AND DOCTORS

THE ARMY WAS a new world, different from anything most recruits had ever experienced before. It separated them from their families and from a familiar way of life. It plunged them into an impersonal environment which obscured, if it did not obliterate, individuality. The lonely, ill-at-ease recruit was unceremoniously assigned to a tent or barracks with dozens of other men, a few women, and some children. Within that tent or barracks he was assigned to a bed shared with another soldier. In place of civilian clothing he was given a uniform which enhanced his anonymity. The use of his time was scheduled, and everything he did, whether he ate, slept, worked, or played, was done with a group.

There were, however, compensations for the loss of personal identity and freedom of choice. A self-contained society, complete with its own "butcher, baker, and candlestick-maker," the army provided for all the physical needs of its members: for food and shelter, for clothing and company, for health and sanitation. No matter that the system often went awry; the assurance of subsistence guaranteed a measure of security which made life in the institution preferable to life in the outside world.

The kind of soldiers whom the army would have preferred in the ranks were those with "Straight limbs, broad shoulders, a good face and every way well made."[1] What it got instead, of course, was great variety. There were tall soldiers and short, fair and dark; some with brutal faces; some surly, coarse, indifferent, placid, proud, or fervorless. Some limped, struggling on aching feet, ragged heads hanging, unhandsome, unwholesome. Except for their uniforms there was little about their physical appearance to distinguish them from the weavers, masons, carpenters, or cordwainers who pieced out a living in small shops in villages and towns in Britain. Despite the risks involved in soldiering, because their daily living environment approximated poverty conditions, soldiers were far more likely to die of disease or of primitive medical treatment than from balls or bayonets.

In theory if not in practice, the army tried to be selective in raising men for military service. In periods of crisis, however, the

legal physical standards set by Parliament were sometimes re-
laxed or suspended, although they were seldom completely abandoned. In their anxiety to fill enlistment quotas, recruiting
officers now and then signed ineligible recruits who, for one reason or another, passed the mandatory physical examination
which was supposed to screen them out.[2] As a result most regiments, even elite or specialist units, contained a certain number
of underaged and overaged, deformed and diseased men. On the
whole, however, the majority of men in all regiments were as
strong and healthy as the times and circumstances would allow.
    The average soldier in the British army was a mature man of
about thirty years of age who had joined the army when he was
around twenty years old.[3] (See Tables 2–9.) The youthful soldier

TABLE 2. The 29th Regiment of Foot, 1782

National Origins		Years Service		Age		Size	
British	427	1–5	96	Under 20	15	Under 5'6"	102
Foreign	58	6–10	273	20–29	187	5'6"–5'8"	292
		11–15	24	30–35	80	5'8½"–5'10"	103
Total	485	16–20	41	36–40	101	5'10½"–6'	18
		21–25	46	41–45	28	Over 6'	1
		Over 25	5	46–50	16	Average size:	
		Average		Over 50	7	5'7"	
		service:		Average age:			
		9.7 years		27.6 years			

Note: There are minor discrepancies in the regimental records upon which the above calculations
re based. Although the total strength of the regiment is given as 485, the numbers listed under the
ge category total 484, those under the category of size, 516.
Source: W.O. 28/10.

TABLE 3. The 44th Regiment of Foot, January 1, 1782

National Origins		Years Service		Age		Size	
British	509	1–5	242	Under 20	25	Under 5'6"	109
Foreign	16	6–10	173	20–29	224	5'6"–5'8"	299
		11–15	52	30–35	186	5'8½"–5'10"	100
Total	525	16–20	29	36–40	52	5'10½"–6'	15
		21–25	23	41–45	20	Over 6'	2
		Over 25	6	46–50	15	Average size:	
		Average		Over 50	3	5'7½"	
		service:		Average age:			
		8.2 years		26.8 years			

Source: W.O. 28/10.

TABLE 4. The 31st Regiment of Foot, 1782

National Origins		Years Service		Age		Size	
British	488	1–5	38	Under 20	22	Under 5'6"	146
Foreign	21	6–10	383	20–29	239	5'6"–5'8"	231
		11–15	38	30–35	172	5'8½"–5'10"	109
Total	509	16–20	34	36–40	46	5'10½"–6'	19
		21–25	15	41–45	23	Over 6'	4
		Over 25	1	46–50	6	Average size:	
		Average		Over 50	1	5'7"	
		service:		Average age:			
		8.9 years		29.4 years			

Source: W.O. 28/10.

TABLE 5. The 8th (King's) Regiment of Foot, 1782

National Origins		Years Service		Age		Size	
British	653	1–5	31	Under 20	14	Under 5'6"	117
Foreign	42	6–10	263	20–29	97	5'6"–5'6½"	131
		11–15	133	30–35	223	5'7"–5'8"	287
Total	695	16–20	131	36–40	198	5'9"–5'11½"	156
		21–25	118	41–45	92	Over 6'	7
		Over 25	19	46–50	54	Average size:	
		Average		Over 50	17	5'8"	
		service:		Average age:			
		14.7 years		36.9 years			

Note: Although the total strength of the regiment is given as 695 in the regimental records, the numbers listed under size total 698.

Source: W.O. 28/10.

associated with modern warfare was avoided by eighteenth-century armies. Frederick the Great deplored the necessity of using "weakly boys" in the Prussian army during the last years of the Seven Years War.[4] When underage recruits appeared on British muster rolls in the early years of the American Revolution, the War Office quickly condemned the practice of signing young boys as "a fraud on the public."[5] On the other hand, men over thirty were not considered desirable recruits either, since their service potential was shorter and "because of the stiffness of their joints they seldom learn to handle their arms with dexterity."[6] Ideally the age limits for recruits were seventeen to twenty-five, by which time most men were physically mature and could, in most cases, be counted on to serve upward of ten years in the army. To be sure, when the manpower shortage became critical, as it did during the American Revolution, the army could not be so selective. The Press Acts of 1778 and 1779, for example, lowered the standards for involuntary draftees to sixteen and fifty.[7]

With relatively few exceptions the typical soldier met and even exceeded the legal criteria for size. Standards for physical proportions were determined by the nature of the service: infantry regiments were not supposed to sign any recruits under 5'6" tall, except "growing lads whom they may take at 5'4"." The average British foot soldier measured 5'7". The "tallest and briskest men" were reserved for specialist units, such as the dragoon guards, trained to fight both on foot and on horseback, and they

TABLE 6. The 1st (King's) Regiment Dragoon Guards, 1775

National Origins		Years Service		Age		Size	
British	275	1–5	105	Under 20	5	Under 5'7"	5
Foreign	1	6–10	102	20–29	138	5'7½"–5'8"	79
		11–15	33	30–35	96	5'9"–5'11½"	187
Total	276	16–20	27	36–40	22	6'–6'1"	5
		21–25	6	41–45	12	Average size:[b]	
		Over 25	3	46–50	3	5'9½"	
		Average		Over 50	0		
		service:[a]		Average age:[a]			
		8.9 years		28.6 years			

[a] Four years later statistics for the same regiment show average age of 26.6, average experience of .7, reflecting the manpower shortage of the Revolutionary War years.
[b] Statistics for 1779 show no change in average height.
Source: W.O. 27/33.

TABLE 7. The 1st (Royal) Regiment Dragoons, 1775

National Origins		Years Service		Age		Size	
British	180	1–5	80	Under 20	12	Under 5'7"	6
Foreign	6	6–10	56	20–29	95	5'7"–5'8½"	82
		11–15	33	30–35	47	5'9"–5'11½"	95
Total	186	16–20	10	36–40	18	6'–6'2"	3
		21–25	5	41–45	10	Average size:[b]	
		Over 25	2	46–50	2	5'9"	
		Average		Over 50	2		
		service:[a]		Average age:[a]			
		8.5 years		28.5 years			

[a] By 1779 average age was 27.4, average experience was down to 5.9.
[b] Statistics for 1779 show no change in average height.
Source: W.O. 27/33.

were supposed to stand between 5′8½″ and 5′10″. The average dragoon fell well within that range, being about 5′9½″.[8] In terms of size the British soldier compared quite favorably with contemporary Europeans and particularly with certain south European armies; in one canton on the Ligurian coast, for example, 72 percent of the recruits signed between 1792 and 1799 were under 5′2″ tall.[9]

Although no European army could afford to be too fastidious in the selection of its members, military manuals sometimes stressed superfluous criteria such as a full head of hair because it was "an ornament and addition to the appearance of a soldier."

TABLE 8. The 4th Regiment Dragoons, 1775

National Origins		Years Service		Age		Size[b]	
British	180	1–5	67	Under 20	12	Under 5′7″	2
Foreign	6	6–10	61	20–29	83	5′7″–5′8½″	46
		11–15	45	30–35	76	5′9″–5′11½″	89
Total	186	16–20	6	36–40	10	6′–6′2½″	1
		21–25	4	41–45	3	Average size:[c]	
		Over 25	3	46–50	2	5′9″	
		Average		Over 50	0		
		service:[a]		Average age:[a]			
		9 years		28 years			

[a] In 1779 the same regiment showed an average age of 28, average experience of 7 years.
[b] Size data are unreliable due to the discrepancy in the total as compared with the totals for age, years of service, and national origins.
[c] Statistics for 1779 show no change in average height.
Source: W.O. 27/33.

TABLE 9. The 7th (Queen's) Regiment Dragoons, 1775

National Origins		Years Service		Age		Size	
British	182	1–5	58	Under 20	5	Under 5′7″	0
Foreign	2	6–10	65	20–29	91	5′7″–5′8½″	28
		11–15	40	30–35	65	5′9″–5′11½″	156
Total	184	16–20	18	36–40	14	Average size:[b]	
		21–25	1	41–45	7	5′10″	
		Over 25	2	46–50	2		
		Average		Over 50	0		
		service:[a]		Average age:[a]			
		9.4 years		28.6 years			

[a] In 1779 the average age for the same regiment was 27.3, average experience 7.6 years.
[b] Statistics for 1779 show no change in average height.
Source: W.O. 27/33.

More realistic, perhaps, was the army's attempt to eliminate before induction men with potentially disabling blemishes or deformities. Regulations provided for a mandatory physical examination of all new recruits by a field officer and a surgeon for "any appearance of a rupture, broken bones, sore legs, scald head, ulcers or running sores . . . old wounds ill cured or any infirmity in body and limb."[10] The quality of recruits of course deteriorated in a ratio corresponding to the increase of the demand. The acute shortage of manpower which forced England to use a press in 1778 and again in 1779 inspired a directive from the War Office to take "any Man that could be made of the smallest use."[11] A general decline in the quality of the troops embarked for America was almost immediately apparent. The worst specimens were rejected at once; thirteen recruits sent to join the 23d, 43d, and 54th regiments in 1781 were declared unserviceable because of ailments ranging from rheumatism to contracted arms and lame hands. Although the recruits for the 2d Battalion of the 42d Regiment in the same year were pronounced "much better" than previous ones, the inspectors report described the men in the front and rear ranks as "of tolerable size," while those in the center ranks were "very low young lads." Old age, youth, "lowness of stature and want of strength" disqualified most of the new recruits for the 98th Regiment; still "because of the necessity of the times and the great diminution that must have happened to their numbers, had the general begun to reject," all were ultimately accepted although forty recruits bound for the 100th Regiment had to be rejected.[12] Sixty recruits sent to Jamaica in the summer of 1782 were returned to England because of "old age, the loss of the use of their limbs or other complaints."[13] Seventy of the eight hundred recruits who arrived a month later were pronounced "absolutely unfit for service," while the rest were "both unseasoned and undisciplined."[14]

Hundreds, perhaps thousands of such recruits, accepted into the army out of necessity, were in fact physically unsuited for infantry service, because they were either too small or too weak to handle the long, heavy musket properly. Two thousand of the troops assigned to the defense of Halifax were, according to Major General James Paterson, "scarcely able to carry much less to make use of their arms."[15] Even elite regiments such as the Royal Artillery were forced at times to accept undersized men. As commandant of the artillery, General James Pattison bitterly wished the 235 drafts and recruits who arrived in 1779 for service with the artillery "back in the bogs from which they sprang." When his attempt to arm the men with carbines, a foot shorter than the flintlock musket used by the infantry,[16] was frustrated by the home government, Pattison offered a contemptuous compromise:

"I will," he wrote to a subordinate, "try how far the strength of these diminutive warriors is equal to carry muskets *cut down*." His aside that "hard times indeed and great must be the scarcity of men when the Royal Artillery is obliged to take such reptiles," and his wistful recollection that "such warriors of 5′5½″ I never saw raised for the service of Artillery" strongly suggest, however, that this situation was exceptional.[17]

Despite all efforts to prevent it, even in normal times many diseased men entered the army undetected. Until the development of modern weapons, perhaps 80 to 90 percent of total army casualties were caused by disease rather than combat. Medical registers for the Seven Years War reveal that the number of men who died from disease was approximately eight times the total battle deaths.[18] Between 1774 and 1780, 10,012 soldiers died in British service in North America and the West Indies.[19] Although the statistics are silent as to the cause of death, in all probability the great majority were victims of disease or of primitive medical treatment.

Although, compared to those of earlier periods, eighteenth-century battles produced heavy casualties, the infrequency of battles combined with the limited range and accuracy of weaponry kept overall combat losses relatively low. The flintlock musket, still in general use during the American Revolution, was accurate only up to eighty or one hundred yards, depending on the bore. Poor workmanship sometimes rendered inoperative up to 50 percent of the weapons in a company; damp and windy weather impaired the musket's action in the field.[20] It was not only that there were relatively few battle casualties, however, but also that the incidence of disease was extraordinarily high; the remote causes for the high proportion of disease-associated losses are traceable to the social and cultural conditions of the times and to the torpid pace of scientific development.

Compared with conditions one hundred years earlier or with the state of affairs in other countries, the health of the general British population had shown marked improvement: an advance in the standard of living, better housing, a more nutritious diet, and a safer water supply had greatly modified the character of infectious diseases and produced a significant decline in the overall mortality rate.[21] On the other hand, however, typhus was still endemic in English towns, and cholera, smallpox, malaria, and dysentery continued to ravage all of Europe. Even though the most destructive effects of the factory system on the health of the English worker were not yet manifest, many crafts had their own peculiar health hazards: weavers were susceptible to chest diseases because they worked their looms with their chests and because they inhaled lint; many painters developed lung and blood disorders from contact with certain toxic chemicals. The steam from the felting process and the dust from the dye made the hatter vulnerable to various respiratory ailments.[22]

The eradication of epidemic diseases was also delayed by a deep residuum of social and cultural backwardness. Although the importance of personal and public hygiene was being advocated with growing enthusiasm by doctors, all classes of society were slow to adopt the most basic sanitary measures. English homes, even of the wealthy, were seldom equipped with bathing facilities, and public baths, once common, had fallen out of fashion, perhaps because of fear of the spread of syphilis. As a result, full immersion in water was a rare experience for the average person. For these and for other reasons disease prevailed unbridled. Medical science, which remained static throughout the century, had as yet achieved no breakthroughs in the pathology of disease, remedial treatment still consisted of bleeding and purging, and drugs and knowledge of their use remained severely limited.[23]

These social antecedents, joined with the improvised nature of army life, increased the degree of probability that the soldier would end his life a victim of disease. An irregular and unwholesome diet, improper and insufficient clothing, and overcrowding in noxious places such as ships, camps, barracks, and hospitals made soldiers particularly susceptible to certain diseases, such as scurvy, dysentery, typhoid fever, typhus, and pulmonary disorders. Many of these "military diseases"[24] were unavoidable, especially where armies in the field were concerned. That many diseases still struck with disabling intensity, however, was in no small measure due to Britain's reliance on an anachronous administrative system to supply its troops abroad.

Practically speaking, having substantially larger numbers of soldiers fighting in distant parts of the world created crises relative to troops' movements, armaments, and supplies for all the great powers of the eighteenth century. These crises were only partly military in nature, inasmuch as military preparedness was and is principally a function of government rather than of the army per se. Although a few states, such as Prussia, had begun to concentrate administrative powers and to develop special functional ministries,[25] antipathy toward strong administration retarded such reforms in England. The inefficiency of the British state bureaucracy,[26] the inadequacy of the commissary system, which was directly responsible for the procurement and distribution of stores and provisions in the field, a critical shortage of land and sea transport, and the routine failure of army purveyors to live up to their contractual obligations made it impossible to supply the army in remote places in a capable, systematic, and economical way.[27]

Although there were no begging wives or starving children, no soldiers dying of hunger, as had frequently been the case with European armies in the seventeenth century,[28] most of the men in the ranks of the eighteenth-century British army were from time to time reduced to actual suffering from want of food. In all probability the average recruit had a malnutrition disorder when he entered the service. A more balanced diet, which added greens, fruits, and vegetables to the basic English fare of meat and cereals, had all but eliminated deficiency diseases such as rickets and scurvy in mortal form, but dietary disorders were still rampant in northern Europe. The standard food allowance in the army was neither a cure nor a remedy. Called "seven rations," the weekly allowance consisted of seven pounds of bread or flour, seven pounds of beef or four pounds of pork, six ounces of butter, three pints of peas, and a half pound of rice or oatmeal.[29] While it was superior to the meat, bread, and alcohol diet of most armies,[30] it still lacked certain essential dietary constituents, such as vegetables and fruit, although to its credit the army made a genuine if inadequate effort to provide a more healthful diet.

In America, gardeners and laborers were hired to cultivate extensive vegetable gardens for the use of the army and navy. The fields and pastures around Boston were sown with turnips and other greens.[31] Virtually all the arable land on Long and Governor's islands in New York, and all the fields around Philadelphia, particularly in the fertile Neck, were fenced in and planted.[32] Seeds sent from England were distributed to garrisons in America and Canada so that the soldiers could plant their own gardens around their huts or barracks.[33] When cabbage was in season, it was issued at the rate of a half pound per man per week; cut fine, salted and fermented with vinegar, it was eaten as sauerkraut, which formed an important dietary supplement.[34] In order to encourage good eating habits, the men were required to cook and eat together in groups of five or six; every pay day each man contributed a part of his subsistence money toward the purchase of fresh provisions. Each "mess" was furnished by the regimental barrack master with a bowl, a platter, six trenchers, six spoons, and a wooden ladle. Noncommissioned officers visited each mess in their squad to see that the regulation was observed.[35] The practice was socially desirable and economically practical. The average out-at-the-heels private could not afford to patronize the local market and was in any case more inclined to spend his extra pennies on alcohol. But the combined contributions of the group enabled them to buy fresh food. Vegetables were plentiful and cheap in the early years of the war, and for a penny each a mess of soldiers could buy a peck of kidney beans, several bunches of turnips, a dozen heads of lettuce, or milk.[36]

Until the development of chemical preservatives provided improved means for preserving the nutrient value of prepared foods, expedients such as these had to suffice. Unfortunately neither the amount nor the kinds of foods needed by the body were available on a regular basis. When vegetables and fruit were not in season the army was afflicted with deficiency diseases such as scurvy, which still survived in a mild form among the land population of northern Europe and in acute form among armies. Shortages of fresh provisions during the winter and spring of 1777 led to an outbreak of scurvy among the men of the 20th Regiment stationed at Isle au Noix in Canada; many of the victims were so severely ill they had to be hospitalized in Montreal. The same year a near epidemic of scurvy struck New York and nearly three hundred cases were treated in Philadelphia. In 1779, British troops in Rhode Island were beset by a siege of scurvy; in 1781 approximately five hundred were sent to New York suffering from scurvy and itch.[37]

Scurvy at sea devoured even greater numbers of men, draining the strength of maritime nations by debilitating its victims and increasing their susceptibility to mortal illnesses. The first account of scurvy at sea was made by Vasco da Gama, who reported losing two-thirds of his men by it.[38] In modern times after the advent of the long sea voyage when sources of Vitamin C were less accessible, its prevalence gained both in degree and in vehemence. Successive centuries of experience had disproved the bizarre theory that sea scurvy was caused by sea air and damp, and in 1753 a British naval surgeon, Dr. James Lind, discovered the real cause as being the sea diet of salt meat and biscuit. Lind recommended the use of citrus fruits and cider as a preventive measure and suggested a process for preserving fruit for consumption on ocean voyages. Antiscorbutics had in fact been in use since the sixteenth century, but the British navy did not order the general consumption of lemon juice or fruit aboard military vessels until 1795, and it was not until 1845 that their use was made mandatory in the merchant marine.[39] The absence of Vitamin C from the common sea fare of "pork and peas, peas and pork, pease and porke, followed by porke and pease," was responsible for the persistence of scurvy in the British fleet and aboard navy transports until the turn of the century.[40]

Another health problem related to the military diet was that there "was not enough to thrive on and too much to die of starvation."[41] Malnutrition disorders suffered by the army in America were associated as much with the scarcity of staple items in the soldiers' diet as with the lack of important dietary constituents. The army there consumed an estimated three hundred tons of food a week, the bulk of it sent from Europe.[42] Bureaucratic ineptitude, venality in purveyance, and crochety Atlantic winds caused frequent and prolonged delays in delivery. In order both to save the salt ration and to supply the troops engaged in ancillary and field operations, the army tried from time to time to live off the land in Napoleonic fashion. But that inchoate venture was doomed from the start, frustrated by the army's failure to develop systematic procedures for the collection of provisions and to establish an equitable system of reimbursement for the livestock and grain confiscated from local farmers.[43] Moreover, the indiscriminate plundering carried out by hungry soldiers discouraged popular support for the Crown.

Even when the army had access to fresh provisions they could not always be readily substituted for prepared items. Rice grew in abundance in the wet coastal plains, but the soldiers found it unpalatable and ate it reluctantly or not at all.[44] A continuing shortage of salt, issued twice a week when it was at hand,[45] made the preservation of fresh meat, even when available, difficult; because of rapid spoilage, especially in the warm South, meat had to be served out immediately or be wasted. To retain freshness most foods had to be cooked soon after they were harvested; but a chronic shortage of cooking kettles, especially in the South and at outposts in the West Indies where the heat made foods more liable to perish, prevented the army from properly utilizing the resources at hand.[46] For all practical purposes, then, the British remained dependent on supplies from overseas. At best, shipping delays meant painful hunger; at worst, the long-continued insufficiency of food led to the enfeeblement of the troops and increased their susceptibility to disease.

The seven pounds of wheat flour, for which the soldiers were charged one penny for baking, made into nine pounds of bread, which formed the principal part of the soldier's diet.[47] An average of nine ounces of salt pork a day, reduced to only six ounces by boiling, was the other staple. Taken in the middle of the day, it was the only nutriment the soldier received until breakfast the next morning.[48] Shortages of flour, pork, or both produced sporadic crises at every major post in North America and chronic scarcity at outlying posts. Shortly after the outbreak of hostilities at Lexington, rebels sealed off the roads leading into Boston. Almost from that moment the British were married to a superannuated supply system. In the long interim before the first victualing vessels arrived with prepared food from England, the ten thousand troops locked in the besieged city lived on livestock collected by foraging parties who combed the area in the general vicinity of New York by transport. Soon even the rich stock from local farms was exhausted and the army began to draw upon reserve stores of salt meat in government warehouses. It was, the men complained, "as hard as wood, as lean as carrion, and as rusty as the devil." The new spruce beer they drank to mask the tainted taste threw them into the "bloody flux." Disease spread. Emaciated by hunger and disease, the army looked like "so many regiments of skeletons." The death toll mounted. Soon the men were calling Boston "the graveyard of England and the slaughter-house of America." Thirty bodies at a time were thrown into a trench for mass burial "like those of so many dogs, no bell being suffered to toll upon the occasion." Between twenty and thirty officers tried to resign their commissions to protest the "inhuman service we are upon . . . the discontent of our army, occasioned by a scarcity of provisions, and the dreadful mortality that has crept upon it."[49] At the height of the crisis an officer wrote his family in anger and despair, "Our distresses accumulate every day; our barracks are all hospitals and so offensive is the stench of the wounds, that the very air is infected with the smell. What in God's name are you all about in England? Have you forgot us?—or are you fascinated?—for we have not had a vessel in three months with any sort of supplies and therefore our miseries are become manifold."[50]

The ungenerous treatment of the army he cried out against proved in fact to be a rooted tendency. In 1776 an officer writing to his sister from Long Island near Charleston complained that the garrison had not "tasted four morsels of fresh provisions for these four months. Broiled salt pork for breakfast, boiled salt pork for dinner, cold salt pork for supper. Even salt beef is now become an object of luxury." For weeks on end the troops sta-tioned in Savannah in 1779 lived on a diet of oysters, "all re-sources of every kind being exhausted."[51] Beginning in 1778 the success of American privateers in capturing British victualers led to critical food shortages and, as in Boston and elsewhere, the army had to improvise in order to survive.

Foraging expeditions combed the area between Long Island and Martha's Vineyard in search of beef and pork, fish and fowl, cheese and potatoes to feed the troops in Rhode Island who were "in great need."[52] In place of meat the troops were given bad fish; to stretch dwindling supplies of flour, bread was made of equal parts of ground rice and wheat flour. When the last of the flour was used, the men were issued two days' supply of bread and three of rice with orders to make it last five.[53]

Although New York was the principal supply depot for North America and was situated in the heart of a very productive re-gion, the late arrival of grain ships caused an acute shortage during the hard winter of 1779. Without a single barrel of flour left in the public stores, the garrison was forced on a diet of bread made from a mixture of fresh and spoiled oatmeal. The fortuitous onset of extremely cold weather, which froze thousands of migrating geese and ducks on the shores of Long and Staten islands, prevented disaster.[54] It was blind fortune rather than purveyance that fed the men at remote stations such as the one on the San Juan River in Nicaragua, which subsisted on an exotic diet of deer and wild hog, teal and partridge, snook fish and crawfish, alligator and shark.[55]

Whether or not deliveries arrived on schedule, prepared food sent from England was all but inedible, sometimes because it was defective when shipped, sometimes because, improperly packaged, it spoiled en route. Collusion between contractors and commissaries, their deputies, and regimental quartermasters, who carried on the actual business of supply, resulted in the shipment to America of tons of adulterated food. Tens of thousands of pounds of contaminated meat, its spoilage clumsily concealed by coverings of better-quality pork and beef, were discovered when shipping barrels were unsealed. Thousands of barrels of flour were found to be "warm and a little sour" and "of a composition . . . consisting of Sweepings of Stores and Bake Houses, Rags, Papers and old Hatts." Casks of musty, molding peas contained dirt and other contaminants and on occasion even live maggots. The sometimes unavoidable necessity of eating sour oatmeal, rancid butter, smelly vinegar, rotten rice, and weevily bread produced diseases arising from parasitic worms.[56]

While it had certain commendable cosmetic qualities, the clothing of the soldier, like his diet, was not the most conducive to good health. The army considered that proper clothing for a soldier should include a cloth coat, a waistcoat, a pair of cloth breeches, a hat, two shirts, two pairs of stockings and two pairs of shoes, with extra soles and heels, one pair of cloth leggings, a pair of woolen mittens, a woolen night cap, a black stock (a stiff, close-fitting neckcloth), and a blanket.[57] What the men actually received was considerably less than that; it was, moreover, totally inappropriate to the work they did.

In fact, the uniform was an anachronism; ill-designed for military operations and ill-provided by the government, it was the cause of numerous nonfatal but debilitating health problems. Responsibility for the selection and issuance of patterns for uniforms rested exclusively with the Clothing Board, set up in 1692 and reconstituted on a yearly basis thereafter.[58] Although minor alterations were ordered by the board and by the Hanoverian kings, who showed an uncommon interest in the details of military dress, the basic design remained unchanged for almost a hundred years.[59] The costume look of the uniform, popular among all European armies in the eighteenth century, was attractive but nonfunctional. The brimless hats were uncomfortable and provided no protection from sun or rain. The "roler," a bandagelike swath worn about the neck, required assistance to arrange; once on it cut blood circulation. The regulation coat, with "the great heap and load of skirts appending to it," served more to limit movement than to fend off the cold. Spatterdashes, the canvas leggings that rode halfway up the thigh and were tightly fastened by two dozen buttons on each leg, not only impeded mobility but on extended marches caused painful swellings of the feet because of their snug fit.[60]

Although the introduction of machinery into cotton manufacture had reduced its cost, coarse, heavy textiles were still used for both uniforms and bedding. Enveloped in wool and canvas, bound by wide buffalo-hide shoulder and waist belts from which hung eleven pounds and eight ounces of accoutrements, hot and weary soldiers fell easy prey to summertime ailments, such as the "prickling heat" rash that pestered British forces in North America. Scores of men were overcome by heat prostration. At the Battle of Monmouth in June 1778, fifty-nine men suffered sunstroke. That same month there was one fatality among the German troops at "Mittletown," New Jersey. Although huts were built to shelter the men from the intense heat, heavy, constrictive clothing continued to cause more casualties. On a single march from Bedford to Flushing in August 1778, nine soldiers died and sixty-three more were struck down by heatstroke.[61]

Standards for personal hygiene, generally quite low in the eighteenth century,[62] were of necessity often lower for soldiers. Regulations required that the men change into clean shirts every Sunday and Wednesday and that bedding be washed at least once a month.[63] Even these minimal conditions were hard to meet in view of the fact that until the nineteenth century there were no bathing or laundry facilities in military barracks. Even when facilities were available in a locality, the woolen coats and ticken or linen breeches were hard to wash and slow to dry. The frequency of "rheumatic complaints" in eighteenth-century armies was probably related to the unavoidable necessity of wearing damp clothing. Certainly itch, the most common filth disease in the army, was caused by the proliferation of the parasitic mites that burrowed into the seams of dirty clothing and foul bed linen.[64] To be sure, even had better hygienic conditions prevailed, a chronic and sometimes acute clothing shortage made it a practical impossibility to require higher standards of personal cleanliness.

The same bureaucratic confusion that crippled the delivery

of food supplies also stymied all efforts to properly clothe the army. The Clothing Board regulated patterns for uniforms but had no authority to make clothing contracts. The Treasury Board did negotiate contracts with private merchants for some articles of clothing, but the real responsibility to do so rested principally with colonels and regimental agents. The actual business of supply, however, was carried out in each regiment by staff officers— usually by a lieutenant who operated independently of any direct supervision.[65] While there were some generally accepted rules governing the operation of the system, the lack of a coordinating head or agency allowed for careless and inefficient performance of duty at all levels of responsibility. Another factor was the poor state of public finance, which forced the army to resort to various penny-pinching methods to outfit the troops.

By the late eighteenth century a few armies had developed sensible rules for the regular renewal of worn-out clothing.[66] In the British army clothing was issued in two cycles: the first issue of clothing was supposed to fit each man out completely; then every year thereafter each private was supposed to receive a new coat, breeches, stockings, shirt, and "the forepart of a waistcoat, the hind part to be made out of that of the preceding year."[67] But there were times, particularly during war, when there was no correspondence between the rules and reality. Such was the case during the American Revolution. Many articles of clothing were made in America by regimental tailors assisted by women camp followers[68] from materials sent from England. That system had its drawbacks, however, most of which stemmed from the flimsy quality of raw goods, and the army was ultimately forced to depend on ready-to-wear clothing bought in England and shipped to America. Because of delays in shipping, the expected replacement period was usually months, frequently years overdue. In Halifax the Royal Highland Emigrant Corps was "almost stark naked," and "all of them barefoot" during the winter of 1775–1776.[69] Although troops in New York were "in great want" of clothing, 1778 renewal shipments were a year late; when they finally arrived on the *Grampus* at the end of April 1779, transshipment still had to be made to woefully neglected troops on the Spanish Main.[70] A year later the soldiers there were reported to be "quite Naked, without shirts, trousers or shoes."[71] Chronic shortages such as these not only made it difficult to carry out operations in the field,[72] but also increased the soldiers' vulnerability to various ailments resulting from exposure. Although the problem was more acute in northern climates[73] troops stationed in the warm, mosquito-infested southern latitudes also suffered from exposure.[74]

Efforts to get maximum wear out of clothing by reissuing usable articles to work parties, or by storing heavy blanket coats through the spring and summer, were sensible practices given the chronic shortages.[75] But the practice, common in all European armies,[76] of passing on the uniforms of retired, invalided, or even dead soldiers to their replacements, without any hygienic precautions, was without doubt a major cause of the spread of communicable diseases.[77]

Among the conditions which favored the spread of disease was the concentration of large bodies of troops in ships, quarters, barracks, or camps where only minimal health standards prevailed. From the moment the soldier boarded a military transport his chances for contracting a contagious or infectious disease increased dramatically. Although there was a recommended pre-embarkation quarantine period of from two to three weeks, it was seldom enforced.[78] The transports were, moreover, ideal breeding grounds for disease. Each vessel carried hundreds of men cramped between decks in tiers of berths lining both sides of the ship.[79] Rural troops, hitherto unexposed to infections, were randomly packed, six men for every ten square feet of space, with men "picked up in the streets" or enlisted directly from the Savoy Prison or other jails. Because of turbulent weather, the ships' hatches often had to be kept closed, cutting off fresh air below decks.[80] Their resistance to infections lowered by malnutrition, exposed to the diseases that flourished in the fetid air of the narrow, poorly ventilated space, soldiers sickened and died at an alarming rate. During the long Atlantic crossing, which took a minimum of six weeks, sometimes four to five months, morbidity rates reached staggering levels: 932 out of 8,437, or 11 percent, of the soldiers embarked for the West Indies between October 1776 and February 1780 died en route. The 91st Regiment, embarked January 1780, and the 94th, a month later, had mortality rates of over 22 and 25 percent respectively.[81]

Those who survived the ocean voyage still had to face the rigors of "seasoning." The ease with which Europeans acclimatized depended to a large degree upon the time of arrival. The cooler months were healthier, and the crossing was safer in the fall and spring, when the sea was less tempestuous. But land transportation in America was poor and the roads practically impassable in winter; therefore military campaigns were rarely planned for the cold months. Instead, most troops were landed in America in time for a summer campaign. Weakened by the long voyage, as many as 75 percent of the new arrivals fell victim to some disorder related to seasoning. Illness was always more com-

mon among recruits than among veterans and among troops stationed in the southern latitudes than among those in the
temperate zones.[82]

Although complete statistics are not available, extant records
suggest that the number of soldiers permanently incapacitated by
service in the South and in the West Indies exceeded that of any
previous British war. Predictably, West Indian–based regiments
suffered the highest losses: nearly 15 percent of the men stationed there died in 1779, compared with 6 percent for Clinton's
army operating out of New York and slightly over 1 percent for
Haldimand's army in Canada.[83] In order to cut losses, efforts
were made to avoid keeping the troops in the coastal lowlands
from late June to mid-October because of "a certainty of their
being rendered useless for some time for military service, if not
entirely lost," and campaigns were planned to coincide with the
healthier seasons.[84]

Exposure in the field, crude sanitation in hastily constructed
camps, and overcrowding in tents, barracks, and hospitals caused
more casualties during war than did battle injuries. During periods of war in Europe, when active military operations were halted
in the winter, armies were usually billeted on civilians. But the
sparsely populated American colonies would not, indeed could
not, accommodate the unprecedented numbers of British and
German troops sent to fight the war.[85] Some of the troops in the
larger towns were housed in makeshift quarters: in public buildings such as the court house and Faneuil Hall in Boston,[86] or the
Bettering House and the State House in Philadelphia;[87] in
churches, including the Old North Church, the South or Old
Dutch Church and the Methodist Meeting House in New York;[88]
or in abandoned houses, outhouses, alehouses, and barns
everywhere.[89]

Other soldiers lived in regular barracks. Despite soaring
prices for nails, cutting tools, and lumber, high wages for artificers and laborers, and a dwindling supply of natural timber in
the immediate environs of occupied towns, the army was forced
to construct barracks.[90] Built in the European style, they virtually
segregated the troops in stinking enclaves. Although there were
local variations, barracks were usually built in a large square, the
rooms contiguous, so that the soldiers could be easily confined to
quarters and isolated from the civilian community.[91] Frame struc-
tures two or three stories high, they were built without foundations. Each building was divided into dozens of small rooms with
few windows, and these half-glazed and half-shuttered. The interiors were as stark and spare as the exteriors. The rooms were
furnished with only the bare necessities: racks for weapons,
stoves, tongs, fire shovels, iron cooking pots, candlesticks, lamps,

coal boxes and berths for sleeping.[92] They were as unhealthy as
they were uncomfortable and unattractive.

Overcrowding in living quarters made a material contribution
to the high rate of infectious diseases in the army. Until the mid-
nineteenth century when the War Office began to construct better
barracks, the recommended amount of barrack space per man
was six hundred cubic feet.[93] In actual practice there was less than
that. The barracks built in Boston in 1775 consisted of eight
rooms with an average of 32 men in a room and 250 men in a
single building.[94] Those at New York had 14 men per room, those
at Point aux Tremble in Canada 20 per room.[95] The fortified barracks on Windmill Hill and on Quaker Hill in Providence, Rhode
Island, were built for 200 men; they housed 245.[96]

Soldiers slept two to a bed in wooden berths six and a half
feet long and four and a half feet wide on straw or horsehair
mattresses. The bedding consisted of sheets made of osnaburg—
a coarse, heavy cotton such as was later used for grain sacks—a
bolster or long pillow, and three blankets, or two blankets and
a rug.[97] Barrack bedding, like everything else, was usually in short
supply, however. Until 1778 most of it was shipped from Devon-
shire, England; after that no more shipments were received, although wear and tear on blankets necessitated about 10,000
replacements a year. A survey taken in 1779 found that 11,700
blankets and rugs were too old and worn out for further use. The
approach of winter forced the Barrack Master General, William
Crosbie, to purchase replacements in America. Chronic shortages
such as these and unsanitary practices such as the passing on of
used bed clothing without proper sanitary precautions, or the
issuance of clean sheets only every thirty days if then, made a
material contribution to the high disease rate in the army.[98]

So, too, did the lack of bathing, laundry, cooking, and dining
facilities in military barracks. Because there were no kitchen facilities, the soldiers prepared, cooked, and ate their rations in the
same rooms in which they slept. In the summer, steam rising
from the boiling kettles heated the small rooms like so many
ovens.[99] In the winter the frame buildings were impossible to
heat. Indeed a chronic shortage of fuel, necessary for cooking as
well as heating, periodically reduced the army to near disaster.
Wood, and coal sent from England, the chief sources of fuel,
were seldom available in sufficient quantities. After 1778, shipments of coal from England ended altogether, due to the cost and
the perennial shortage of shipping.[100]

There was a severe fuel shortage in Boston in the winter of
1775 after supplies were cut off by the rebels. In order to heat the
living quarters of the army until a coal ship finally arrived in
January, a number of houses, wharves, stores, and vessels belong-

ing to rebels were cut into firewood.[101] During the winter of 1776 the troops in New York were supplied with coal from England and from Spanish River on Cape Breton Island, and with wood cut on the east end of Long Island or purchased in New York and in the Jersies.[102] All of the wood on the neck of land south of Philadelphia, between the Delaware and the Schuylkill rivers, was appropriated to fire the army in Philadelphia during the winter of 1777–1778.[103] Until they were evacuated to New York in the fall of 1779, the six thousand troops in Rhode Island consumed about three hundred cords of wood a week, most of which was cut on Shelter and Connonicut islands, on Commonfence Neck and at Lloyd's Neck some fifty miles from New York. During the bitter winter of 1778, with those supplies virtually exhausted, the regulated fuel allowance had to be cut to two-thirds, although snow lay ten inches deep on the ground and the port wine issued to the army froze in its bottles in the frigid living quarters.[104]

The main army in New York, almost entirely dependent on wood obtained locally, was nearly destroyed during the winter of 1779–1780. The winter was unusually severe, with snow falling almost daily from early November through mid-March. By December, high fuel consumption by the twenty thousand troops and dependent refugees had exhausted the forests in the environs of the city and on Long and Staten islands and had reduced reserves in military magazines to only seventy cords of wood and eighty chaldrons of coal. To stave off disaster, Barrack Master Crosbie ordered wood parties out on sleds and in bateaux to bring in wood from Brooklyn and from Bergen; ships and hulks in the harbor and ornamental and fruit trees in gardens, courtyards, lanes, and avenues were cut down and distributed to the various regiments.[105] The indigent poor and the army suffered most from the energy shortage. At the height of the crisis the fuel allowance for officers and men was reduced by half; many of the soldiers living in barracks run down by hard use and poor maintenance were frostbitten in their quarters. "It was," wrote a Hessian officer, "real misery." [106]

As a rule, camps cannot have been a great improvement over regular barracks. During the warm months and when the army was in the field, the troops lived in tents. Although the size of officers' tents varied according to rank and even from regiment to regiment, the standard size of privates' tents was six and a half feet square and five feet high. Five men lived in each tent in conditions highly inimical to health.[107] In the first place, most tents were much the worst for wear due to constant use and infrequent replacement.[108] Rotten or damaged, they offered little protection from the rain, the heat, or the cold. A shortage of frames to elevate the thin, straw sleeping mats often forced the soldiers to sleep directly on the hard, damp ground, which contributed to chronic disabilities of the joints or muscles.[109] A scarcity of straw for stuffing the sailcloth bed cases made it impossible to renew the straw regularly; the lice and bedbugs which infested the stale bedding encouraged the spread of scabies, typhus, and various other filth diseases.[110]

Wigwams made of brush or palmetto were cooler than the heavy canvas tents and were used in their stead in most of the South. More substantial sod houses were built by the soldiers themselves in Jamaica, Hempstead, Bedford, Brooklyn, Flushing, and other northern communities. Although they offered more protection from the elements, they too were crowded, with from twelve to twenty-four men per hut. The single pane of glass allowed each hut limited fresh air and light, while the thatch roofs leaked and the clay and brush chimneys were highly inflammable.[111]

Although army sanitarians like Sir John Pringle, Richard Brocklesby, and Donald Monro had begun to explore the association between environment and disease, bad living conditions continued to have a significant influence on sickness and mortality in the army. It was the "fevers," which caused approximately one out of every eight deaths during the century, that made the saddest havoc in the army. Dr. Brocklesby estimated that eight times as many men died of fevers of various kinds as died of wounds in battle.[112] Because there was no systematic classification of fevers and because records of clinical descriptions are often confused as well as confusing, it is difficult to distinguish between the several types that flourished in the period. Typhus, typhoid, and dysentery all shared common clinical symptoms; typhus and typhoid were not in fact recognized as distinct diseases until well into the nineteenth century. Nor was typhus reported separately from the other fevers until 1840.[113] Since both typhus and typhoid are carried by lice and are characteristic of overcrowding, their distinction historically is not perhaps of great significance. In any case, it was an army physician, Sir John Pringle, who made the first successful attempt to classify fevers. As physician general to the army from 1744 to 1752, Pringle had the opportunity to observe at first hand the clinical course of various fevers. His experience produced careful descriptions of symptoms as well as a general discussion of etiology which placed heavy emphasis on environment as a factor in the incidence of disease. His *Observations on the Diseases of the Army*, published in 1757, recognized two major categories of febrile diseases.

The first category, the vernal or inflammatory fevers, including coughs, pleurisies, peripneumonies, rheumatism, and inflammations of the brain and bowels, were never a serious health factor in the Revolution, largely because the government had already implemented some of the preventive measures recommended by Pringle, such as the issuance of blankets for every tent and the requirement that soldiers wear underwaistcoats, watch coats, and sturdy shoes while standing guard duty.[114]

The second category, the so-called putrid and bilious fevers, had a far greater impact on the course and the outcome of the Revolution than is generally recognized. Collectively they were regarded by army sanitarians as "the most offensive and loathsome of all military diseases . . . the most mortal . . . or hardest to be cured."[115] Malaria, known variously as ague or intermitting and remitting fever because of its two-cycle annual wave in the late spring and early fall, was the most common type of fever in the semitropical heat of the South, which offered attractive breeding grounds for the insect vector. Malignant forms survived and even increased in virulence in the South throughout the eighteenth century.[116] As newcomers to the colonies, British soldiers were usually nonimmunes.

Dysentery, in its most virulent form known as the "bloody flux," was, like malaria, also endemic to America and appeared in virulent form from New England to Georgia. Both because they were newcomers and because as a communicable disease dysentery was easily spread in hospitals and camps, British soldiers proved more susceptible to dysentery than did the American troops.[117] On the other hand, typhus was never a health hazard in America until the Revolution created conditions favorable to its development.[118]

The majority of the wounded at Bunker Hill succumbed to dysentery, and only an estimated 50 percent of the survivors were declared "cured fit for service," an indication that the disease usually recurred in less acute form. In 1779–1780, a "pernicious fever," later identified by a medical board as intermittent fever and dysentery, struck New York in epidemic proportions. Beginning in July, it spread rapidly to Staten and Long islands, where it raged unchecked through October. Over five thousand soldiers were stricken, and fatalities ranged from twenty-five to sixty men per English regiment.[119] At one point every soldier in von Donop's German regiment was infected. Although the epidemic waned during the winter months, it recurred with less intensity during the same months of the following year.[120]

Despite the fact that the army used mosquito nets in the South,[121] military returns from southern bases, such as Ebenezer, Georgia, indicated that two-thirds of the troops were disabled by malaria every week. Posts there and at Abercorn were eventually closed and the troops moved to Savannah because of the crippling effects of the disease. When two-thirds of the 71st Regiment, stationed at Cheraw Hill, South Carolina, were certified unfit for service, Cornwallis was forced to abandon that post, a decision which had important military repercussions, since the rebels interpreted the move as evidence of British timidity and "the whole Country between the Pedee and the Black River, openly avowed the principle of Rebellion."[122]

British forces at Camden, Georgetown, and Savannah were ravaged by fevers during the course of the Southern Campaign; wagons carried four hundred sick and wounded on Cornwallis's march through North Carolina; at Guilford one-third of the army was ill or wounded. It was the health of his troops which dictated Cornwallis's move to "the upper parts of the Country, where alone I can hope to preserve the troops from the fatal sickness, which so nearly ruined the Army last autumn."[123] His final decision to occupy Yorktown was at least partially dictated by health factors.[124]

Regiments ordered to West Indian and Central American service faced the most inimical health conditions. The hostile tropics were a literal graveyard for the Europeans; entire regiments in Barbados, Grenada, and Tobago were permanently invalided after a tour of duty there. In Nicaragua, fevers and fluxes decimated whole corps. Lieutenant Colonel Stephen Kemble's cheerless reports to the home government describe with poignant simplicity the awful reality of tropical service: "The sick in a miserable, shocking condition, without anyone to attend them, or even to bury the dead who lay on the beach shocking to behold; the same mortality raging among the poor soldiers aboard ship, where accumulated filth had made all air putrid; officers dying daily, and so worn down with disorders, lassitude, etc. that they are even as filthy and regardless where they lay, as the Soldiers, never stirring from their beds for days."[125]

Although modern medical research has established the cause of smallpox as a virus, its diffusion was aided by the same overcrowded and unsanitary environments which bred the "fevers," itch, and various other filth diseases. Smallpox was endemic in nearly all of Britain's major cities in the late eighteenth century. To counteract the exceptional mortality produced by this disease, the army adopted the practice of inoculation. At the beginning of the Seven Years War, seven out of every nine soldiers in infantry regiments had smallpox, and nearly one in four who contracted it "in the natural way" died.[126] By the beginning of the Revolution, smallpox rarely occurred in epidemic proportions among army personnel. However, colonial laws, especially in New England, proscribed the use of variolation because of the risk factor and because, even in the milder form induced by the procedure, patients could transmit the disease. As a result, the Revolutionary period witnessed fresh outbreaks of smallpox, striking the American army with virulent force during the invasion of Canada.[127] A serious epidemic struck the British in Boston in 1775 and reportedly killed an average of three soldiers a day for a month before it could be checked.[128] As a result, a voluntary inoculation program was immediately begun in the army; soldiers who refused to participate were quarantined so as not to communicate the disease.[129] In the summer of 1780 smallpox struck the troops at Charleston and in the fall the base at Camden.[130] Although statistics on the death rates are not available, it is highly probable that on balance the fatality of smallpox was lessened by inoculation.

Among contagious diseases, syphilis and gonorrhea, communicated either by contact or congenitally, were, as one regimental surgeon put it, "so prevalent that no reproach follows it, either from their comrades or from many of their officers." According to the estimate of Dr. Robert Hamilton, a regiment of four hundred men had an average of three hundred cases of venereal disease a year. The actual number of cases cannot be ascertained, first, because as Hamilton notes "many men were infected two or three times a quarter," which means that the same case was counted several times a year. On the other hand, many cases were probably undetected, since some regiments deducted "venereal money" from the pay of soldiers with reported cases; the money was then divided "among the Good men of the Company who are obliged to do their duty for them."[131] The fines did little to discourage soldiers from associating with "lewd and disorderly women," and the army ultimately had no recourse but to try to keep women known to be infected away from the camps and out of the barracks and to treat reported cases of syphilis or gonorrhea with mercury.[132]

The average British mortality from musket or rifle fire was considerably less than that from disease; nonetheless many of the wounded died who might have been saved. Because there was no ambulance service or medical corps, many soldiers bled to death or died of exposure before they could be removed from the field on provision or ammunition wagons. Most of the 706 men wounded at Bunker Hill were not brought to the hospitals in Boston until evening; a great many died in the meantime, of shock or by hemorrhaging; others developed gangrene.[133] Those wounded in the operations against Ticonderoga in July 1777 were left in bark huts, without medical attention, until regimental surgeons could reach them later. Two days later, when the army moved on to Skeensborough, the wounded were left behind under the charge of Sergeant Roger Lamb.[134] "It was," Lamb re-

called, "a distressing sight to see the wounded men bleeding on
the ground; and what made it more so, the rain came pouring
down like a deluge upon us. And still to add to the distress of the
sufferers, there was nothing to dress their wounds. . . . The poor
fellows earnestly entreated me to tie up their wounds." Lamb tore
up his own shirt and with the help of a soldier's wife made bandages, dressed their wounds, and carried them in blankets to a
small hut a few miles away where they remained another seven
days.[135] The wounded at Saratoga were left out on the field of
battle all night; at daybreak they were finally brought in and
placed around campfires; since "we were almost froze with cold,"
Lieutenant William Digby remembered, "our wounded who lived
till the morning must have severely felt it."[136] Those wounded at
Guilford Court House remained on the field through the night;
nearly fifty died before morning. When the army moved on,
seventy of the worst wounded were left behind at a Quaker meeting house.[137]

Even when the army was able to remove its wounded, there
was little demonstrable benefit to the patients. Field hospitals,
which were supposed to provide emergency treatment, were as a
rule understaffed and ill equipped to care for major battle casualties. Regimental and even general hospitals were not always
better, although they were probably on a par with contemporary
clinics in London. Because they were less crowded and so theoretically enjoyed a lower mortality rate, regimental hospitals
took care of the majority of patients requiring hospitalization.
Most were located in barns, stables, granaries, churches, and
large public buildings, which were frequently ill adapted to their
use.[138] Some techniques of disinfection, in use since the Middle
Ages, were being used successfully in military hospitals, at least in
regard to certain types of infections. Army rules required that
every hospital be thoroughly cleaned before occupancy, the walls
and floors scraped and washed with soapy water and vinegar, and
the interiors fumigated with wet gunpowder and aromatics such
as incense, juniper wood or berries, or steams of vinegar, sulphur,
and gunpowder.[139] Advances in theory as to the nature of infection and contagion also produced a policy of segregation derived
from the ancient practice of isolating lepers. Because it was believed that infection was carried by effluvia given off by a sick
person, flux or fever patients were kept in separate wards, victims
of smallpox or "pestilential disorders" were vigorously quarantined in "as private and remote lodgings as can be had," and
visiting was strictly prohibited.[140]

Despite these advances, hospital standards were on the whole
quite primitive. Many were dirty, particularly field and regimental hospitals at remote posts. Because they drew supplies from the

general hospital at New York and transportation was at best unreliable, military hospitals in Florida, Georgia, Carolina, and the West Indies were chronically short of brooms, spades, shovels, rakes, and other implements for keeping the premises clean.[141] Most were badly overcrowded. Only the critically ill had single beds; all other patients shared narrow straw pallets with bolsters, spaced at intervals of six feet.[142] The wounded who survived long enough to receive treatment in a general hospital had still to face the risks of surgery. Although opium and cinchona bark were used to relieve pain, there were no anesthetics, and many surgical patients died of shock. Surgical treatment, even of conventional wounds, was crude and dangerous. Balls and extraneous matter, such as wadding or cloth lodged with them, were located and removed by probing with the finger. If the ball was beyond the reach of the finger it was left, in the hope that, in time, it would work itself to the surface.[143] The lack of knowledge of aseptic procedures greatly increased the danger of infections, such as tetanus, which caused death in a high percentage of surgical cases.

Moreover, the iron balls and lead bullets then used caused more extensive damage than modern steel balls. Although musket balls were highly lethal, cannonball wounds were almost always worse. Even for those hit in the limbs the chances of survival were slight. During the rebel cannonading of Roxbury in July 1775 a British artilleryman was hit in the thigh and died soon afterward.[144] A year later, when the British cannonaded Roxbury on the anniversary of the Boston Massacre, an American officer was shot in the thigh by a cannonball, "which so fractured the bone that the leg had to be removed near the body. His pain was so exquisite occasioned by the bone being shivered to pieces quite to his hip joint, that he died about nine o'clock in the morning."[145] During the American cannonading of Saratoga, Baroness von Riedesel and two female companions took refuge in an abandoned cellar, which was called into use as a temporary hospital. She tells how a wounded soldier, whose leg was then being amputated, was struck in the other leg by a cannonball during surgery. Forsaken by his friends, he rolled into a corner of the room to die. Shortly after that an officer, the husband of one of the women, was brought in "after a cannon ball had taken off his arm close to the shoulder." All night the women "heard his moans, which resounded fearfully through the vaulted cellars." The next morning he died.[146]

The circumstances of war sometimes produced outright acts of cruelty which greatly intensified the suffering of the wounded. At Bunker Hill, for example, the provincials charged their muskets with old nails and angular pieces of iron, and directed them at the legs of British soldiers so as not to kill them but "to leave them as burdens on us, to exhaust our provisions and to engage our attention, as well as to intimidate the rest of our soldiery."[147] Wound surgery for injuries to the extremities such as these usually consisted of amputation. A skilled surgeon could remove a limb in twenty minutes, but the procedure sometimes took up to forty minutes, and the mortality rates were appallingly high.[148] Most of those wounded at Bunker Hill who had to have both legs removed died either of shock or of loss of blood.

In treating wounds or disease, medical men were of course handicapped by a lack of knowledge of bacteriology, antibiotics, and modern surgical techniques. As a result, they had to depend on popular remedies of the day such as purging and bleeding. Bleeding was routine therapy for virtually all illnesses. Unfortunately, the procedure was neither clinical nor scientific. Since leeches could not be easily transported, most surgeons used venesection; seldom equipped with bleeding cups, which would indicate a specified measure, they drew copious amounts, allowing the blood to flow freely onto the ground or into a basin.[149] If a man had already lost blood in the field, further bleeding in the hospital could prove fatal. Extreme vomiting and purging induced by emetics and laxatives such as ipecacuanha intensified the suffering of the gravely ill without having any real therapeutic value.

Army doctors did have certain helpful drugs, such as quinine against malaria. However, throughout most of the century the dosage of quinine given was too small to be effective.[150] Moreover, scarcity and inflation caused the price of cinchona, the bark from which quinine was isolated, to quadruple between June 1776 and September 1777. Both the British and the American armies were forced to use substitutes including wine or botanicals indigenous to the colonies, such as Virginia snakeroot. Prices of all drugs rose between 500 and 600 percent during the course of the war, and Americans, cut off from customary English sources, began to prey upon British supplies until importation procedures established by Congress and French aid eventually relieved the shortage.[151]

Both scientific knowledge and circumstances peculiar to war set limits to the effectiveness of medical care in the army. Even within those limits, however, the quality of care varied considerably. For one thing, the decentralized nature of the British medical service militated against consistently high standards. Unlike the French service, which was operated by private enterprise under the general supervision of a *commissaire de guerre* and a medical staff appointed by the Crown,[152] British military medicine was organized almost exclusively on a regimental basis. Until 1795 an annual allowance of thirty pounds sterling was granted to each regiment to establish its own hospital; the medical officers who staffed the hospitals were attached to the regiments themselves and were paid as regimental officers.[153] It was not until 1756 that the first distinct administrative medical organization, the Hospital Board, was set up to direct the army medical service. The board, composed of physicians and chief and master surgeons, met regularly to appoint medical personnel, certify soldiers as invalids for discharge, and approve the purchase of hospital supplies.[154]

In the spring of 1779 a new office, that of Superintendent General of Hospitals in North America, was created in an effort to centralize authority and thereby improve the quality of health service. Subordinate only to the commander in chief, the Superintendent General had theoretical control over all British and German hospitals in North America. In actual practice his duties seem to have been principally clerical and supervisory: he collected statistical information on the numbers of sick and wounded and on the medical staffs of the regimental and general hospitals; he examined accounts and supervised the operations of the purveyor's office; he was general supervisor of the inspectors of regimental hospitals; and he made recommendations to the commander in chief regarding the filling of vacancies.[155]

Apart from administrative defects, the most critical weakness in the medical service was in the practitioners themselves, who in many cases did not know enough to take care of people and in some cases did not care to do so. Even by the standards of the time, army medical officers were poorly trained. There was no army medical school in England until 1858, and until then no civil medical school in Britain taught military surgery or clinical and military medicine. Medical education at Edinburgh or at one of the continental universities was excessively long and expensive. Few recipients of the coveted degree of doctor of medicine were willing to give up the prestige of a lucrative private practice in exchange for ten shillings a day as an army physician. Conscious of that fact, the War Office tried to revise the salary scale upward; the Treasury Board refused, however, to grant the recommended pay increase, although it did certify army doctors as eligible for a regular military pension.[156] As a result, the medical staff during the Revolution consisted chiefly of surgeons, there being only ten physicians employed at any one time in North America and the West Indies.[157]

The empirical nature of the surgeon's training made him more of an artisan than a scientist. After completion of a period of apprenticeship, most surgeons went to "London or Edinburgh a few months in winter, to walk the hospitals, return home and

set up for themselves; and this forms the whole of their medical
education."[158] In order to compensate for the informal nature of
their training, the War Office, traditionally responsible for the
day-to-day operational activities of the medical branch, tried to
establish suitable standards for army service. All surgeons were
supposed to pass a qualifying examination at Surgeons Hall before appointment.[159] Although the sale of commissions, even of
chaplaincies, was common, the practice was forbidden in the
medical branch. The War Office discovered the sale of a surgeon's
commission in a New York hospital, which had apparently been
accomplished by deception, and immediately ordered it rescinded.[160] The policy of promotion based on merit was not without results, since about half of the British army surgeons in
America during the Revolution had also served as regimental
mates prior to winning a surgeon's commission; several went on
to do university work after the war.[161]

Apprenticeship in a hospital and on-the-job training in the
field might conceivably prepare a surgeon for his work, which
was "the cure of external diseases, such as properly require the
knife or plaister, and a manual neatness in bandages."[162] But low
status and poor pay made many of them indifferent to their
suffering patients. As staff officers, surgeons were outranked
even by ensigns, quartermasters, and adjutants. Although they
differed in educational background, skill, and character, as a
group they were looked down upon by everyone.[163] When staff
vacancies opened at the general hospital in New York, the War
Office declined to fill them with regimental surgeons because "the
charge is of too serious a nature to be entrusted to the surgeons
of regiments, who have very rarely had opportunity of acquiring
great skill to perform the great operations of surgery, or sufficient judgment to decide upon the necessity of performing
them." Their lack of diagnostic skill was also impugned by the
Secretary at War, who added, ". . . it is well known that the Company's surgeons have very little physical knowledge, and are totally ignorant of medicine and the proper method of treating
dysenteries and intermittent fevers."[164]

Passed over by the state that employed them, they were
mocked and scorned as well by their peers. In a biting piece of
satire, as contemptuous of medical practice as of surgeons' skills,
an anonymous critic scoffed at the whole profession: "The principal part of your job is to bleed and dress sore backs," he wrote.
Jeering at the surgeon's lack of diagnostic skills, he continued, "If
you are ignorant of a soldier's complaint first take blood, then
give him an emetic and a cathartic—to which you may add a
blister. This will serve, at least, to diminish the number of your
patients." In a bitter thrust at the venality of army surgeons, he

exhorted them to treat patients roughly who did not pay for the cure of venereal disease; if they did "observe nearly the same conduct . . . besides," he added, "as the ladies of the camp or garrison are pretty much in common, these men may, by circulating the disorder, procure you some practice among the officers." [165]

Unfortunately for the patient with a burning and mortal ague, or with wound gangrene or blood poisoning, many surgeons lived up to the harsh characterization. Because at six shillings a day before deductions pay was low and the cost of living in America was high, many surgeons augmented their incomes by engaging in surreptitious traffic in regimental medicines, which could yield as much as £130 a year in extra income. [166] Medicine money, partially derived from a penny-a-month deduction from each soldier's pay, was often used to buy "the cheapest and coarsest articles" for the regimental medicine chest; the difference disappeared as "a perquisite to the surgeons." Knowledge of such practices was common, even among private soldiers, who as a result often chose to have prescriptions filled by a local apothecary, "rather than be subjected to swallow the medicine which their own physician prescribes for them." [167]

The effectiveness of medical care was also influenced by a morale problem with regimental and hospital mates, who shared the surgeon's responsibility for administering therapy. [168] Although subordinate to surgeons, mates were theoretically required to pass the same examinations in surgery and pharmacy. Actually the meager pay scale of three shillings a day—which, less deductions, yielded slightly over four pounds a year profit—discouraged most mates from incurring the heavy expense of medical education. As a result the great majority were "almost totally ignorant of what is passing in the medical world," as one surgeon put it. [169]

As a result of these and other problems, including ignorance and confusion about disease, primitive therapy, and shortages of essential supplies and medical personnel, [170] military hospitals frequently did the patient little good and in many cases positively did harm. This was particularly true of regimental hospitals, whose staffs were as a rule inferior to those of general hospitals. In a harsh indictment of regimental hospitals, Superintendent of Hospitals J. Mervin Nooth reported to Commander-in-Chief Henry Clinton finding desperately ill men who had been left lying for days on lice-infested straw until they "are frequently so shamefully nasty and lousy and so much in want of necessaries that it is out of the power of the persons attending them to clean them." [171] Patients admitted to regimental hospitals for treatment of minor problems faced the risk of contracting more serious, often fatal illnesses. Some patients in a regimental hospital in Jamaica, under treatment for minor complaints, were permanently disabled as "men having trifling sores are become ulcers of the worst kind, thro' want of care—some of whom have had their legs amputated to the eternal disgrace of those who were the cause of it." One physician estimated that seven out of the ten soldiers who died on West Indian service could have been saved with proper medical care.[172]

On the other hand, there were a few first-rate medical officers in the army, like the conscientious regimental surgeon Robert Hamilton, or the brilliant physician John Pringle, whose achievements in military medicine cut the path for advances in civil medical practices in a number of significant areas. Pringle's emphasis on environment as a factor in the incidence of disease stimulated interest in the concept of public health. Soon after his research demonstrated that camp dysentery was spread by improper sanitary arrangements, the army adopted his preventive measures regarding the location of latrines—although educating the soldiers to use them remained a problem. His association of malaria with stagnant water influenced the army practice of locating campsites away from marshy areas. His common-sense rules regarding diet and clothing make his name pre-eminent in the origins of modern public hygiene. Dr. James Lind's rules for the prevention and treatment of scurvy and for ship hygiene as well as his pioneer work in the study of tropical diseases mark Lind among the precursors of the public health movement.[173]

Although remedial treatment was never what it should have been—at times was not even what it could have been—on the whole the soldier probably received as good or better health care than the average British citizen. Under the influence of scientists like Pringle, the army began to take the first halting steps in the direction of preventive health care. Noting that "if the operations of war are checked by sickness, the instructing soldiers how to live will then be as necessary as to teach them how to fight," military manuals began to stress the need for personal hygiene.[174] Regimental orders frequently exhorted the soldiers to bathe, preferably in the early morning or late evening when bathing was said to be least prejudicial to health, to change personal linen twice a week, and to wash and comb out the elaborate "clubb'd" hair style decreed for infantry by George III, which the men were wont to leave "for some days together without opening and combing it," causing scabs, ulcers and "an accumulated mixture of filth, dirt, and Vermin."[175]

Given the high disease rate of the period, the peculiar hazards of army life, and the state of scientific development and contemporary attitudes toward personal cleanliness, the British medical service during the Revolution left a creditable record. During the first six years of the war, 23,520 soldiers were sick. Between 1775 and 1780, there were 6,107 deaths, or an average of 1,018 per year (2.6 percent).[176] Although there is no absolute basis for comparison, when these figures are contrasted with the mortality rates of contemporary hospitals, the military medical record is favorable.[177]

Change in both the theory and the practice of medicine occurred slowly in the eighteenth century. So far as the military was concerned, better than three-quarters of a century was to elapse before a major effort was made to radically reorganize the medical department. The push for reform did not achieve success until 1857–1860, when the first code defining the duties and responsibilities of medical officers was adopted and an army medical school was established in Chatham to train men for service in the medical department. Shortly thereafter an army hospital corps was set up to provide orderlies to be permanently attached to regimental hospitals. In 1861, the New Purveyors Code and Regulations reorganized the medical department.[178] Developments in the understanding of anatomy and physiology, the cause and cure for septic wounds, and the discovery of anesthetics ultimately sent the death rates plummeting. In the meantime the medical service worked with what it had and what it knew, and it did perhaps almost as well as could reasonably have been expected.

3 REWARDS AND RECREATION

THE ARMY WAS a paternalistic society which provided relief from ordinary social competition for the goods of life. Although it did not guarantee a decent, even an adequate standard of living for its members, it did give them equality of income. Low wages, erratically paid, represented an acceptable substitute for a hitherto chaotic existence. To some, if not to all, the army awarded a small pension and a primitive form of disability relief. Meager and limited though such benefits were, they made the military profession special, since civilian occupations were still without these protective features. Totally dependent upon the institution, soldiers soon came to identify with it and to look to it for all their personal, social, and psychological satisfactions.

Once in the army, men of different social origins merged into a special social status in what was in fact a reconstructed society. Life for them was bad—austere, squalid, harsh. Penniless bachelors most of them, unable to afford life's basic necessities, much less such luxuries as a wife and family, they lived bored and lonely lives in uncomfortable proximity to bored and lonely neighbors. Propertyless, entirely dependent on income from wages, they looked to a bleak future when, too feeble to fight, many would be discarded by the state without economic security. In spite of it all, existence for them was no worse and was in some respects somewhat better than for the great majority of the urban lower classes.

Soldiering as an eighteenth-century occupation anticipated some of the problems which became general for industrial workers in the nineteenth century.[1] As wage workers, without any job security,[2] their existence was totally dependent on the state—a fact which most of the great powers, as employers, were slowly if reluctantly beginning to grasp. Confronted with a situation already desperate, most of them had begun to develop social programs to relieve the soldier's distress. But the inability of their national economies to support such programs, combined with the social and cultural backwardness of the times, hindered real progress.

Based on a comparison of annual income, only country laborers ranked below common soldiers in the social structure of eighteenth-century England.[3] The soldier's per diem of eight pence a day was set by Parliament in 1660, according to the wages of common laborers, the strata from which foot soldiers were then drawn.[4] That figure was, however, only a nominal wage, since in most cases it was substantially altered both by deductions and by various pay supplements.[5] Numerous deductions severely depressed the soldier's real income. The only portion of his gross per diem that went directly to him was subsistence money, the rate of which was regulated at six pence. The difference between total pay and subsistence, which amounted to two pence, was termed "off-reckonings," which part of his wage was liable to legal deductions. Sometimes additional deductions were also authorized. During the Revolution, two and a half pence a day was withheld for provisions in the field.[6] There was a one-penny deduction to cover the cost of baking the soldier's flour allotment in the regimental ovens. Soldiers paid three pence a month to have bed linen laundered.[7] Although in the late seventeenth century the state assumed responsibility for the clothing and equipment of the troops, soldiers still paid through deductions for certain articles of clothing, such as shoes, buckles, or cockades.[8] Those who required hospitalization paid a deduction of four pence a day.[9] Beginning in 1684, twelve pence per pound was withheld from the pay of the whole army for the support of the Royal Hospital at Chelsea.[10] What remained after assorted illegal and semiauthorized deductions were made was nominally, though not actually, six pence a day, which represented all the soldier had to live on.[11]

There were of course fringe benefits, such as free postage[12] and a maximum of twenty days' leave every six months, unless longer leave was approved by the regimental colonel or another field officer,[13] as well as other special forms of remuneration, including the gratuity or bounty given for extraordinary valor in battle and prize money taken in the form of enemy spoils, but such windfalls were both capricious and limited. Normally needy and enterprising men who wanted to supplement their wages did so by volunteering for extra work assignments. Privates received no compensation for routine work, such as bridge and road repair, but the construction of forts or other public works was compensated at the rate of nine pence a day.[14] Because the men had to pay for their own provisions in America, skilled workers such as artificers were paid as much as one and a half shillings a day for work formerly regarded as duty.[15] While on furlough or during off-duty hours, many soldiers earned extra money working at their own trades, although in America the economic competition from soldiers taking jobs in the community was so bitterly resented that, in the interest of civil-military relations, the army banned the practice. Thereafter soldiers in American cities huckstered food they bought from farmers in the locality, lumber they summarily appropriated from fences, barns, wharves, or ornamental trees, and in some cases even their own weapons.[16]

Various payments in kind, such as free quarters, subsidized clothing, and free rum also added to the soldier's total income but probably did not markedly improve his economic condition relative to civilian workers, since payment in kind was fairly common; it was, for example, customary in agriculture and coal mining for the employer to provide his workers with free or low-rent cottages, and beer and ale were distributed to all coal workers and to field workers at harvest time.[17]

During the eighteenth century, social and cultural backwardness kept all working people on the hard edge of poverty. Wages were deliberately held down under the prevalent assumption "that the lower classes must be kept poor or they will never be industrious."[18] A similar premise that "poverty will agree better with subordination than wealth" kept the soldier's per diem stable at eight pence for a century and a quarter.[19] To compound the problems of the working poor, the shrinkage by inflation of already inadequate government income made it impossible for most of the great powers to meet their fiscal obligations on a regular basis; armies suffered the worst effects, with wages frequently six months to a year in arrears.[20] Delays in payment did not necessarily mean outright loss to the troops, of course, since cumulative wages were eventually paid in a large lump sum. Although no one starved in the meantime, most soldiers had no cash either for necessities or for the small comforts that made life sufferable.

If the present was capricious, the future was precarious. Although none of the great powers had a legal obligation to provide economic security for aged and disabled veterans, most were slowly beginning to recognize a moral obligation to do so. By the eighteenth century tentative steps toward establishing a policy of social security for veterans had been taken by several countries. In the late seventeenth century, France and then Germany began to offer old age and invalidism benefits to veterans.[21] The first rude form of relief for disabled soldiers appeared in England during the reign of Elizabeth I and was continued in subsequent reigns. Annual pensions, of an amount determined at the discretion of county officials but limited to £10 for privates, were paid out on a weekly basis to those who qualified by reason of war-related disabilities. The pension was not then regarded as the defined right of a disabled soldier, and all benefits stopped when his connection with the service ceased, no matter what the rea-

son.[22] Indeed, the consequence of being found unfit to serve was
often to be cast off as a privileged beggar, licensed by the state
to ask for charity from the point of one's discharge until one
reached home or a place of legal settlement.[23] It was only in 1806,
in Wyndham's Act, that permanent government support was finally accorded as the soldier's right.[24] The act was, however, subsequently amended to make disability rather than length of
service the major criterion for a state stipend. The pension list
burgeoned, augmented in many cases by simulated disabilities,
self-inflicted injuries, or falsified records. An investigation by
a special pension board finally produced significant changes in
pensioning procedures. A new Pension Warrant based veterans' benefits upon length of service, wounds received in action,
and condition of health determined by a medical examination.
Among the liberal features of the Pension Warrant of 1833 was a
small increase in the daily rate of pension.[25]

The establishment of eleemosynary institutions to care for
veterans until they died was another significant step in the evolution of a policy of social security. The founding of the Maison des
Invalides by France in 1671[26] was followed in England by the
institution of the Kilmainham Hospital near Dublin in 1684 and
the Royal Hospital at Chelsea in 1690. The broken and infirm
veterans of the Restoration struggles were the first pensioners of
these state asylums.[27] Only a small minority of veterans were actually cared for in such institutions, even though privates were
required to contribute twelve pence per pound from their salary
toward the support of the Royal Hospital. Most of the in-pen-
sioners were over forty-five years old, although a few were in
their early thirties. The majority had long service records, extending in some cases up to thirty years. Although most had
legitimate war-related disabilities, some were obviously admitted
at the intercession of powerful patrons, even though in a few
cases there is no indication that they had served a single day in
the army.[28]

As the number of claims to admission increased far beyond
the capacity of the institutions to support them, a system of out-
pensions emerged; veterans whose disability was certified by the
Surgeon General and the commander in chief were awarded pensions in lieu of admission. In 1694 there were 127 out-pension-
ers from the rank and file.[29] Although Americans from provincial regiments like the Queen's Rangers applied for the royal
bounty during the Revolution, they were denied permanent state
support.[30]

The establishment of companies of invalids was another way
in which eighteenth-century powers gave grudging recognition to
the soldier's economic dependence upon the state. Service-worn

veterans of twenty years or more were designated as enrolled
pensioners; those who had the physical competence were assigned to garrisons such as Windsor, Hampton Court, and Chelsea. In America, British regulars certified as unfit for field service
by their regimental surgeons were organized into independent
companies of invalids, commanded by half-pay officers, and assigned to garrison duty.[31] State support for them consisted of a
biennial issue of clothing and a small stipend of five pence a day.[32]
In January 1786 the whole number of forces on the British establishment was 17,638, including 2,030 invalids.[33] Three years later
the number of forces held steady at 17,448, but the number of
invalids was down to 1,620, reduced presumably by death.[34]

The principle of the right to relief, still in gestation for soldiers, was not even conceived of for their dependents. Except for
a begging certificate allowed wives not permitted to embark with
their husbands on foreign duty,[35] women and children had no
legal claim on the state for support. Those who were permitted to
accompany their husbands on duty were ordinarily allowed a half
ration, plus a quarter ration per child from government stores.[36]
Although provisions were made for officers' survivors, the family
of a soldier who died or became an invalid was not entitled to any
benefits whatever.[37] If he was killed on active duty the most a wife
could then expect was wage arrears or a small "donation" from
the government or private charity and return passage to England.
In order to collect even that from the government, the family had
to plead destitution.[38] Those found to be "proper objects of charity" were placed on the Compassionate List and were awarded a
sum usually ranging from £4 to £10.[39]
Army orphans were particularly pitiful. Although some were
taken in and cared for by foster parents in the army, large numbers were simply abandoned. If both parents died on foreign
service or if the children were of Scottish or Irish descent, they
were ineligible even for parish aid and were thus left with no
place to go but into the vast and helpless ranks of the casual
poor.[40] In 1779 a small orphanage was set up in New York City,
under the direction of Lieutenant William Browne of the 60th
Regiment, to care for children orphaned by the Revolution. Because it was entirely dependent upon charitable contributions for
support, it accepted only a small number of children, all of them
bereft of both parents. Motherless children were not eligible for
the army orphanage, which meant that those without friends or
benefactors in the service were left alone in the event the father's
regiment was called to duty.[41] There were probably hundreds of
children abandoned at the end of the war. As the last British
troops were being withdrawn from America, thirteen army or-

phans were discovered in the poor house in New York; rather than leave them alone and destitute, Commander-in-chief Carleton ordered them sent to Halifax to be bound as apprentices to a Reverend Mr. Breynton.[42]

Not until well into the nineteenth century did the state finally establish a system of family allowances in the army.[43] Until then the fate of widows and orphans was largely at the mercy of private charity. In the early years of the American Revolution, public support for the war inspired a number of philanthropic actions on their behalf. The popular tract by Jonas Hanway, *The Soldier's Faithful Friend*, which went through at least three editions, was printed to benefit the widows and orphans of soldiers killed in America. Committees were formed in London and in Bristol to collect and disburse money.[44] In the first years of the war a number of charitable organizations in several English cities raised funds for the relief of needy army families: the "people of England" donated a pair of shoes and stockings and some tobacco and cheese to every soldier who had served in the Boston campaign of 1776; women whose husbands were killed in military operations then received a pair of shoes and stockings for themselves and for each of their children "as some recompense for their suffering."[45] In February 1776 a donation of goods sent by "friends in Bristol" arrived on the *Renown*.[46] The Committee for the Relief of the Soldiers, Their Widows and Orphans sent a substantial cash donation in May 1776, followed by two shipments of goods, one in the spring, another in the fall of 1777.[47] A group of London merchants raised money to award a ten-dollar bounty to soldiers or sailors wounded in service in America and a five-pound bounty to widows of soldiers killed there.[48]

As public enthusiasm for the war waned, however, donations fell off. The grotesque nature of existence of the army poor thereafter became primarily a matter for internal relief. Sporadic efforts helped little or not at all. In 1777 proceeds from the sale of hides and tallow from oxen slaughtered to subsist the troops in Canada were sold and the proceeds distributed to needy families.[49] During the winter of 1778 the Barrack Master General ordered that damaged blankets be distributed among refugees and soldiers' wives and children.[50] Occasionally officers sponsored events, such as the benefit plays staged in New York and Philadelphia during the Revolution, and donated the profits to army families.[51] Although Theatre Royal in New York was the most successful of such efforts, after two years of almost weekly performances the enterprise paid only about £300 to the army poor.[52] Burdened by the knowledge that death or disability would rob their families of all means of support, some noncommissioned officers and privates organized their own benefit societies to provide for their survivors. Each society set up a fund into which every subscriber made regular payments; in the event of his death a member's accumulated savings were paid to his widow if she could furnish proof of widowhood.[53]

The insecurity of the present and bleak prospects for the future made marriage very difficult for the professional soldier. Indeed, the hand-to-mouth existence that was normal for most working people disposed even the civilian population to marry late in life; a high percentage of Western Europeans never married at all.[54] A single soldiery was typical for Europe in the eighteenth century. Although the mercenaries of the seventeenth century had been free to arrange legal or common-law marriages, the steady increase in the size of armies, with potentially tens of thousands of additional dependents requiring some public support, influenced European governments to develop policies restricting the soldiers' right to marry.[55]

The British army deliberately recruited unmarried men. While there were no legal restraints on marriage after enlistment, for prudent and expedient reasons the army discouraged it. The extra cost and inconvenience to the public of feeding and housing entire families, together with the prevalent assumption that the common soldier's predilection for "women of abandoned characters and behavior" would undermine morals and discipline, led to the adoption in the late seventeenth century of a rule forbidding a soldier to marry without the approval of his captain. At the time of the great demobilization of 1697, all married men were summarily discharged.[56] Although married men were later accepted, commanding officers continued to exercise oversight responsibilities to keep their numbers at a minimum. Only if the woman seemed to be of sound moral character and to be industrious and able to earn her bread should permission be granted; if not it should be denied. It was, of course, still legally possible for the couple to marry, but it was highly unfeasible for them to do so, since the soldier faced possible disciplinary action for disobedience of orders and the couple could be refused permission to live together. On occasion, military authorities arranged with local ministers to refuse to perform a ceremony which was not officially sanctioned.[57]

Since "honest, industrious Women were rather useful in a Company," the army did permit the marriage of a limited number of noncommissioned officers and privates by making provisions for their families on the basis of six women per company. Even for these, however, marriage was a blind bargain. Only a few couples were privileged to live in private huts;[58] the rest, like the family of the celebrated eighteenth-century novelist Laurence

Sterne, were forced to share communal life in the barracks.[59] Moreover, army rules and regulations often discriminated against the married couples; if, for example, a soldier was admitted as a patient to the hospital where his wife worked as a nurse, she could be dismissed or have her pay suspended.[60] Women with children were not allowed to work as nurses in military hospitals.[61] Although medical care was legally guaranteed to every soldier, regimental surgeons were under no obligation "save that of charity" to treat any member of his family. As a consequence, sick women and children were often left to their own resources, moving one regimental surgeon to observe that "the misery of a soldier's sick family exceeds all others."[62]

The military family, like most contemporary families from comparable strata of society, was small. Until the beginning of the twentieth century the mean household size in England remained more or less stable at under five persons, although family size varied both regionally and according to social status. Generally speaking, laborers and paupers had the fewest children, followed by tradesmen and craftsmen, and it was from these last groups that the army was formed.[63] Since the state did not begin to require the keeping of regimental registers until 1824,[64] it is impossible to ascertain precisely the average size of army families. A regular diet of salt rations and a high level of venereal disease conceivably reduced fertility among soldiers and held the birth rate down. In time of peace in Britain there were approximately eight children born in each company annually, or an average of only about fifty births per regiment each year.[65] As a rule during war the birth rate drops sharply, which may or may not have been the case during the American Revolution. All the statistics reveal is that there were roughly 12,000 children with the army in America and an average troop strength of 39,196.[66] In any case, because of the extreme poverty of many families, the brutality of life during war, regular exposure to the elements, and the increased risk factors caused by communal living in army barracks, infant mortality was higher in army families than in other segments of English society.[67] The deaths of four of the six Sterne children, all below the age of four, in Irish barracks, were unexceptional for the times and for the occupation.[68]

Discouraged by the state and seeing at what level of privation and humiliation most army families lived, the majority of soldiers remained single. A contemporary estimate put the ratio of single to married men at roughly five out of six.[69] Except for the Hessians in America, who were welcomed with extraordinary warmth in German-American communities in Pennsylvania and Virginia, soldiers lived in near total isolation from society. Treated with contempt or looked upon with fear, they had few opportunities to meet agreeable marriage partners from the settled community. As a result their sexual lives were extremely precarious—a condition which constantly threatened the marital integrity of army households.

Although there are few explicit references to sexual misconduct in surviving documents, these indicate widespread extramarital activity. Communal living arrangements encouraged if not promoted promiscuity; because of limited space on transports two or three couples were assigned to the same bed, although "to prevent misbehavior as much as possible, every three pairs were separated." [70] For the sake of convenience, space in barracks and tents was measured out in similar fashion. Although monogamy was probably still the ideal of behavior for the soldier as it was for the English people in general, there were apparently frequent departures from the norm—particularly at popular fêtes, such as the German celebration of Johannes Tag, or St. John's Day. Intoxicated revelers treated observers to "many very strange occurrences," not the least of which was "what promiscuous exchanges were made with their wives," as one shocked witness put it. [71] Young female children who lived in this kind of atmosphere were particularly vulnerable to sexual advances. Because of the nature of the crime, most cases of sexual abuse of children were probably unreported, but military court records show that rape of army children was a not uncommon occurrence. [72] In the majority of reported cases, the child victim also contracted venereal disease and the family was eventually forced to seek medical help; in that way the crime came to the attention of military authorities.

No matter how extensive adulterous behavior was, the number of promiscuous wives was nonetheless limited, and most soldiers formed liaisons with women from the superfluous ranks of society. Women from the growing body of the useless poor attached themselves to the army and lived off its hospitality. Since only legally married women were permitted to board military transports, [73] a substantial percentage of the five thousand camp followers who traveled with the British army in America were just such wayside accretions. [74] Many of them were the unfortunate daughters of humble families who lacked the money and the means to survive independently. In exchange for government rations they did useful work for the regiments, cooking, cleaning, caring for the sick and wounded. Quite a few of them came from local brothels, such as the "holy ground," in New York City, so named because it occupied the property of St. Paul's Church, or Canvas Town, the area between Great Dock and Water streets, where drunks, runaway slaves, derelicts of every description, and countless prostitutes maintained a bitter existence in the skeletal remains of burned-out buildings. The most engaging women were soon appropriated by officers—many of whom "lived openly with their whores." A few "kept mistresses" appeared in the plays staged by officers in New York, Philadelphia, and elsewhere.[75]

The majority did not make it into the elevated ranks of the *demimondaines*, however, but had to content themselves with the company of common soldiers; they became, in the euphemism of the day, "artillery wives." Spurious unions such as these in fact vitiated the whole purpose of a single soldiery. They reduced the numbers of legitimate dependents, but produced broods of bastard children for whom neither the state nor anyone else assumed responsibility. The high infant mortality rate in the army was in many cases directly related to "the want of care in the men" and "the profligacy and debaucheries of the women."[76] The illicit unions diffused the biological impetus for marriage and at the same time wreaked havoc with traditional familial attitudes; after having "married" sixteen "loose women of the town" by persuading a chaplain from a different regiment to perform each ceremony, a sergeant from the 38th Regiment of Foot admitted an ambition to improve his record many times over "before making up his mind to take the last one in earnest."[77]

In the witty Restoration comedy, *The Recruiting Officer*, George Farquhar, in dramatizing his own experiences as a recruiting officer in the time of Queen Anne, confirmed the practice common among soldiers of marrying frequently and fraudulently. Urged by Captain Plume to marry a woman who had just given birth to a child, Sergeant Kite protested, "I'm married already." Asked by Plume "To how many?" Kite replies, "I can't tell readily. I have set them down here upon the back of the muster roll. Let me see. Mrs. Sheely Snicker-eyes; she sells potatoes upon Ormond-Key in Dublin; Peggy Guzzle, the brandy woman at the Horse-Guard at Whitehall; Dolly Waggon, the carrier's daughter in Hull; Mademoiselle Van-Bottomflat at the Buss. Then Jenny Oakham the ship-carpenter's widow at Portsmouth, but I don't reckon upon her, for she was married at the same time to two lieutenants of marines and a man of war's boatswain."[78]

Such cynicism was probably not typical, but a high degree of skepticism about the merits of monogamy was bound to follow as a consequence of the army's restrictive policies toward marriage. Casual and indiscriminate sexual practices, moreover, demoralized the troops and undermined discipline. Numbers of camp followers drifted from regiment to regiment, giving "promiscuous embraces without any fidelity to the man with whom they lodge, and leave him as their fickleness prompts, or their conveniency serves. They encourage rioting and drunkenness . . . theft and other villanies . . . and an unclean disease."[79]

The extraordinary incidence of venereal disease in fact temporarily but regularly incapacitated large numbers of men.

Poor, alone, beset by sexual difficulties, his existence a game of chance—in retrospect the eighteenth-century soldier's life seems bare and desolate, but it should be recalled that most of the lower-middle and lower classes of the world shared the same wretched conditions. Work and the destructive amusements that passed for recreation filled their waking hours. In part this was the result of contemporary social attitudes. The emphasis on social distinctions which characterized eighteenth-century England carried over into leisure activities. Some recreational forms were gradually opening up to middle-class participation, but by and large recreational and cultural pursuits remained the preserve of the upper classes, who alone could afford their cost.[80] There was, moreover a deep residuum of ignorance as to the social value of recreation and a rather firmly held belief among the upper classes that recreation produced undesirable effects on the health, industry, and frugality of working people. These precepts of traditional social theory were bequeathed intact to the military.

Drunkenness was an accepted mode of relaxation for all classes in the eighteenth century; indeed it was for most people the basic form of recreation. The social conditions of working people—long hours, low income, job insecurity—together with the rituals of daily life habituated them to drinking as the basic medium of social intercourse. Public houses offered the only place of recreation available to workers. For many trades they served as employment agencies; wages were frequently paid in alehouses on Saturday nights, and workers in many occupations were partially compensated in alcohol.[81] The army perpetuated these social customs and adhered at the same time to the popular belief that persons engaged in physical labor functioned better with generous amounts of spirits. Because of its medicinal properties and its alleged regenerative powers and because soldiers had come to regard a daily ration as their right, beginning in 1777, rum was issued daily, at the rate of a quart for each six men, to entire garrisons as part of the regular ration.[82] Over and above that, working parties were usually allowed a half pint a day; in cold or damp weather, guards were sometimes issued an extra quarter pint.[83] Through authorized allotments such as these, the army in America consumed more than 360,000 gallons of rum a year, which represented the single largest item of expense among government provisions.[84]

In addition to the regular allotment, soldiers were able to buy intoxicants from regimental canteens operated by licensed sutlers who set up shop in regimental quarters,[85] or surreptitiously from camp followers who concocted their own poisonous swill and sold it from stalls located out of the line of camp or beyond the limits of military jurisdiction.[86] Many soldiers, accustomed to beginning each day with a strong tot of rum, became heavy drinkers. Some, said a disgusted army officer, were "not contented with pints; those led to quarts, and quarts to gallons; and some swill as much as a hog."[87] Frequent and even daily intoxication had of course severe physiological and psychological effects. Much of the rum consumed by the army was not only highly intoxicating but also toxic.[88] Either the distillation process itself or materials used in the processing caused immediate illness in many cases, and in rare and extreme cases death.[89] Eighteenth-century medicine had not yet linked alcoholism to specific diseases, but chronic excessive drinking presumably precipitated organic damage to the liver in advanced alcoholics; heavy, regular use certainly contributed to nutritional deficiencies, chronic gastritis, and other disturbances of the body.

The effects of intemperance on military efficiency cannot be measured in absolute terms, but they can hardly have been inconsequential, since at even low and moderate blood alcohol levels physiological functions such as sensory perception, reaction time, and motor performance begin to be impaired. Almost every regimental memoir refers to the inability of soldiers to perform routine military tasks, such as parade exercises and guard or sentry duty, because of intoxication. Drunkenness was a major factor in the failure of soldiers to report for duty; according to the testimony offered in military courts it was one of the most important causes of desertion.[90] The rum distributed to help soldiers bear the fatigues of campaigning instead reduced operational efficiency. On the march, as one army physician observed, "the men are constantly seen mixing their rations of rum with the drinking water." A march of the 52d Regiment in 1778 described by Lieutenant Colonel Christopher French suggests the consequences. To overcome fatigue or fear excited by the prospect of battle, or perhaps simply from habit, the soldiers began to drink soon after the regiment moved out at a quarter of six in the morning. The warm May weather combined with too much alcohol "occasion'd the men to fall back terribly," French wrote. A quarrel broke out which quickly erupted into a fight with fixed bayonets, leaving one soldier dead.[91]

The rising scale of behavior problems alarmed military authorities in America, and steps were taken to curb excessive drinking. In Boston, Philadelphia, New York, and Providence, unlicensed dram shops were raided, their stock seized and de-

stroyed. Retailers, most of them army retainers, were arrested
and confined aboard military vessels in the harbors. Curfews
were established, officers were ordered to sleep with their men in
the barracks, and the number of evening patrols was stepped up.
As a last resort, local distilleries were temporarily closed.[92] Although there was still widespread belief in the medicinal effects
of rum, there was at the same time a growing awareness, particularly among physicians, of the need to control its promiscuous
use. In 1777 Dr. Benjamin Rush, Physician General to the Continental Army, published a pamphlet entitled *Directions for Preserving the Health of Soldiers*, in which he argued that drinking
alcoholic beverages aggravated fevers, jaundice, and other diseases.[93] Other army physicians began to warn of the harmful
effects of overindulgence.[94] Although these early published reports stimulated debate on the subject, no permanent restrictions
on liquor rations were adopted until late in the nineteenth century. In a series of articles and books calling for numerous army
reforms, Henry Marshall, a senior army medical officer, successfully challenged the traditional assumptions about the wholesome
qualities of liquor. Impressed by Marshall's arguments against the
venerable practice, Parliament adopted measures giving division-
al commanders discretionary authority to limit the issue of alcohol.[95] Even afterward, drinking remained a perennial problem.

If drinking served as an escape from the physical ordeals of
life for many people in the eighteenth century, gambling was
their addiction. Despite laws against cockfighting and bullbaiting
and a strict licensing policy, gambling was a conventional form of
recreation in contemporary England. In 1778 it was institu-
tionalized when the State Lottery became a regular method of
raising revenues. On the wheels at Guildhall and in the numerous
private lotteries rode the dreams of countless carpenters and bar-
bers, grinders and gunsmiths, hatters and jewelers, braziers,
butchers, maidservants, and wives of industrious journeymen.[96]
This too was part of the soldier's social inheritance.

A passion for gambling permeated all ranks of the army as it
did all classes of English society. In nightly sessions of faro and
other forms of "high gaming," fortunes were made and lost by
officers; the gambling clubs formed in Boston, New York, and
Philadelphia played for such high stakes that some officers were
forced to sell their commissions to settle their losses. In an effort
to shame the Boston group, General Thomas Gage organized an
Anti-Gambling Club, and placed a limit on wagers.[97] With the
hypocrisy characteristic of the upper classes, General William
Howe ignored his own well-publicized affinity for gambling and
its preponderance in the officer corps and deplored it as a social

evil among the men in the ranks; "such Instances of idleness and depravity," he sternly warned, "are always and particularly at this time to be prevented and suppressed." [98]

But testimony before a committee of the House of Commons revealed that gambling debts provided an impetus for "the scandalous heights to which plundering was arrived at in the army." [99] In the march through the Jersies, "Many of us received a great deal of booty," confessed the Hessian Adjutant General Major Carl Leopold Baurmeister to his landgrave: "then the passion for gambling inherent in the British offered an opportunity to gain money. Nonetheless, it cannot be denied but that few of the Hessians are without debts, and considerable ones." [100] Duels over gambling were common, especially among the Germans, who fought savage contests in which the duelists, stripped to the waist, slashed and cut at one another with knives until blood was drawn and honor assuaged. [101]

Drinking and gambling in the army served to relieve the soldiers' perennial boredom. As in civilian life, they facilitated the forgetting of self and the release, perhaps, of impulses to self-assertion and aggression. For another seventy-five years they continued to be the principal if not the only social outlets for enlisted men. In the interim before the great advances of the Age of Reform, only a few isolated and groping efforts were made to introduce new forms of socialization. Most of them were the work of compassionate or self-interested officers or of a few progressive regiments.

As was the case in all eighteenth-century armies, the British officer corps was dominated by the upper ranks of society. The laws of primogeniture, which cut younger sons off from inherited property, forced many young aristocrats to earn a living in government service, business, or the professions. The sale of army commissions, the cost of which varied according to rank from the elite corps to the infantry, also gave a clear advantage to those with means. As the century progressed, more sons of middle-class families secured commissions as ensigns, lieutenants, captains, and majors. But widespread use of patronage and political connections guaranteed the preeminence of aristocrats from the rank of colonel up. [102] Urbane, sophisticated, and desperate for entertainment in provincial America, they tried to reproduce the cultural life their social peers enjoyed in Europe's urban centers. Small groups of enlisted men participated, at least in a peripheral way, in most of their undertakings.

Because they were accustomed to art and concert music and to compensate for the limited cultural offerings in America, groups of British officers organized their own concert series. During the brief occupation of Boston they staged several concerts.[103] From the occupation of New York in September 1776 until its evacuation in 1783, army and navy officers held regular concerts and even established a subscription series. The performers were amateur musicians drawn from the officer corps and from the ranks of the army and navy, probably from the military bands.[104]

Simultaneously, with the construction of defense works, British officers organized *corps dramatiques* in virtually every occupied American city. On December 2, 1775, the military theatre opened in Faneuil Hall in Boston with *Zara*, the prologue for which was written by General John Burgoyne. A subsequent performance of a farce written by Burgoyne called *The Blockade of Boston* was ironically interrupted by an American bombardment of the city just as the curtain was drawn.[105] From that inauspicious beginning the military theatre grew and spread, reaching its zenith in New York. In January 1777 the *New York Gazette and Weekly Mercury* announced the opening of the Theatre Royal for the "charitable purpose of relieving the Widows and Orphans of Sailors and Soldiers who have fallen in support of the Constitutional Rights of Great-Britain in America." The theatre, managed by Dr. Hamond Beaumont, Surgeon General of the army, was housed in an unsightly red wooden building located directly on Broadway.[106]

Five days after the British began the occupation of Philadelphia, they began offering performances at the Southwark Theatre on an almost weekly basis, except during Passion Week, when all entertainments were suspended in deference to the religious feeling of the Quaker community.[107] A small theatre established by "Gentlemen of the Garrison" sprouted briefly from September to November 1781 in Savannah. Even the little post at St. Augustine had its own company of military players.[108] A company of English prisoners of war taken with Burgoyne at Saratoga built a "Comedy House" in Staunton, Virginia, and acted some "very fair plays" there on a biweekly basis.[109]

Despite the exigencies of war, the British theatre functioned more or less like a repertory company, preparing a number of plays and producing them alternately. The repertoire of the players included English standards familiar to American audiences. Except for George Farquhar's *Beaux Strategem* and *The Constant Couple*, the low comedy of the Restoration period was avoided in favor of the Shakespearian plays then in vogue in London. *King Richard III*, *Othello*, *Macbeth*, *Henry IV*, and *The Taming of the Shrew* were performed in the New York theatre, though in adulterated and abbreviated form.[110] Several tragedies popular with London audiences, such as Nicholas Rowe's *The Fair Penitent* and the more recent *Douglas* by John Home were offered in America. But comedy dominated the military stage. Henry Fielding's *Tom Thumb*, which broke records for long runs in London, Susanna Cent-livre's *The Wonder: A Woman Keeps a Secret*, which kept the English stage for over a century, and other proven audience pleasers, such as Richard Cumberland's *The West Indian* and Richard Brinsley Sheridan's elegant comedy *The Rivals*, were the usual bill of fare.[111] In addition to the conventional works, the prisoners who organized the Staunton theatre offered improvisatory pieces, most of which were apparently political satires aimed at Americans, who consequently boycotted the theatre. The efforts at playwriting were also a response to the boredom of confinement and represented, as one amused officer noted, "the soldier's desire to show that he can laugh at everything and in himself can find means to make life endurable and comfortable." The soldiers themselves made the point rather emphatically: on the drop curtain they painted a harlequin, his wooden saber pointing to the words "Who would have expected all this here?"[112]

Although leading parts were almost always played by officers, enlisted men made up the supporting casts of most productions. The actors played both male and female roles; wigged and robed in women's clothing, young drummers "were transformed into queen's and beauties"[113]—which is perhaps what inspired Ensign Thomas Hughes's captious remark that New York plays were "vilely enacted."[114] Soldiers also took minor parts in the afterpiece, usually a short dramatic work such as Fielding's *The Mock Doctor*, which was performed after the major piece. Between acts, singers, dancers, or musicians from the military bands entertained the audience with musical selections, such as songs or "catches" and instrumental music.[115]

Although admirable in conception, the best that can be said for the military theatre in practice is that it bridged the cultural hiatus in America caused by the war.[116] It did little to relieve the distress of widows and orphans, and though it briefly provided an alternate form of recreation, it reached only a handful of soldiers whose talents or abilities singled them out for special treatment. A more disinterested effort to ameliorate the hard conditions of army life was the institution of regimental schooling. Although eighteenth-century England enjoyed an adult male literacy rate of about 60 percent,[117] the rate of illiteracy of soldiers was comparatively high. Presuming the literacy of individuals able to sign their names and conversely the illiteracy of markers, extant records show an average literacy level of less than 35 percent in the army. The estimate is based on a deposition list and on the payroll books of two regiments, the 84th Regiment of Foot and the 71st Regiment of Foot.[118] The fact that both regiments were Scottish does prejudice the results. Moreover, because literacy was still linked to occupation and wealth, a high proportion of farmers, laborers, or workers employed in the spinning and weaving trades—groups generally inferior in literacy—would have a substantial negative effect on the overall average.[119] Inasmuch as the army recruited heavily from these groups, it is highly probable that that fact is reflected in the average.

Since noncommissioned officers were expected to be able to read and write in order to carry out various clerical functions, and since many of them rose from the ranks, the army was slowly beginning to recognize the utilitarian value of education.[120] A few schools were created by regiments, some time before the Revolution. There was one functioning in a corps of Scotch Highlanders, for example, and Chudleigh's Regiment of Foot must have had one as well, since Laurence Sterne recalled in his memoirs that he learned to write in the Dublin barracks.[121] Little is known about the organization of these first schools, but they were apparently supported by voluntary contributions from officers and were conducted by regimental chaplains or literate veterans.[122] At best they were no more than grammar schools, giving elementary instruction in reading, writing, and arithmetic.

While they did not succeed in eliminating illiteracy, these early schools were significant for the future to the extent that they helped to focus interest on the need for providing soldiers with the essentials of learning. During the Revolutionary era a few service manuals began to urge the necessity of education for soldiers. Lamenting the fact that soldiering was popularly censured "as an idle profession, that requires little intellectual ability and less application . . . the sure retreat of ignorance and indolence," Lewis Lochée, master of the military academy at Little Chelsea, advocated the establishment of garrison libraries, or at least "that every regiment [be] furnished with a small collection of the best books as part of its common baggage."[123] Although Lochée did not explain how illiterate soldiers might read the classics, other military writers encouraged the foundation of more regimental schools. Moved by the poverty and lack of opportunities for social improvement for military families, they called for the training of army children, "who from the poverty of their parents must ever remain in the state of ignorance."[124] Nothing came of these early plans, however. Although the tradition of army education had been planted, official indifference and public apathy hampered its development. In the years before the Age of Reform only a few regiments established adult schools. Under the auspices of the Duke of York, army schools were authorized during the Napoleonic Wars, only to be discontinued in the 1820s as an economy measure. Twenty years later Henry Marshall revived the idea. Pleading the cause of the common

soldier in an important book entitled *Military Miscellany*, Marshall
called for the creation of regimental schools as a means of im-
proving the social condition of the soldier and his family. Perhaps
as a result of his work, or as part of the general climate of reform, beginning in 1846 a series of reforms for the enlisted man
were enacted, including the creation of a Corps of Army School-
masters and a system of regimental libraries.[125]

At the time of the American Revolution, however, those improvements were in the distant future. For nearly three-quarters
of a century longer, social conditions in the army did not improve
substantially. Ill-fed, ill-housed, poorly paid, uneducated, bored,
diseased, depressed, the vast majority of common soldiers continued to live poverty-stricken lives with their wives or whores
and their crying children. Some officers recognized their misery;
those with a sense of social responsibility pitied them and tried to
help. What they did or tried to do was not much; it was certainly
not enough; but it was something.

4 CRIMES AND COURTS

THE ARMY WAS a new social environment which detached men from their homes and families and loosed them from the social controls which had formerly regulated their behavior. It thrust them instead into almost completely masculine surroundings, where a different set of values predominated. Freedom from civilian society's taboos and controls and the encouragement of powerful group sanctions for certain types of behavior such as gambling, drinking, sexual promiscuity, and looting brought out primitive aspects of personality in soldiers and stimulated the development of behavior patterns which tend to have a peculiar association with the military life. In an effort to control the worst excesses, the army leaned heavily on a system of punishment, coercion, rewards, and incentives.

In the contemporary mind and in the view of recent scholarship, soldiers in earlier times came from the scrap heaps of society. The need to rely very heavily on records of criminal activity to discern the character of the common soldier has tended to weight the balance conspicuously on the side of criminality. The most comprehensive source of information dealing with the conduct of the army is the records of the Judge Advocate General, which comprehend only serious violations of the law and so emphasize deviant behavior. The men of Britain's army were not uniformly decent; there was a criminal element in the army, but it was not an army of criminals. Moreover, the delinquent tendencies apparent in army behavior were typical not only of armies of the times but of armies of all times. The soldiers' aggressiveness was largely due to environmental influences arising both from the general culture and from the army subculture.

There were, and indeed still are, elements in army life that are conducive to certain types of behavior. Drinking, for example, was culturally sanctioned in the eighteenth-century army, where it served to relieve boredom and to release tensions and aggressive impulses. Gambling, which was widespread in the army as it was in civilian life, prevailed primarily because no other kind of recreation was so readily available. Moreover, because most of their physical needs were provided by the institution, soldiers probably did not value money in quite the same way as did civilians. Certain crimes, such as desertion, were clearly motivated by the desire to escape the constraints imposed by military life and discipline, or to escape from a difficult and dangerous situation such as an enemy prison.

Until the mid-nineteenth century, desertion was a major disciplinary problem for most European armies.[1] In most wars, including the American Revolution, there was a considerable amount of movement between belligerent armies. Official British figures show a total of 3,701 desertions in North America and the West Indies,[2] but if one takes into account pardons which lured deserters back, the total should certainly be much higher. Even then, however, given the number of British troops who served in North America, desertion was apparently not a significant problem. From an estimated 60,000 in 1776, British troop strength in North America, the West Indies, and Florida reached a peak of 92,000 in 1780–1781. In 1782, it declined to 82,000 and by 1783, it was down to 70,000.[3] Considering the inducements and the opportunities to desert, the actual number of desertions seems an insignificant portion of the whole.

Since desertion was a capital crime, the majority of those retaken were tried by general courts martial—which alone among military courts were legally empowered to order the death penalty. Eighteenth-century records kept by general courts reveal that there were several kinds of deserters. A significant number were habitual deserters, men who deserted not only from one army to another, but frequently from one regiment to another, presumably to collect the bounty money offered to new recruits.[4] Many of those who deserted, however, had specific grievances. A great number ran away to avoid punishment or because they had already been severely punished or abused, usually by a noncommissioned officer.[5] Many left because of personal problems, such as bad health or family difficulties; some were disturbed, others were drunk.[6] A large category of deserters was made up of very young soldiers, most of them new recruits, or of veterans with good service records and no history of previous offenses.[7] For one reason or another—despair, boredom, adventure—they left the chronic misery of army life and tried to escape to something better or at least different.

Almost half of all deserters in the American Revolution (as probably in most eighteenth-century wars) ran away from specific situations where conditions were unbearable or life was at stake. Nine hundred and nineteen men deserted from West Indian posts. The severity of the climate, the remoteness of the islands from the main supply routes, and a predictably high disease level produced the highest fatality rates in the hemisphere and gave the Indies a reputation as the graveyard of European soldiers. Rather than waste its best troops there, the War Office sent the worst; most of the men forced into the army by the press were dispatched to tropical duty.[8] Destined for death in a hostile environment, they deserted at the first opportunity.

Eight hundred and ninety-four of the men classed as deserters were actually prisoners of war taken with Burgoyne's Convention Army at the Battle of Saratoga. During most of their confinement, conditions were intolerable. In the winter barracks at Cambridge thirty to forty men were crowded together in tiny huts without foundations. Wearing the same threadbare uniforms issued three years earlier, without blankets or bedding, on short fuel allowance because of the scarcity of wood, they survived the winter by burning the rafters.[9]

Hoping to encourage desertions, the American Congress ordered the prisoners moved south to points in Virginia, Maryland, and Pennsylvania. Once again they were confined in overcrowded, unplastered log cabins; termites ate through the rafters and beams, rats gnawed the bedding and uniforms. Half-naked and half-starved, separated from their officers in violation of the capitulation terms, the men of the Convention Army deserted "rather than endure such distress."[10] In keeping with contemporary military practices, several hundred of the captives were released to live and work in nearby communities on condition that they not fight again. Finding a change for the better, a large number of them settled permanently in America.[11] Many of them, not caring on which side they fought, joined American regiments.[12] Not all of those who switched sides switched loyalties, however. At least 250 of the British soldiers who left their regiments did so as a means of escaping prison and as a way of returning sooner to British service. Called by Burgoyne "honorable deserters," they abandoned the new service at the first opportunity, escaped to New York, and rejoined Clinton's forces there.[13]

During the era of the American Revolution, and indeed through much of the eighteenth century, mutiny as an organized, collective action was rare. Only a scattering of obviously organized incidents involving numbers of men occurred. Like desertion, however, they reflected the unsatisfactory conditions of military service. The pay mutiny, the soldier's counterpart of a strike for unpaid wages, was the most common. In the beginning of the century, during Queen Anne's War on the continent, pay mutinies had occurred with almost rhythmic regularity.[14] Although the number of incidents declined over the years, the problem of nonpayment of wages continued to precipitate occasional mutinies, threat of mutinies, and numerous cases of individual insubordination. In 1777, five privates from four different regiments serving in America led fifty of their comrades in refusing to obey orders until their claims for clothing and pay arrears were satisfied.[15] In 1778 the 78th Regiment, or Seaforth's Highlanders, mutinied over arrears of pay and bounty money and over rumors that the regiment was being sold to the East India Company.[16] In 1783, the 77th and 83d regiments mutinied at Portsmouth over reports of an impending tour of duty in the East Indies and over high stoppages brought on by "innovations in dress, feathers and fobberies" made by the regimental colonel. The impoverished mutineers refused to return to duty until the officer in question agreed to sell his commission to pay off regimental creditors.[17]

A combination of factors, including delays in pay and provisioning, also contributed materially to the problem of looting. The fact that soldiers were underpaid encouraged them to take what they needed; so too did the thriving black market in American towns, which found civilians willing to pay high prices for scarce items such as fuel. Although looting was officially frowned upon, there were powerful group sanctions for the legal despoiling of the enemy. Traditionally, pillaging the enemy had been regarded as a quasi-legitimate supplement to meager pay. Because it was detrimental to discipline and alienated the civilian population, however, beginning in the sixteenth century belligerent powers had attempted to inhibit the excessive abuse of civilians by adopting articles against killing draft animals and dairy cows. In the seventeenth century the articles were expanded to include arable fields, meadows, and gardens.[18] Despite these efforts to limit and control plundering, throughout the eighteenth century there were periodic reversions to the older, more sinister tradition. During the Seven Years War, for example, French troops indulged in an orgy of looting in Hanover, and as late as the 1790s allied armies invading France pillaged with seventeenth-century abandon.[19]

The logistical inefficiency of Britain contributed to another relapse during the American Revolution. The Treasury Board, which was responsible for the supply of food, clothing, and some equipment, tried both to feed the army from America and to feed it from Britain.[20] Because neither system worked adequately, soldiers often took by force what they needed to survive. The changeover to a wartime morality was apparent immediately following the outbreak of hostilities. During and after the Lexington engagement, soldiers, convinced that pillaging the enemy was a legitimate act of war,[21] looted and destroyed everything they came on. At Lexington they were "so wild and irregular that there was no keeping them in order." After Bunker Hill "they destroyed everything they could come at without scruple."[22]

Fearing the effects of indiscriminate plundering on public support for the Crown, military commanders instituted tight controls. Since most thefts in occupied towns were committed in the evenings, soldiers were confined to their barracks after 8:00 P.M.; public houses were closed at 9:00 P.M., and regular checks were made by the provost guard to apprehend "night adventurers."[23] Most looting, however, occurred during military exercises, when the mobility of the army made absolute control difficult if not impossible. To cut down on the number of incidents, restrictive policies were employed when the army was on the march: officers were ordered to march at the rear of their units and to accompany all foraging parties; on approaching settled areas the army was marched without rest breaks, and guards were posted at private homes along the route. As a final deterrent, the order was given to summarily execute any soldier caught marauding.[24]

Despite these measures, during the New York campaigns in the summer and fall of 1776, on the march, during skirmishes and even battles, soldiers strayed away on looting expeditions. There was wanton destruction of some private and public property, such as the pillaging of Hackensack and Princeton, which left both the college and the church in ruins; but most of the damage done was to crops and to slaughterable animals, products which were directly consumable and therefore had more immediate value to troops who subsisted on a diet of salt and dried rations. In the beginning at least, British regulars participated with enthusiasm in this private war on the countryside; soon, however, disciplinary measures began to take effect, and the number of complaints against British infantrymen tapered off.

The German mercenaries, on the other hand, continued to plunder with the kind of ferocity that usually distinguishes religious or civil wars. Like ancient Huns, "the Hessians destroy[ed] all the fruits of the Earth without regard to Loyalist or Rebel, the property of both being equally a prey to them." With single-minded zeal they "threatened with death all such as dare[d] obstruct them in their depredations."[25] British officers, while deploring the behavior of their own troops, were appalled at the ravages committed by the Hessians: "It is impossible to express the devastation which the Hessians have made upon the houses and country seats of some of the rebels: all their furniture, glasses, windows, and the very hangings of the rooms are demolished or defaced."[26] The sight of the swarthy German, his hair so tightly queued that it stuck out from his head like the handle of a skillet, was said to terrify most Americans: "The dread which the

rebels have of these Hessians is inconceivable: they almost run
away at their name. Indeed they spare nobody, but glean away all
like an army of locusts."[27]

It is difficult to explain the rapacious eagerness with which
the Germans razed the country. Part of the explanation probably
lies in the circumstances under which they came to America.
Many were temporary private mercenaries; although Britain paid
about eight million pounds for their services, they received no
extra compensation for foreign service and so perhaps looked on
plunder as a legitimate perquisite. Others were compulsorily
drafted to satisfy quotas stipulated in the treaties. Many of these
involuntary recruits were arbitrarily arrested and detained under
heavy security until the transports sailed for America.[28] The cruelty of the Germans, so frequently commented upon by British
officers, may well have been a manifestation of the frustration
they experienced at being forcibly separated from their homes
and families. To some extent their destructiveness was encouraged by their officers. Many German officers were openly permis-
sive about plundering. Some "publicly permit[ted] or rather direct[ed] these depredations to be made."[29] The Hessian General
de Heister reputedly put up for public sale the house he had
appropriated from a New York loyalist.[30]

Possibly because German discipline became more rigorous or
because the soldiers' initial hostility was leached out by a deliberate propaganda campaign initiated by the American Congress
and by the sympathetic treatment they received from German-
American communities, reports of Hessian abuse of civilians declined after the New York campaign. Instead there were growing
numbers of complaints of extreme ill-use by camp followers and
blacks. This was especially true in the South.

The mobile nature of the war in the South provided an almost ideal setting for plundering, particularly for the camp followers, who ordinarily walked at the rear of the line of march or
at the head or on the flanks of the baggage train, where supervision was minimal. From those relatively inconspicuous positions a
"swarm of beings—no better than harpies" slipped from the
ranks to "distress and maltreat the inhabitants infinitely more
than the whole army, at the same time they engross, waste
and destroy at the expense of the good soldier, who keeps his
ranks."[31] During the Southern Campaign a distraught Cornwallis
fumed that the women were "the source of the most infamous
plunder." So numerous were the complaints against them that he
was obliged to institute new disciplinary measures to hold them in
line. Company commanders were ordered to have frequent roll
calls at irregular hours to discover absentees; routine inspections
and a running inventory of possessions were made to turn up

stolen property. Unless proof of purchase could be shown, all items unaccounted for were burned in the presence of the assembled company. Still reports of "the most grievous and intolerable irregularities" continued to reach headquarters. Desperate, Cornwallis ordered all women to attend executions and floggings, a spectacle that was apparently enough to starve the thieving impulse in most, because ten days later the order was rescinded.[32]

The thousands of blacks who sought British protection during the Revolution also joined the camp followers in straggling from the ranks to plunder and "use violence to the inhabitants." Commanding officers of regiments were regularly ordered to exercise close discipline, and threats of severe punishment were repeated almost as a matter of course. Finally an order was given to execute on the spot any black taken plundering.[33] The zeal with which blacks plundered their former masters can be explained in terms of a reaction to their previous status as slaves and their new-found freedom. Once secure behind British lines they considered themselves "absolved from all respect to their American masters, and entirely released from servitude."

By and large, however, American blacks did not take full advantage of the opportunities offered by the Revolution to engage in organized rebellion. Although there was no general servile uprising in the British Caribbean, guerrilla bands of runaway slaves joined with British deserters to terrorize whites as they burned and looted plantations on Tobago and St. Kitts.[34] Armed and organized, these insurrectionists and maroons were usually native Africans, or "new Negroes," who had only recently been imported to the New World as slaves. Because they retained cultural cohesiveness and because the nature of the islands' plantation organization allowed them to exercise a measure of control over food, markets, and heritable property, they had the unity and the self-sufficiency to take advantage of the chaos produced by the years of war and revolution. By contrast, the North American plantation organization, with the dominating presence of the master, robbed mainland slaves of their tribal cohesiveness. Without either food or property, in an area torn by ferocious internecine warfare, the vast majority of North American slaves manifested their rebelliousness by defection to the British and by plundering their former masters at every chance.[35]

Undoubtedly much of the looting by all elements in the army was inspired by greed as well as need. The wealth of the country and the lack of adequate controls by the military invited offenses against property. By and large, however, plundering as well as mutiny and desertion were the predictable results of the lack of proper maintenance. When wages were paid, when there was enough food, most soldiers behaved well. When wages were delayed, when the army was not properly fed, when conditions were intolerable, the end was always the same—a precipitous rise in the rates of military crimes.

By contrast there were comparatively few serious crimes against persons committed by soldiers.[36] During the Revolution only a handful of murder cases were brought before general courts martial, which had jurisdiction in all capital cases, and few of these were returned as homicides. In ten out of fifteen cases sampled, a general court decided for acquittal; in one case the accused was pardoned; in two more cases the court found the defendant guilty of the lesser offense of manslaughter; the death penalty was given in only two cases.[37] The most significant fact that emerges from these verdicts is that the officers who comprised all military courts, like their social peers in contemporary England, tolerated and even condoned a high level of personal violence among the rank and file if it was confined largely to the military community; the murder of a civilian, on the other hand, which had potential political repercussions, was usually punished by death.[38]

Because the army lived in a relatively closed community environment, most victims of personal violence were in fact associated with the army—soldiers, their wives, and their children. In over two-thirds of all reported homicides the assailant and the victim were members of the same regiment, a fact which indicates prior acquaintance. Wife-killing composed roughly 20 percent of reported homicides. Other victims were soldiers of other regiments, sailors, and, in strikingly few cases, civilians.

The specific circumstances that motivated most homicides reveal that, like military crimes, violence against persons was largely a function of living conditions in the army. Trial accounts show that adultery and alcoholism were prime contributing causes. For example, William Norrington was acquitted in the stabbing death of another soldier because the deceased was "trying to lay with Norrington's wife." Patrick McGuire killed James McCullough in a fight over McGuire's wife. John Lindon killed his wife when she attempted to leave him for another soldier. Alexander Monroe beat his wife to death because she was drunk. John Whitebread killed a private and Michael Kelly a sergeant; both were pardoned after they pleaded intoxication at the time of their crimes.[39]

Fewer rapes were detected than were committed; even fewer rapists were actually tried and convicted, and only a part of those were ever punished. The embarrassment of a public trial and the dread of community censure led to the suppression of most sexual crimes. In testimony before the House of Commons, General Howe claimed that only one incident occurred under his command;[40] but in a private letter to his uncle, Francis, Lord Rawdon, a young officer with a bright future, observed of the Howe-led operations on Long and Staten islands that "the fresh meat our men have gotten has made them as riotous as satyrs. A girl cannot step into the bushes to pluck a rose without running the most imminent risk of being ravished."[41] Although a committee of the American Congress investigating British conduct of the war concluded that sexual abuse of American women was general and extensive, corroborative evidence is lacking both in official records and in personal accounts.[42]

Although rape was a capital crime, it is of course entirely possible that reported rape cases were tried illegally by regimental courts, which frequently exceeded their jurisdiction. Trial records of general courts martial show that very few rape cases involving American women as victims were reported. Four out of five soldiers convicted of raping American women were in fact members of loyalist regiments: two from Oliver De Lancey's regiment were conducted in irons to the spot where the crime was committed and there were gibbeted for public scorn.[43] Two of Simcoe's Rangers were executed for the rape of a Virginia woman.[44] Apparently only one British regular, a Sergeant Boswell of the Volunteers of Ireland, was executed, for the rape of a New York woman.[45]

The majority of reported rape cases were not of civilians but of army wives and children. The most common victims were female children under ten years of age who lived in army barracks. Sentencing of child molesters shows, moreover, a surprising degree of tolerance for the sexual abuse of army children: one rapist was given the death penalty but was subsequently pardoned by General Howe "because of his youth and the very good character given of him by the field officers of his regiment"; two others, who were also convicted of communicating venereal disease to the victim, were given 1,000 lashes, another received 1,100 lashes, and a fifth was acquitted of raping a four-year-old child. A soldier accused of raping the wife of another soldier in Gibraltar received only 600 lashes, a comparatively lenient penalty for the times.[46]

There were some half-hearted and largely unsuccessful efforts to exert moral influence on the soldiery through religion. For the most part, however, the British army, like all contemporary armies, relied on a harsh system of discipline to control behavior. Although there was probably less of it in the British army than in other European armies, the arbitrary use of force by officers continued to be an informal instrument of discipline. Officers were not required to report all rules infractions to a court

martial;[47] as a consequence many minor offenses were punished
with the swift, summary, savage discipline of the cane. Perhaps
because subalterns and noncommissioned officers had more regular, personal contact with the men than did field officers, complaints of physical abuse by them figure more prominently in trial
records, particularly in accounts of desertions. Many privates tes-
tified that they deserted after they were beaten with sticks, clubs,
or gun butts by a sergeant or an ensign, as punishment for some
infraction such as being late for roll call or missing drill.[48] Some
complained of frequent and regular abuse.[49] One, Thomas Slack,
deserted after an officer beat him black and blue with the scabbard of his sword.[50] Another, James Cairns of the 18th or Royal
Irish Regiment of Foot, objected when his wife was stolen by his
company officer, for which objection he was beaten with a whip;
because Cairns tried to defend himself he was brought to trial for
insubordination and sentenced to 800 lashes; after taking 500,
Cairns deserted.[51]

There was, however, a wind of change in the army. The privilege of personal abuse traditionally enjoyed by officers over private soldiers was slowly being eroded everywhere. In most of
Western Europe, attitudes regarding the common soldier as an
individual had already taken a turn. Even in absolutist Germany,
military literature began to advance the idea of the soldier as a
human being capable of rational motivation.[52] The same theme
runs through British military literature. In *The Regulator*, the pro-
lific Thomas Simes admonished officers not to manhandle their
subordinates: "The men are to be treated with humanity and
respect, and on no account to be struck *with sticks* or ill-used." In
place of the rule of the cane, Simes advocated the rule of law:
"If they commit a fault deserving of punishment, recourse must
be had to the articles of war, or the standing orders of the regiment." Noting that personal brutality was detrimental to morale
Simes quoted regimental standing orders against the practice:
"To see a man struck under arms, or when paraded for guard or
other duty, is so unmanly, unsoldierlike, and so lessening of the
consequence of a soldier and the service, that officers who shall
presume to do it hereafter shall be tried for disobedience of
orders."[53]

A less important factor, and one which was probably unique
to the British army and perhaps even to a small part of the officer
corps, was the idea that personal violence was repugnant to the
spirit of the national constitution. In an earlier work written especially for young officers, Simes observed that "The spirit of
equality *on which British youth are brought up*, makes it disagreeable
for the one to exert, or the other to submit to so much servility."[54]
Certainly no eighteenth-century soldier believed in equality in an

absolute sense, least of all an officer. Nonetheless, trial records of
the century clearly show a reluctance on the part of the common
soldier to submit to personal abuse. Although soldiers still had no
formalized right of complaint against abuse, they returned violence with violence with surprising frequency, given the fact
that insulting, threatening, or striking an officer was a capital
offense.[55]

The decline in the use of physical force was accompanied by
growing reliance on the military legal system to control behavior.
Judicial power was vested in a court martial system, the origins of
which are not entirely clear. There is little positive evidence of
any judicial procedure for the enforcement of military discipline
during the Middle Ages. Minor offenses were probably disposed
of by summary course, although Henry V's Ordinances of War
suggest that serious offenses may have been subject to regular
proceedings. Moreover, extant ordinances or articles of war expressly empowered the holding of courts martial, indicating that
courts of the same nature as the modern court martial enforced
military discipline.[56]

The articles of war of 1685 recognized the existence of two
types of courts, although they may have existed earlier.[57] General
courts heard only capital cases. Regimental courts were supposed
to try only misdemeanors and impose no penalty other than corporal punishment. In practice, however, because the rules and
procedures governing regimental courts were vague and imprecise and because their jurisdiction was ill-defined, they administered military law in a cruel and capricious fashion, disregarding the traditional legal procedures observed by general
courts, in order to punish soldiers with severity excessive even
by the standards of the day.[58]

Although it had long been customary in all English courts,
both civil and military, to swear members in order to insure an
impartial hearing, after 1718 the oath was usually eliminated in
regimental courts. Beginning in the reign of Charles II the articles of war had expressly stipulated that members of all military
courts serve under oath and that all testimony be given under
oath. But the ambiguity of wording of the rules of 1718 allowed
regimental courts to ignore that provision with impunity.[59] In
order to limit the discretion of military courts by forcing them to
follow established procedures and adhere to certain fixed principles, the rules of war, beginning in 1685, required that a sworn
clerk attend the general courts to "make true and faithful records."[60] Regimental courts, however, had no regular clerk to keep
records of court proceedings.[61] Minutes, if they were kept at all,
were taken in a careless, even haphazard fashion. Testimony was,
as one officer complained, often misconstrued because "one or

some, or all the members of the court, take the deposition of a witness or prosecutor contrary, reverse or otherwise than what I suppose they may design or mean."[62] In some cases misrepresentation of the facts was probably deliberate; more often than not it was the result of ignorance and inexperience. Most officers preferred to avoid the boring routine of court duty; as a result "often very young gentlemen just come in the army are members or compose the whole court martial."[63] Moreover, while royal review of general court martial proceedings was mandatory, regimental courts were not required to obtain Crown approval for all sentences; punishment for minor offenses could in fact be inflicted by order of the commanding officer of the regiment.[64]

Their flagrant disregard for due process allowed regimental courts to inflict crippling punishments for a great variety of offenses, minor as well as major. Although murder, rape, mutiny, desertion, and other serious crimes were cognizable before general courts, regimental courts frequently retained jurisdiction by reducing the charge from a major offense such as desertion to a lesser offense such as absence without leave or neglect of duty.[65] This encroachment on the jurisdiction of the general courts was usually done with the approval of the regimental commanding officer when, in his personal judgment, "a regimental court may probably inflict as great a punishment as the other might judge necessary."[66] Few records of regimental court proceedings survive, but these suggest that the penalties imposed by regimental were often more brutal than those pronounced by general courts. Certainly they were more varied in cruelty.

Although sentences by regimental courts were not supposed to exceed one hundred lashes without express royal approval, in reality they were often greater than that.[67] Moreover, because regimental court sentences were not subject to royal review, there was little chance for a mitigation of the sentence; courts were free to inflict the most sadistic forms of punishment without threat of royal interference. In 1722/3, as part of a futile effort to force regimental courts to conform to the legal standards practiced by general courts, Edward Hughes, Judge Advocate General of the army under George I, reported to the secretary at war that regimental courts routinely "inflicted such unmerciful corporal punishments which would have made even death more desirable."[68] Six years later Hughes was still objecting to "the immoderate corporal punishments not previously inflicted on the most notorious offenders."[69] That kind of brutality, as he had warned on another occasion, was not only a disgrace to military law but "if known and complained of by the enemies of His Majesty's government," would discredit the military reputation of Britain.[70]

By and large, little came of Hughes's efforts to reform regimental court practices until early in the nineteenth century. Until then only minimal standards of justice were observed by those courts. Harsh and archaic punishments, including the use of torture devices, continued to be given even for petty crimes. Although contrary to English civil law, the wooden horse, an ancient torture device which strained and dislocated the joints of the thighs and legs by forcing the victim to straddle it with muskets or weights tied to his legs, remained in use throughout the century. An unsigned report on the wooden horse which bears no date but is filed with papers for the period January–May 1781 claims, moreover, that in the British army, as in the armies of France, Holland, Sweden, and Switzerland, it survived as a form of summary punishment.[71]

By comparison, general courts administered justice with a degree of restraint and with regard for judicial procedure unusual for army justice anywhere in the eighteenth century. Beginning in 1718, a series of reforms, many of them initiated by Hughes, most of them paralleling developments in contemporary civil justice, began to transform the general court martial system. By the era of the American Revolution the distinct outline if not the actual form of the modern military justice system had been set forth by Parliamentary statutes, by the rules and articles of war, and by directives from the Crown and from the Judge Advocate General of the army.

One of the most significant developments was the emergence of an awareness of the importance of procedural exactitude. Due process of law is a recent term for an ancient tradition, the concept of which dates back to Magna Carta, the Petition of Right, and the English Bill of Rights. During the eighteenth century, however, the concept was refined to mean the employment of proper forms of indictment, hearing, and trial. Although there were differences, both procedural and substantive, by and large military law and practice coincided in most respects with contemporary judicial trends.

By English common law all prisoners were privileged to bail unless charged with treason, murder or in some cases manslaughter, counterfeiting, or arson. Military law made no provision for bail for common soldiers, who were in fact sometimes held without charge for long periods.[72] In 1753 that practice was finally barred by the rules of war, which limited pretrial confinement to eight days and provided that the provost martial submit to the commander in chief the names of all prisoners and the charges against them within twenty-four hours of their arrest.[73] There were violations of the law, but when they were discovered the prisoner was usually given a royal pardon or else his sentence was commuted.[74]

In England common law defendants were not allowed the benefit of counsel in felony cases; neither were soldiers, although the judge advocate, who also served as counsel to the court, was supposed to assist each defendant in the conduct of his defense.[75] The incompatibility of the two roles was lessened somewhat by the fact that the judge advocate exercised no judicial power.[76] Throughout the eighteenth century criminal trial procedure was weighted in favor of the prosecution. This was particularly true in military courts, perhaps because treasonable activities by the army or by individuals in it render the state especially vulnerable. In case of insufficient evidence to convict, for example, French military courts could order that the accused "be put to torture in order to make him confess his crime."[77] English military law stopped short of that extreme, but a distinction was made in the soldier's legal rights. Although common law required two witnesses for conviction for treason, military law accepted "one positive evidence to facts," and even "strong presumptive proof has been deemed sufficient to condemn a criminal though he absolutely denies the fact."[78]

Nevertheless, after 1715 there was a marked tendency to expand the rights of the accused. The rules of war of 1718 required that an oath be administered to all members of general courts and that all witnesses be examined under oath.[79] Although this was in conformity with practices in English common law courts, it was not customary in other European armies to so bind court members. In French and Spanish military courts, for example, members served only under the royal injunction to give judgment according to conscience and in conformity with the rules of war.[80]

Perhaps because the burden of proving his defense was on the accused, late in the century general courts began to recognize the defendant's right to postponement.[81] While it was seldom invoked, the prisoner's right to challenge members of the court began to be acknowledged at about the same time.[82] Occasionally a defendant claimed his right to cross-examine a witness or to challenge the credibility of a witness with a criminal record or a previous conviction on a charge of treason, piracy, or perjury.[83] Frequently the accused exercised his right to address the court in the reply and rejoinder, which constituted the summation of the prosecution's case and the final plea of the defense. Few if any soldiers were competent to argue legal technicalities, so most simply begged the mercy of the court or pleaded extenuating circumstances. In exceptional cases the defendant presented a prepared, written defense to the court.[84]

Parliamentary statutes also extended legal guarantees in several important particulars: Section 8 of the Mutiny Act of 1753 provided that upon request every defendant must be furnished with a trial transcript within three months of its conclusion. Section 10 secured the defendant against double jeopardy within the military system, although it did not exempt a soldier from being proceeded against in ordinary courts of law.[85] But it was the Crown, exercising its prerogatives in military affairs, which did the most to insure a fair and impartial hearing for soldiers. Royal review of general court martial proceedings dates back at least to 1685, when the rules of war provided that a sworn clerk attend the general court to keep records. The systematic supervision of the general courts' performance, however, was begun by Edward Hughes. In 1716 Hughes introduced a regular form to promote uniformity in the reporting of trial proceedings.[86] Periodically over his long tenure in office he insisted on the inclusion of more detailed information. In 1716 he ordered that trial records contain an account of the evidence given by witnesses.[87] In 1734 he demanded that the records show all the circumstances considered mitigating by the court.[88] Full reports of every trial, each bearing the signature of the president of the court, had to be submitted to Hughes for review before being passed on to the king. When they were found to be deficient in detail they were returned to the board with instructions to submit a more complete version. When on occasion a major procedural violation was discovered, the Crown, under the exercise of the prerogative of mercy, could and usually did remit or reduce the penalty.[89]

The more meticulous adherence to technical detail which resulted from these efforts helped to establish the rule of law in the administration of justice by general courts martial. At the same time the Crown aimed at making soldiers more aware of the law and at creating the habit of rational obedience to the law. All European armies made some attempt to familiarize their troops with the rules of war; the Prussian army, for example, required a biannual reading of the articles of war.[90] In 1716 a communiqué from Whitehall to commanding officers of regiments declared that in the future no sentence of death would be confirmed by the Crown unless it was positively sworn and recorded that the articles of war had been read to each defendant.[91] Article 46 of the rules of war of 1718, which specified that the articles must be read at the head of every regiment, troop, and company, at regular two-month intervals, established this as a fixed principle.[92]

By the late eighteenth century the shift away from fear and force as weapons of control toward "instruction and government" as instruments of correction had been fully formulated by military spokesmen. Military handbooks began to preach a doctrine of positive discipline. Knowledge and understanding of the articles of war and of standing orders of the regiment were, as one manual on discipline reasoned, "an absolute condition necessary to give all possible laws their due force. . . . As it is contrary to equity and justice to condemn and punish men for doing, or omitting to do anything which they did not know to be criminal, so it is a rule that no laws of human institution can be obligatory, before they are made known to those whom they are designed to govern."[93] Another manual urged that all regiments adopt the practice, then in use in some, of requiring all off-duty soldiers to attend court proceedings so that "they may not only distinctly hear the proceedings of his trial read, and see the punishment executed, but that it may also be explained to them the steps which have been taken to reclaim the offender, before severity was used."[94]

There were of course powerful and persistent attempts to resist change, particularly by the regimental courts. Nonetheless, royal review of general court martial proceedings insured at least minimal compliance with the new techniques of discipline. General courts were obliged to ask all defendants "whether they have heard the articles of war and standing orders of the regiment read to them and whether they did not know the fact of which they were accused."[95] In the majority of cases, prisoners who could demonstrate to the satisfaction of the court that they had not heard either the articles of war or standing orders read were acquitted by the court,[96] were pardoned,[97] or had their sentences commuted by the Crown.[98] Only in exceptional cases and for reasons that are not entirely clear was ignorance of the law rejected as a defense.[99]

Despite all the impediments raised against the accused, legal procedures observed by general courts martial were more or less in line with those practiced in all other English courts. They contributed at least to the possibility of a fair trial for soldiers who ran afoul of the law. Conviction, however, still resulted in harsh, even brutal punishment. English law, both civil and military, continued to be among the most severe in letter, although in execution both types were becoming more moderate as the century wore on. In England as elsewhere in Europe, the Enlightenment served as a forcing bed for changes in criminal codes and punishments. There were reductions in the number of criminal offenses and limitations of capital offenses. Beginning in the 1760s, restrictions in the use of torture were adopted in a number of countries; the *peine forte et dure*, death by starvation and pressing, was abolished in England in 1772.[100] Under the burgeoning influence of an advanced section of public opinion, the harshest laws were deliberately weakened by the liberal interpretation of the courts.[101] These developments were translated, in modified form, into military justice. The effect was to abolish the more oppressive features of punishment, without, however, abandoning either the concept or the practice of tough retributive justice.

Like English criminal law, military law lacked graduated punishments. In fixing punishments general courts were more or less limited to death and corporal punishment. As a result, until 1718 the death penalty was ordered by general courts martial in three out of five cases sampled. However, over a third of the men in the sample received royal clemency, and another 5 percent escaped death through a perverse form of mercy which allowed the condemned men to cast lots for their lives. Nonetheless, over 30 percent were executed, either by a firing squad or by hanging, which was then considered a more shameful form of execution.[102] (See Table 10.)

A series of changes in the law, however, produced a marked decline in the rate of executions over the course of the eighteenth century. The most important factor was the steady reduction in the number of capital offenses until they roughly corresponded with modern military codes. The rules of war of 1642 recorded no less than twenty-one separate capital crimes, ranging from treason to dishonorable references to the Lord General of the Army. The rules of 1673 reduced the total number but at the same time designated new offenses, such as the theft of church ornaments or abuse of churchmen or civilians, as capital crimes. The list remained more or less constant until 1718, at which time several ceased to appear as capital offenses: traitorous language and the malicious destruction of cornfields or meadows were now to be punished "according to the nature of the offense"; resisting or striking an officer, sleeping at or abandoning a post, and selling or destroying arms carried penalties of corporal punishment or fines instead of death.[103] The rules of 1722 shortened the list further by giving the court discretionary power to assign punish-

TABLE 10. Disposition of Capital Cases by General Courts Martial, 1666–1718 (Size of Sample: 524)

	Number	Percentage
Executions	166	31.68
Corporal punishment	81	15.46
Cast lots	24	4.58
Pardon	206	39.31
Acquittal	47	8.97

Source: See note 102.

ments or substituting corporal punishment for crimes such as destruction of church property, disclosure of the watchword, and embezzlement of government stores.[104]

Although mutiny, plunder, and aid to the enemy were still classified as capital crimes, the rules of 1753 gave the courts freedom to order some other form of punishment if there were mitigating circumstances.[105] The rules of 1789 offered still another alternative to the death penalty for desertion: service at a foreign post for life or for a stipulated number of years, depending upon the gravity of the case.[106] The practice had already been used informally and infrequently by the Hanoverian kings to man garrisons at remote and inhospitable places, such as Georgia, Jamaica, the Leeward Islands, and Minorca.[107] Successive changes such as these increased the courts' discretionary power to lighten penalties, and the rules of war of 1786 unequivocally circumscribed their right to impose the death penalty except for crimes expressly designated capital by the articles of war.[108]

The effect was to produce a drop in the rate of executions together with a rise in the rate of other forms of punishment. The most conspicuous change was the increase in the use of corporal punishment: from just above 15 percent of my sample to nearly 50 percent by the end of the American Revolution. The rate of pardons declined significantly, but acquittals and the substitution of other forms of punishment easily made up the difference. (See Tables 11 and 12.) Measured by modern standards, these advances were modest indeed; seen in the context of the times they appear more substantial.

Early disciplinary codes punished various offenses with un-

TABLE 11. Disposition of Capital Cases by General Courts Martial, 1719–1753 (Size of Sample: 644)

	Number	Percentage
Death	140	21.74
Corporal punishment	257	39.91
Service at a foreign post	137	21.27
Other punishment	2	.31
Pardon	60	9.32
Acquittal	33	5.12
Release without trial[a]	15	2.33

[a]6 (.93%) were released because the Articles of War were not read to them, 9 (1.40%) because of illegal confinement.
Source: See note 102.

TABLE 12. Disposition of Capital Cases by General Courts Martial, 1754–1782 (Size of Sample: 893)

	Number	Percentage
Death	206	23.07
Corporal punishment	411	46.02
Service at a foreign post	1	.11
Other punishment	4	.45
Pardon	41	4.59
Acquittal	230	25.76

Source: See note 102.

speakably inventive torture. The primitive disciplinary code published by Richard I in his expedition to the Holy Land in 1189 punished theft by pouring boiling pitch and then feathers over the shaven head of the thief, who was then abandoned and left to his own resources.[109] The rules of war proclaimed by Richard II allowed for beheading, drawing and quartering, and various forms of mutilation.[110] The rules adopted in 1586 by the Earl of Leicester to discipline the troops serving in the Low Countries ordered that quarrels and brawls be punished with "loss of life or limb at the discretion of the general or marshal"; treason or conspiracy was punished by "death with torments."[111]

The rules laid down by Robert Devereaux, 3d Earl of Essex and Lord General of the Army in 1642, directed that any soldier who lifted his hand against "any of the great officers of the army . . . shall lose his hand."[112] In the seventeenth century, religious fanaticism produced hideous forms of punishment for moral transgressions. The rules of war of 1642 made the penalty for blasphemy to have the tongue bored through with a red-hot iron.[113] Disabling punishments such as these were of course prohibited by the Bill of Rights of 1689, which proscribed cruel and unusual punishments. Perhaps because of the importance of rigid discipline during hostilities, particularly to a military establishment which used close-order formations, military law remained anomalous. The rules of war of 1722, for example, still sanctioned the use of potentially disabling penalties such as the wooden horse. It was not until 1753 that the rules were altered so as to implicitly prohibit such exorbitant punishments. Even after that, mutilation was sometimes ordered by general courts. Two privates convicted of manslaughter in Minorca, one in 1775, the other in 1780, were branded on the hand.[114] Three Indian soldiers convicted of desertion in 1782 were first beaten and then had their ears cut off.[115] These were exceptional cases, however, and apparently reflect the practice of importing into court martial proceedings the laws of the colony where the trial was being held.[116]

Flogging was the last vestigial barbarity practiced by general courts. Stripped to the waist and tied to crossed halberds, the hapless flogging victim was whipped in turn by regimental drummers, a "fresh drummer" taking over every twenty-five strokes. The infamous cat-o'-nine-tails actually consisted of six lines, each two or three times the thickness of ordinary whipcord, each with several hard knots tied into it. In the ritual of whipping, the drummer swung the cat twice around his own head, gave a stroke and then drew the tails through the fingers of his left hand to rid them of flesh and blood.[117] The knotted lines bruised, blistered, and lacerated the naked flesh, disabling the victim, often for days, sometimes for weeks.[118] Running the gauntlet and lashing by each man in the guards were variant and perhaps even more savage forms of flogging. One German soldier who was made to run the gauntlet was, an officer noted afterward, "quite pitifully cut and beaten and he had to be led all day by two non commissioned officers because he could not walk."[119] Most flogging victims in fact ended up in regimental hospitals, where, because of the suppurating nature of their wounds, they were kept in single beds separated from the other patients.[120]

Sadistic and savage though it was, measured by the standards prevailing then, such flogging was not untypical. Throughout the eighteenth century and through most of the nineteenth, physical chastisement was everywhere, both privately and publicly, an accepted form of correction. Even though nineteenth-century penal reforms helped to humanize punishment, corporal punishment was imposed on women until 1817[121] and on men decades longer. Under English criminal law for a number of noncapital felonies male prisoners convicted by a jury were liable to be publicly or privately whipped.[122] In 1858 in England and Wales 83 males were sentenced to be whipped by Courts of Assize or Quarter Sessions; in the same year 502 males were sentenced to be whipped by summary conviction by justices. Although the majority of these were juvenile offenders, more than 50 were adults over twenty years of age.[123]

Moreover, everywhere in the Western world flogging was still commonly regarded as necessary to restrain the criminal element in the army; no army had as yet abandoned its use. The knout was widely used in the Russian army; in the Prussian army it was the stick.[124] The American articles of war drawn up by the Continental Congress legalized corporal punishment in the newly created Continental Army, and although the articles established a

maximum of 100 lashes, in actual practice the law was circum-
vented by military courts, which customarily ordered 100 lashes
for each charge.[125]

Although for another century there were no formal restrictions on the number of lashes British general courts could impose, by 1740 they had already begun to use more discretion in
awarding punishments. In earlier years, penalties of course varied from crime to crime and even from case to case; often, however, the number of lashes ranged up to several thousand for
conviction on a single charge. Until around 1740 it was common
practice to punish desertion, the most frequent infraction of the
disciplinary code, by having the offender run or walk from two to
sixteen times up and down several companies, a whole battalion,
or even one or more regiments, sometimes carrying a fifteen- or
eighteen-pound weight in his hands, while his comrades whipped
him with rods or halberds, as the court directed.[126] In a typical
case, Private James Chivers, a first-time deserter, was sentenced in
1722 to walk six times through his regiment and be whipped with
halberds.[127] Even if the regiment were only at half strength
Chivers's sentence added up to at least 1,500 lashes; at most he
received 3,000. In 1716 John Carrison was sentenced to run six
times up and six times down, through two regiments on the same
day.[128] A month later John Brooks and James Cole were ordered
to run six times up and down the entire regiment while carrying
an eighteen-pound shot.[129] In 1721 Roger Bryan and William
Jones were sentenced to run through a regiment, six times up, six
times down, on each of four days and three days respectively.[130]

Beginning around 1740, penalties of a comparatively lenient
character were handed down by general courts. With few exceptions the maximum number of lashes given for serious crimes
such as desertion became more or less fixed at 1,000,[131] and these
were administered at intervals of several weeks under the supervision of a regimental surgeon, who was held responsible for the
death or permanent injury of the victim.[132]

Coincident to these developments was a conspicuous increase
in the number of acquittals in capital cases. From 1666 to 1753,
the rate of acquittals fluctuated only slightly, averaging around 7
percent for the whole period. In the three decades after 1754,
however, the rate increased abruptly to nearly 26 percent. Contemporary practice required that a charge once made must be
brought to trial unless retracted by the accuser; apparently the
convening authority was not empowered to dismiss the charges
even if they were groundless or trivial.[133] Presumably the statistics
cited here reflect that situation to some extent. They also reflect a
growing aversion to the drastic nature of punishment.

No one in the eighteenth-century army challenged the basic

contention that retribution was necessary to deter soldiers from
breaking army rules; nor for that matter did anyone yet deny that
corporal punishment should be the principal instrument of discipline for major offenses. By the era of the American Revolution,
however, a few military writers were beginning to question
whether it should be the only instrument of discipline. Their
opposition to the flogging system was based both on practical and
on humanitarian grounds.

   Penalties, wrote Thomas Simes in 1777, that were so disproportionate to the offense as to shock the moral sense defeated
their own purpose. The provost and even officers, Simes pointed
out, were reluctant to report soldiers apprehended in the commission of a crime such as plundering, because "every person is
unwilling to be the cause of the death of a poor fellow whose
belly perhaps was craving for hunger." [134] Instead, he noted, "out
of a sense of humanity, [they] turn their eyes when they see
marauders." [135] In his important work *A Treatise on Courts-Martial*,
Captain Stephen Adye, judge advocate to the British army in
America, went further to question whether the whip was the most
effective method of discipline; he proposed instead a number of
substitutes for it. "Let us," Adye began, "consider that every soldier is a human creature, susceptible to the same feelings and
passions with others, and as such every method should previously
be taken to deter them from vices rather than to trust to reforma-
tion by punishment." He recommended that punishments be
proportioned to the crime; confinement, fines, or double duty
assignments were, he reasoned, appropriate penalties for minor
offenses. He advocated less emphasis on retribution and more on
reform. Although the Order of the Bath was a citation of merit
reserved almost exclusively for officers, Adye suggested that it be
conferred on common soldiers as well as a means of encouraging
good behavior. [136] Like Adye, Captain Bennett Cuthbertson was
also convinced that the whip as a remedial measure was ineffec-
tive. In order "to render the necessity of applying to a courts-
martial less frequent," he proposed in 1776 the creation of a
special citation to reward good conduct. The order of merit proposed by Cuthbertson would be given to every soldier who served
at least seven years without censure by a court martial. As an
added incentive, medal holders were to be "preferred in all
things" and "given every indulgence." [137] Only a few regiments
had medals, which were usually awarded by the commanding
officer, and these were to honor heroism in battle. Apart from the
silver Waterloo medal, the first medal conferred upon all ranks
was issued after the Afghan war of 1839–1842. Good conduct
badges, of the type advocated by Cuthbertson, and good conduct
pay were first instituted after 1832. [138]

Whether Simes, Adye, Cuthbertson, and others like them mirrored or molded the attitudes of other officers is not clear. In any case it is less important than the fact that from such criticisms a more humane system of discipline slowly began to evolve. For another century the army clung to the vicious system of flogging. Although there were efforts early in the nineteenth century to abolish it, they were beaten back by the opposition of army authorities and their conservative supporters in Parliament. The first restrictions on the number of lashes were not imposed until 1812, when flogging by order of a regimental court was limited to 300 lashes. All forms of corporal punishment were finally abolished in 1881.[139]

In the meantime, discipline continued to be maintained by severe and brutal punishments. Nevertheless, advances made during the eighteenth century gave military law a dynamic thrust which pushed the entire justice system in the direction of change and in the process improved by degrees the condition of the rank and file. The eighteenth century did not witness the completion of these developments—only their beginnings. By the same token, the celebrated reforms of the nineteenth century did not bring about sweeping changes but rather accelerated tendencies already in motion.

5 TRAINING AND CAMPAIGNING

THE ARMY WAS an authoritarian organization with rigid and inflexible patterns of authority and subordination. Discipline, designed to produce obedient personalities, pervaded every aspect of the soldiers' lives. From reveille to tattoo, formal rules and regulations laid out by the institution told them what they must do, when and how they must do it, and with whom it must be done. Daily work was characterized by the constant repetition of dull details and the performance of menial tasks, such as digging latrines or burying offal, which emphasized their low position in the hierarchy. Close-order drill, borrowed from the Prussians, formal guard mounts, parades, and personal inspections all helped to generate conformity. The intent and the effect of the military regimen was to inhibit if not destroy ingenuity and initiative and to substitute instead dull, automatic responses. Being drawn from the lower levels of a stratified society and accustomed to conformity, discipline, and routine tasks probably made adjustment to army culture comparatively easy for most of Britain's soldiers.

A soldier's life was hard and short. Like the great mass of manual workers in eighteenth-century England, the soldier worked long hours doing repetitive, unimaginative work, in conditions which were at best dismal, at worst dangerous. Soldiering was more than an occupation, however; it was a way of life. Most of the soldier's working hours were spent in the field or in preparation to take the field. His social isolation, the detailed regulation of his life, the rigors of his training were supposed to make him a better fighter, skilled in the art of war, disciplined to accept its dangers. Although violence was commonplace in the eighteenth century, it occurred in particularly concentrated form for the soldier. Those who did not bleed to death on the battlefield or die under the surgeon's knife lived to see their comrades mutilated by balls and blades or ravaged by fevers and burning agues. Although arduous by modern standards, the soldier's normal nine-hour work day compared favorably to that of most working people in the eighteenth century and was actually shorter than that of urban industrial workers in the nineteenth century. It

began at daybreak with the sound of reveille as drummers beat
through the principal streets of garrisons and camps. It ended at
8:00 P.M. when tattoo ordered everyone into quarters.[1] The daily
work was tedious and exhausting, but it was intermittent. Unless
the army was in the field, regular working hours were between
6:00 and 8:00 A.M., 9:00 A.M. and 12:00 noon, and 2:00 and 6:00
P.M.[2] Taken singly, military chores were boring and monotonous;
still there was a certain variety of employment unknown to factory operatives after the Industrial Revolution.

A part of every soldier's day was devoted to "fatigue duties,"
routine, dreary, dispiriting work. While a sanitary detail burned
or buried old meat, refuse, and rubbish, parties of men clad in
striped overalls loaded and unloaded provisions, collected and
transported fuel, or swept out garrison chimneys to prevent fires.
In the bitter cold of northern winters they shoveled snow and
learned to march about on snowshoes. In the humid heat of the
lowland South they bound "bundles" for laying on the marshes to
make them passable. In preparation for taking the field, fatigue
men made fascines, or cut and built abatis. Seasoned veterans
made cartridges, exacting work which demanded watchful, conscientious effort, and then packed them in bladder or leather for
preservation. There was no remuneration for these routine
chores because they were considered part of the soldier's obligation. Only those with special training, such as masons or carpenters whose skills were urgently needed to repair redoubts,
barracks, and storehouses, received extra pay.[3]

Among the regular assignments none was more bitterly despised than guard duty. On the average during peace time each
soldier mounted guard every three or four days. In periods of
war, however, the need to provide security against a surprise
enemy attack made it a much more frequent and burdensome
occurrence. Daily the main guard, from which all other guards
were detached, assembled at the quarters of the respective captains to be marched to the parade; from there small details were
sent to man posts at the military hospitals, the markets and magazines, the prisons and commissaries. Others were assigned to
guard the tents or quarters of general officers and regimental
colonels or to man the numerous sentry posts that protected garrisons and camps and prevented enemy infiltration of the lines.
Conditions at those advanced posts were highly favorable to desertion, and hundreds of men escaped through that avenue.[4] Because of the custodial character of the work, only the most trusted
soldiers were assigned to the provost guard, whose regular police
functions included the constraint of war prisoners, spies, and
deserters, the control of camp disorders, the regulation of markets that formed in the camps, the prevention of illegal sales of

alcohol by unlicensed sutlers, and the execution of capital punishment.[5]

Important as they were, cleanliness, order, and security were peripheral duties; the central work of the soldier was preparation to take the field. All other activities simply supported it. This was perhaps more true for the eighteenth-century soldier than for any other before or after. European wars before the French Revolution were fought for a limited objective, usually advantageous position. The tactics used were determined by the size, composition, and armament of military forces. Although there was great interest throughout the century in tactical innovations, most armies still used the tactics developed by Frederick the Great. The Prussian attack was built around infantry supported by cavalry and artillery. Like the ancient Greeks, opposing armies came on the field in columns, in an order of march which corresponded to the order of battle. The battle itself usually occurred after one of the opposing generals took up a position which he believed to be defensible against enemy attack. After reconnoitering, his opponent decided whether he had the preponderance of power necessary to risk attack; because the stakes were so high, the prospects for success must be good. As they prepared for engagement, the deep marching columns shifted into long, shallow lines of attack or defense, so as to exploit the greatest number of muskets for the volley. Because the very thinness of the formation could easily lead to breakthroughs, the battalion had to be deployed in practically continuous lines, which limited maneuverability. Moreover, once set in motion, the extended lines must advance with little or no interruption.[6]

Close-order tactics reflected of course the state of technological development; in a sense they also reproduced the attitudes of contemporary European society. The sublimation of the individual through discipline and subordination, which were necessary prerequisites for harmonious action in the field, were the foundations upon which the entire social structure rested. The social and political convulsions of the American and French revolutions ultimately refashioned conceptions of the individual. As the effects resonated throughout Western society, corresponding changes in the conception of the individual soldier produced a military revolution beginning in the 1790s. As a consequence, the solid phalanx which characterized close-order tactics was broken; from the fragments a new infantry was built whose form and functions could be adapted to suit diverse conditions. Until that time, like all the great powers, Britain continued to rely upon traditional drills and exercises to prepare troops to fight conventional warfare.[7]

The stylized maneuvers that armies used in battle were the

final results of an endless repetition of exercises learned during drill. In principle, officers were responsible for the preparation of their troops. In actual practice, because they found the monotonous routine tiresome and demeaning, they usually passed the responsibility on to noncommissioned officers, most of whom had themselves risen from the ranks.[8]

As a consequence of their indifference toward training, both their own and that of their men, the reputation of the officer corps has suffered. Their elevation of personal dignity to the first place, even above the development of proficiency in performance, was characteristic of their class, however, and was consistent with contemporary standards of professional conduct.[9] In fact, professionalism in the modern sense of the word was not yet part of the military vocabulary. It was still common practice in all European armies to purchase commissions and to use political influence to win promotions.[10] The average officer was a professional only to the extent that he made a living by soldiering; no officer corps in any army anywhere in the world was adequately trained in military science. Only a few military schools existed, and these offered a minimal amount of technical instruction. It was not until 1818, with the establishment of the Prussian War Academy and the Ecole d'Application d'Etat Major in France, that officer training began to concentrate on military science. Although the Royal Military Academy at Woolich, which trained men for the artillery, was established in 1741, it was not until the Staff College was detached from the Royal Military College in 1857 that officer training in England began to concentrate on military science.[11]

There was, however, a great deal of interest in military art, and a number of treatises appeared in Britain over the century.[12] There was, moreover, considerable progress toward standardization of drill and formations in the British army, as evidenced by the publication of tracts dealing with the practical training of infantry, cavalry, artillery, and engineers. By 1775, Major General Humphrey Bland's *A Treatise of Military Discipline in which is Laid down and Explained the Duty of the Officer and Soldier Thro' the several Branches of the Service* had been officially adopted by the Adjutant General's Office. In the second half of the century, tracts dealing with light infantry tactics, such as M. de Jenny's *The Partisan* and Andrew Emmerich's *The Partisan in War*, were being studied and discussed. Separate training manuals for cavalry, such as Campbell Dalrymple's *Military Essay*, and Captain Hinde's *Discipline of the Light Horse*, began to appear, indicating growing recognition of the distinct functions of specialized units.

As a result of the interest generated by these military writers, a formal program of practical training for recruits was fairly well developed by the Revolution. Preparation of new recruits and drafts for service in America apparently began soon after enlistment. While waiting to embark from Cork, Ireland, young Thomas Sullivan and other recruits for the 49th Regiment "were marched to a back-yard in Blarney lane and also several days to the South Mall, where we learned to march and go through the different facings, which we fully learned in Cork."[13] In Halifax, Nova Scotia recruits for the Royal Highland Emigrants were drilled twice every day.[14] Even veteran troops were regularly exercised during peace and in preparation for war. In the years before the outbreak of hostilities, British regulars stationed in Boston were drilled daily on Brattle Square, much to the annoyance of John Adams, whose house was directly opposite the square. Adams complained bitterly that "the spirit stirring drums and the earpiercing fife aroused me and my family early enough every morning."[15] In preparation to take the field in 1777, Burgoyne's troops in Canada were "kept in continued exercise," although snow lay deep on the ground and the parade and field exercises had to take place on an ice-covered field.[16]

Because of the exacting nature of the infantry exercise, each of the three daily drill sessions was limited to two hours. The first session was devoted to conditioning exercises, such as running, to prepare the men for rigorous field operations. Under normal conditions an army in the field usually marched about fifteen miles a day; but a forced march could cover twenty-five to thirty miles a day.[17] The vastness of the American theatres of war made long marches inevitable, and so all British troops, even artillerymen, were required to run from a half hour to an hour every day during the training period.[18] Off-duty regiments, fully armed and accoutred, were sometimes marched several miles into the countryside to build up their endurance for campaigning.[19] A second drill period was usually spent practicing facings, wheelings, and the other complicated motions that made up both the infantry and cavalry exercises. During the parade exercise the various maneuvers learned at drill were performed either by companies or by platoons.[20]

Drill sergeants, armed with a cane or a stick, carried as a symbol of their authority, presided over these sessions. Their first responsibility was to teach the soldiers "character," which for all intents and purposes meant to make them subordinate. In the status-conscious world of the eighteenth-century army, the most important principle of discipline was deference to superior officers. It was, moreover, an exaggerated form of deference which reflected not only the hierarchical nature of military society but also the customs, traditions, and values of English society. The salute, for example, is in modern armies a mutual exchange of respect expressed by raising the hand to the headgear. In the eighteenth century it was performed only by enlisted men and consisted of the removal of the hat in a single sweeping motion which brought it to rest against the thigh. The uncovering of the head was symbolic of submission, not only to the rank of the officer but to his social station as well.[21]

The complicated evolutions that allowed a whole body of troops to change form and disposition, either to attack the enemy or to improve a defensive position, demanded a high degree of formation discipline. To achieve the necessary precision, the training program in the beginning concentrated on marching. The British used a stiff-kneed marching style similar to the German goose-step of more recent years.[22] The rate of stepping varied according to the nature and the purpose of the maneuver. To cover great distances or to traverse uneven ground, a steady, measured pace of seventy-five steps a minute was used because it helped to maintain the line in solid form and allowed it to present regular volleys. Certain types of offensive actions, however, called for a more rapid disposition of the troops, and in those cases the pace was quickened to 120 steps a minute, a gait apparently peculiar to the British army.[23] The problem of synchronizing the movements of large numbers of men, an inevitable consequence of linear tactics, was only partially solved by the use of drum or musical accompaniment both in training and in field operations.

Once a certain level of competence in marching was reached, training progressed to the more sophisticated tactical exercises which the army employed to change posture or position. Although drill manuals made no reference to fighting in loose formation, during the Revolution British troops were especially instructed in different tactics suited to the conditions of American terrain and to the nature of the opposition. During operations on the Canadian frontier in the summer of 1776, British forces under Sir Guy Carleton's command were "trained to the exercise calculated for the woody country of America, with which they were totally unacquainted."[24] Because fighting in line was practically impossible in the Canadian wilderness, General John Burgoyne's troops were trained in different tactical combinations in preparation for the British invasion from the north. Burgoyne himself reviewed the troops in Montreal and as Lieutenant Thomas Anburey, a volunteer in the 29th Regiment, reported, watched them perform "common manoeuvres" plus "several new ones, calculated for defence in this woody country."[25] In the broken country between Montreal and Saratoga, rowing was as much a job for a skilled soldier as fighting in line, and the men in Burgoyne's expedition were alleged to be "all expert at rowing, having been ordered to practice frequently."[26] On the other hand, because "the nature of service in America makes them almost useless," several maneuvers practiced by British troops in Europe were eliminated from the training of troops bound for America.[27]

Aside from these minor departures from conventional tactics, the British army remained wedded to the practice of engaging infantry in battle in line form. The disciplined line represented the structural framework of the linear system; musketry provided the firepower. After 1710 all infantrymen were armed with a flintlock musket whose barrel measured three feet, eight inches, to which the stock added another foot. The weapon carried a lead bullet, .550 inch in diameter. A leather scabbard suspended from a crossbelt over the right shoulder held a seventeen-inch bayonet of the socket type, which allowed the weapon to be discharged while the bayonet was attached.[28] Due to poor engineering and craftsmanship, the flintlock was inaccurate, undependable, and often defective.[29] But until the open-order tactics of a later period finally made the faulty musket obsolete, the British preferred it to the rifle. Spiral grooves cut into the gun barrel of the rifle gave the bullet a rotary motion which made its flight more accurate. The weapon had long been in use and was first introduced in America by Germans as early as 1709; some German jaeger regiments serving in the Revolution carried rifles, although they were not especially skilled in their use. Major Patrick Ferguson of the 71st Highlanders designed a breechloader called the Ferguson rifle and equipped his special corps with them. Apart from that, however, the rifle was not generally used by the British, although American-made rifles, especially those produced in Pennsylvania, were used very effectively by American forces against the British.[30]

The manual exercise for infantry was designed to train soldiers in the loading and firing of muskets and to condition them to act in conformity with the rest of the line so as to produce a massive, though not necessarily accurate, volley. In combat, once the advancing lines fired the initial volley, the muskets had to be reloaded and primed as the lines continued to move forward in the face of enemy fire. The complex loading drill consisted of twenty-four separate motions, beginning with opening the pan, removing the cartridge from a pouch worn at the waist, biting the top off the cartridge, shutting the pan, and pulling the hammer down on it. The next series of motions was related to loading the barrel with powder and paper from the cartridge and ramming home the lead bullet with an iron ramrod.[31]

The complicated process of loading and priming meant that even highly trained and disciplined soldiers could at best achieve no higher rate of fire than two rounds a minute.[32] In actual combat in America the rate may have been slightly better, however, since soldiers did not charge their weapons in the prescribed fashion with rods; instead they drove home the powder and shot by striking the butt end of the piece on the ground before it was fired.[33]

Because it took so long to charge the musket, aiming was prohibited in most European armies, since it would have further retarded an already slow rate of fire.[34] But long years of Indian fighting in America had produced a great deal of emphasis on marksmanship in the British army.[35] During the Revolution there was frequent practice in firing with balls at marks, including life-size wooden targets and objects floating in the water. Even in inclement weather regiments were urged to "get any places in their barracks or elsewhere under cover [where] young and inexpert soldiers may be there perfected in the manual [arms]."[36] As an incentive to develop accuracy in firing, competitions were held and prizes were given to the most accomplished marksmen in each regiment.[37]

In the eighteenth century the firelock had a peculiar, almost symbiotic relationship with the bayonet. For one thing, the main attack often culminated in a bayonet charge. For another, because of bad design the serviceability of firelock and bayonet was conterminous. Although there was an established caliber for all firelocks, there was no standard size for the muzzle. Neither was there an established gauge for the sockets and fixtures of bayonets, which meant that a given bayonet would not fit any musket except the one for which the bore of the sockets of the bayonet and the fixing grooves were matched. During the approach in combat the firelock, with fixed bayonet, was carried shouldered. If either one or the other was damaged by artillery or infantry fire, as was frequently the case, it could neither be replaced nor exchanged.[38]

For all that, the British used the bayonet with devastating proficiency, which was the product of long training. Originally issued only to dragoon regiments, by the 1680s the hollow dagger had become general issue. During the Revolution, to compensate for American superiority in wilderness fighting, the British military command emphasized the battlefield value of the bayonet as a shock weapon. As he launched the Long Island campaign in September 1776, General Howe reminded the troops under his command of their effectiveness with the bayonet against the rebels, "even in woods where they thought themselves invincible," and recommended to them "an entire dependence on their bayonets."[39] After acknowledging the American advantage in wooded country, Burgoyne warned his troops that British success in any engagement in the Canadian wilderness "must greatly rest on the bayonet." His orders urged officers to "inculcate that idea into the minds of the men."[40] Lieutenant Colonel Stephen Kemble's order to the British troops on the Nicaraguan expedition to use the bayonet "whenever it can be done in good order" stressed the extraordinary psychological effect of face-to-face, hand-to-hand combat; "nothing," Kemble observed, "strikes such a damp on foreign or undisciplined troops as coming to close quarters."[41] The swift, vicious Paoli Massacre of 1777 was the most dramatic demonstration of the special character of the bayonet attack. In drill-book fashion British regulars, carrying unloaded muskets, fell upon the sleeping camp of Mad Anthony Wayne at midnight; with blows and thrusts they quietly killed or wounded over two hundred Americans.[42] A bayonet charge by Ferguson's provincial troops temporarily repulsed the attackers at King's Mountain.[43] The Highlanders' charge with fixed bayonets sent General Nathanael Greene's North Carolina militia fleeing in terror at Guilford Court House.[44]

Despite the conditioning exercises and the long hours of drill in tactical exercises and the manual arms, various factors complicated the performance of armies in the field. More often than not soldiers entered battle worn out by the physical and mental ordeals of campaigning. Long marches, exposure, hunger, thirst, discomfort, and loss of sleep severely tested their stamina and endurance. Anxiety excited by the prospect of battle and depression brought on by the death or injury of friends and relatives tested their willpower and patience.

Without mechanized land transport, eighteenth-century armies were forced to make long, strenuous marches to engage or to escape the enemy. Although batmen carried the personal belongings of officers, privates marched under the weight of their weapons and accoutrements. Fully assembled with iron rammer and sling, the five-foot-two-inch-long musket weighed sixteen pounds, seven ounces. The tin or wooden cartridge box worn at the waist, together with cartridges, balls, bayonet and scabbard, flints, and cleaning materials added up to eleven pounds, eight ounces of accoutrements literally "hanging on the man's body."[45] Nor was that all.

On his back each soldier carried a well-filled kit on top of which were his great-coat and blanket roll, a canteen, a camp kettle, and a haversack stuffed with sundries such as leather and tools for repairing shoes, a hatchet, and a three-day supply of beef and ship biscuit.[46] Thus encumbered, his head held down by the weight on his neck, the soldier was, as a seasoned veteran complained, "half-beaten before he came to the scratch."[47]

In addition to the fatigue caused by carrying sixty pounds of gear most of the time, the soldiers were hungry, cold, and wet into the bargain. Lieutenant William Digby of the 53d Regiment of Foot, a veteran of both the Carleton and the Burgoyne campaigns in the north, made the point in a graphic way: "The idea of service to those who have not had an opportunity of seeing any, may induce them to believe the only hardship a soldier endures on a campaign is the danger attending an action." But, Digby continued, "there are many others, perhaps not so dangerous, yet in my opinion very near as disagreeable—remaining out whole nights under rain and almost frozen with cold, with very little covering, perhaps without being able to light a fire; fearing the enemy's discovering the post, and not knowing the moment of an attack, but always in expectation of one. . . ."[48]

En route to Saratoga, the climax of Burgoyne's invasion from the north, the army suffered all of the insidious cruelties described by Lieutenant Digby. The campaign began on June 3, 1777, when the troops moved from winter cantonments to assemble at St. Johns.[49] Departing daily at dawn, they marched by brigade, averaging at first seventeen to twenty miles a day.[50] But natural impediments and American forces operating in the area slowed the advance. Most of the march was through dense woods, across land broken by creeks and marshes and cut by deep morasses. In the sultry summer heat, devoured by swarms of flies and mosquitoes, the troops labored by day to clear away the woods for encampments and to repair roads and construct some forty bridges to span the numerous creeks, ravines, and gullies.[51] Beginning in August, thunderstorms regularly flooded the primitive roads and soaked through the canvas tents where the men lay at night to rest from the fatiguing work of the day. In the meantime the salt rations, sufficient to feed an army on a rapid march, were quickly depleting due to the halting pace of the army. When bread supplies ran out, the soldiers resorted to flour cakes, made with water and baked on stones before the campfires.[52]

On the nineteenth of September, Burgoyne's severely weakened army, suffering from deprivation and discomfort, engaged an American force under General Horatio Gates at Freeman's Farm. Between one and two o'clock the signal guns sounded the order to advance. At three o'clock the action began with a vigorous attack on the British line. The stress of the action was felt by the 20th, 21st, and 62d regiments, most parts of which were continuously engaged for almost four hours without interruption.[53] The fighting continued until dark. That night the men slept with their accoutrements on, being under constant harassment from American gunfire. "We are now," noted Thomas Anburey, "become so habituated to fire, that the soldiers seem to be indifferent to it, and eat and sleep when it is very near them."[54]

Once the shock of battle was over, the survivors had still to suffer the spectacle of the battlefield. The sights and sounds of the dead and the dying produced in many soldiers the severe emotional stress which in recent wars has come to be called battle shock. The survivors' feelings of helplessness and frustration are conveyed in Lieutenant Anburey's description of the aftermath of Freeman's Farm. After leading a burial detail through its grim chores, Anburey wrote:

> [The] friendly office to the dead, though it greatly affects the feelings, was nothing to the scene of bringing in the wounded; the one was past all pain, the other in the most excruciating torments, sending forth dreadful groans. They had remained out all night, and from the loss of blood and want of nourishment, were upon the point of expiring with faintness; some of them begged they might lay and die, others again were insensible, some upon the least movement were put in the most horrid tortures and all had near a mile to be conveyed to the hospitals; others at their last gasp, who for want of our timely assistance must have inevitably expired. These poor creatures, perishing with cold and weltering in their blood, displayed such a scene, it must be a heart of adamant that could not be affected by it.[55]

On the third of October, provisions now dangerously low, the salt allowance was reduced by half. On the seventh, Burgoyne ordered his hungry, travel-worn troops to occupy Bemis Heights. The bitter fighting, which continued until nightfall, produced heavy casualties, especially among artillery units. At 9:00 P.M., in a heavy downpour, the British army began to retreat toward Saratoga.[56] From that day forward the soldiers were without tents in an incessant rain that fell until the surrender. When they reached Saratoga late in the evening of the ninth, the army was "in such a state of fatigue, that the men had not strength or inclination to make fires, but rather sought rest in their wet cloaths and on the wet ground, under a heavy rain that still continued."[57] But, as Lieutenant Digby recalled, "it was impossible to sleep, even had we inclination to do so, from the cold and rain, and our only entertainment was the report of some popping shots heard now and then from the other side of the great river at our Battows."[58]

Because of the state of the army Burgoyne decided on the tenth to retire to the heights of Fort Edwards, and a detachment was sent out to repair the bridges and open the roads leading there. As the army prepared to march, however, intelligence was received that the enemy possessed the road to Fort Edwards and surrounded Saratoga.[59] That avenue of escape closed, the British prepared to maintain the post. Throughout the night the soldiers worked, throwing up entrenchments and dragging up the heavy cannon in anticipation of an attack at daybreak. But the Americans, aware that sooner or later Burgoyne would be forced to move, declined to hazard a battle.

Inside the works the situation was grave. Provisions were almost exhausted. An inventory was taken on the twelfth and "they were found mostly consumed."[60] Thirty English officers, "who could endure hunger no longer," begged food from Baroness von Riedesel, campaigning with her husband, General Frederick von Riedesel.[61] There was a severe shortage of water. Prevented by American rifle fire from reaching the river, the troops had to drink from a muddy spring where cattle watered, or catch rainwater in their caps "to render their provisions more palateable."[62] A continuous cannonade with rifle and grape shot forced the men to "lay constantly upon their arms," so that in addition to hunger and thirst they were "harassed and fatigued beyond measure from their great want of rest."[63] On the seventeenth of October Burgoyne's proud army surrendered, "a prey," Lieutenant Digby concluded, "to want and hunger which then stared us fully in the face."[64]

It was in the southern theatre of war that the most excessive physical demands were made on the army. The vastness of the southern theatre made occupation of territory impractical; as a result, action there took on many of the features of guerrilla warfare. Instead of the slow, regular close-order movements of linear warfare, the southern campaigns of 1780 and 1781 were often characterized by the rapid and unpredictable rhythms of independent actions. Strenuous forced marches through country intersected by rivers and creeks, abounding in swamps and morasses, without either shelter or regular meals, debilitated Britain's soldiers, many of them verging on middle age.

In June 1780, the American Congress commissioned General Horatio Gates to lead a southern army to drive the British from the South. Gates's first attempt to do so culminated in the Battle of Camden in August. His crushing defeat there sent Gates retreating in advance of his army into North Carolina. As the American armies fled from the scene of battle, "the road for some miles was strewed with the wounded and killed, who had been overtaken by the legion in their pursuit. The number of dead horses, broken wagons and baggage, scattered on the road, formed a perfect scene of horror and confusion,"[65] wrote Commissary of the Army Charles Stedman. But the victorious British, commanded by Lord Cornwallis, remained at Camden, paralyzed by a lack of supplies. In a report to the home government Cornwallis explained his failure to destroy Gates's army: "the Corps with me being totally destitute of Military stores, Cloathing, Rum, Salt and other Articles necessary for troops in the operations in the field, and provisions of all kinds being deficient, almost approaching to a famine in North Carolina, it was impossible for me to penetrate into that province before the harvest."[66]

A month later, strengthened by stores and reinforcements from Charleston, Cornwallis on the eighth of September launched the British invasion into North Carolina, advancing with the main body of the army through the hostile settlement of Waxhaws to Charlotte, while Patrick Ferguson and the loyalist militia moved along the frontier, and Banastre Tarleton, with cavalry and light and legion infantry, pressed up the west bank of the Wateree. Despite the unfriendly disposition of the inhabitants, the army was able to draw supplies from the numerous flour mills in the vicinity of Charlotte. But on the seventh of October the operations of the campaign received a major setback with the defeat of Ferguson at King's Mountain, where the small band of rangers and loyalist militia had been compelled by a superior American force to take refuge.

For more than seven months Ferguson's corps had been carrying out partisan operations under the worst possible conditions. In an effort to cut off the activities of enemy border partisan corps before the onset of winter, the loyalist troops were forced to make daily marches and countermarches through swamps where the water was two to three feet deep, to ford numerous streams (one, the winding Cane Creek, had to be crossed nineteen times in four miles), and to make frequent halts to repair bridges or to collect livestock for the use of the army. From the first of October until the sixth, when they took their ground on the rocky summit of King's Mountain, the corps had marched fifty-two miles and forded four streams.[67] Outnumbered two to one, with some detachments being out of ammunition, the command surrendered after an hour of desperate fighting.

The defeat and dispersion of Ferguson's corps, combined with the unsuccessful attempt to recruit militia in the Cheraw Hill region and sickness in the army, obliged Cornwallis to abandon the plan to reduce the province of North Carolina and to fall back into South Carolina. The retreat, which began on the fourteenth of October, lasted fourteen days and was one of the most arduous of the entire campaign. Rain fell steadily for several days without interruption, swelling the streams and flooding the roads until the soldiers were "over their shoes in water and mud." At night, without tents, they encamped in the woods on the damp, cold ground. Without rum and virtually destitute of provisions, "sometimes the army had beef and no bread, at other times bread and no beef. For 5 days it was supported upon Indian corn, which was collected as it stood in the field, 5 ears of which were the allowance for 2 soldiers for 24 hours. They were to cook it as they could, which was generally done by parching it before the fire." In riding through an encampment one evening Commissary Stedman observed the soldiers grating their corn, which was done by "breaking up their tin canteens and with a bayonet punching holes through the tin" which made a kind of rasp, on which they grated the corn in preparation for cooking. The water the men drank was, as Stedman described it, "frequently as thick as puddle." Few armies, he observed sympathetically, "ever encountered greater difficulties and hardships"; yet "the soldiers bore them with great patience, and without a murmur."[68]

On the twenty-ninth of October the army headquartered at Winnsboro, both to provide cover for the western frontiers of South Carolina and because the spacious plantations situated between the Broad and Wateree rivers could supply flour, forage, and livestock for the army while the sick and wounded recuperated.[69]

At Winnsboro, Cornwallis waited for reinforcements to renew the North Carolina campaign. General Alexander Leslie, delayed by swamps and high water, finally arrived from Charleston in December with a large detachment and the advance began on the nineteenth of that month.[70] In the meantime General Nathanael Greene, who took command of the southern department for the Americans on the third of December 1780, in seeking to avoid a direct operation against Cornwallis and to provision his troops, divided his army, sending Daniel Morgan with light troops to threaten the British post at Ninety-Six while the rest of his army marched under Greene to the vicinity of Camden.[71] Leaving garrisons at Augusta, Savannah, Charleston, Camden, and Ninety-Six, Cornwallis divided his remaining forces into three parts— his own, Tarleton's, and Leslie's. He ordered Tarleton to strike at Morgan's force while he led the main body of the army northwest between the Broad and Catawba rivers.[72]

Tarleton led a 1,000-man detachment on a difficult and circuitous march over the Ennore and the rapid Tiger rivers and numerous creeks and ravines all swollen by autumnal rains. Pushing forward, he crowded Morgan over the Pacolet, finally driving him back to the Cowpens, a pasture ground near the Broad River. At seven in the morning on the seventh of January, the British attack began. Although the field was well chosen for the movements of mounted men, Tarleton's troops were physically exhausted by the rigors of the previous weeks and worn out by a march through swamps and broken ground that began at three in the morning on the day of battle.[73] After a brief contest the militia gave way and the British approached the main body of Continentals. Although the American line gave way under the shock, the British infantry, exhausted by the fatiguing march in the morning and by their exertions in action, were unable to take advantage of the opportunity.[74] Tarleton then ordered the 71st Regiment with two hundred dragoons to charge. When the infantry and cavalry were within thirty yards, the retreating Americans rallied, faced about, and began firing. The unexpected counterattack stopped the tired British, threw the cavalry into disorder, and spread panic along the whole line.[75] The British sustained a severe loss, as almost all the infantry engaged were either killed, wounded, or made prisoner.[76]

In an effort to redeem the rout at Cowpens, Cornwallis attempted to intercept Morgan, who, with his infantry and British prisoners taken at Cowpens, crossed the Broad River and forded the Catawba on the twenty-fourth of January. His offensive operations impeded by baggage and carriages, Cornwallis halted at Ramsours Mills on the twenty-fifth to collect provisions and to destroy superfluous baggage, including tents, rum, and supplies. On the twenty-seventh and twenty-eighth, heavy rains raised the waters of the Catawba, so that when Cornwallis reached its banks on the twenty-ninth, it could not be crossed. In the meantime Morgan, incapacitated by rheumatism, was replaced in command on the Catawba by Greene. As Morgan made his way to Salisbury, Greene, with Morgan's division and a force of militia, prepared to dispute the British passage of the Catawba.[77]

At one o'clock in the morning on the first of February, Cornwallis, with the main body of the army, marched to McCowan's, a private pass six miles south of Beattie's public ford. The river, a rapid stream a half mile wide at the point of crossing, was almost four feet deep with a very rocky bottom. On the high, steep hills of the opposite shore a detachment of the enemy waited to contest the passage. As soon as the light and grenadier companies entered the water, the Americans began a constant and heavy fire, which the British were unable to return, as their cartouche boxes were tied at the back of their necks. In his journal, Sergeant Roger Lamb recalled the details:

> Let the reader only for a moment consider what a situation the British troops were placed in while they were wading over this ford, upwards of 500 yards wide, up to their breasts in a rapid stream, their knapsacks on their backs, 60 or 70 rounds of powder and ball in each pouch tied at the pole of their necks, their firelocks with bayonets, fixed on their shoulders, 300 of their enemies (accounted the best marksmen in the

world) placed on a hill as it were over their heads, keeping a continued and very heavy fire upon them.[78]

Once out of the water, the light infantry quickly formed and, charging with bayonets, drove the enemy from the ground, forcing them to retire precipitously across the Dan River into Virginia on the fourteenth of February.

The Continentals now being driven from North Carolina, the militia awed and prevented from collecting by Tarleton's destruction of a small retreating American force rendezvoused at Tarrant's Farm near Salisbury, Cornwallis retired from the Dan and proceeded by easy marches towards Hillsborough, the capital of the province, to rest his exhausted army and hopefully to recruit reinforcements from the inhabitants between the Haw and Deep rivers.[79] After the long and rapid pursuit of Greene, over bad roads and deep creeks, through wild and unsettled country, in heavy rains, without tents or the usual baggage, the barren country around Hillsborough, already exhausted of supplies, yielded no stores. Although small stocks of salt beef and pork and some hogs were found in the town, extreme necessity finally forced Commissary Stedman with a file of soldiers to go from house to house requisitioning food from the nearly destitute inhabitants; ultimately the half-starved troops were forced to eat the army's draft horses and some draft oxen confiscated from area farmers.[80]

It was the inability to support the army at Hillsborough that forced Cornwallis to withdraw to a camp near Allamance Creek, a tributary of the Haw. But inhabitants of the area assumed that the move was precipitated by Greene's return to North Carolina from Virginia,[81] and local support for the Crown melted away. In the meantime, Greene's command, strengthened by the junction of the divided Continental armies, formed for battle near Guilford Court House. Despite the fact that since the departure from Hillsborough the British troops were in great need of food and clothing and that they were outnumbered two to one, Cornwallis decided to attack the American army wherever it offered battle.[82]

The action at Guilford Court House began at half past one in the afternoon on the fifteenth of March. For better than a month prior to that time the British troops had suffered uncommon hardships. They had been hungry during much of the long campaign. "Sometimes," Sergeant Lamb recalled, "we had turnips served out for our food, when we came to a turnip field; or arriving at a field of corn, we converted our canteens into rasps and ground our Indian corn for bread; when we could get no Indian corn, we were compelled to eat liver as a substitute for bread, with our lean beef." [83] For over six weeks they had been without tents during a cold and rainy period. On the morning of the day they came to action, they had marched several miles starting at daybreak. They had had no provisions of any kind whatever on that day, nor did they receive any until four o'clock on the afternoon of the following day—and then only a quarter pound of flour and a quarter pound of lean beef. [84]

The action at Guilford Court House lasted two hours and was one of the most severely contested battles of the war. The remarkable discipline of the British troops and the superb tactical leadership of Cornwallis overcame the American advantage in numbers and position and won for the British a Pyrrhic victory, since the effectiveness of the British army was considerably impaired. [85] With nearly four hundred wounded and almost one hundred killed, Cornwallis's army was virtually prostrate. On the evening of the day of battle a torrential rain fell on the wounded and dying redcoats, who lay all night on the battlefield without tents. Their agony disturbed the rest and marred the victory for the survivors: "The cries of the wounded and dying," wrote a moved Commissary Stedman, "who remained on the field of action during the night, exceeded all description. Such a complicated scene of horror and distress, it is hoped, for the sake of humanity, rarely occurs, even in a military life." [86]

To add to its difficulties, the army was for all practical purposes destitute of food. A third of the men were sick or wounded; the rest were without shoes and completely exhausted. Under such circumstances, despite the victory, a retreat to secure supplies was necessary. On the eighteenth of March the British departed Guilford Court House. Although Cornwallis had anticipated a friendly reception and ample provisions at Cross Creek, the inhabitants of the high bluffs along the Cape Fear River were hostile, and supplies were scarce, forcing Cornwallis to push his weary army further south to Wilmington, a seaport town, to obtain supplies. [87] The sanguine expectations of loyalist support in North Carolina never materialized. That fact, coupled with a near total lack of an internal navigation system, persuaded Cornwallis to abandon North Carolina and strike into Virginia, where the death agony of the army ended at last. [88]

By the time of the American Revolution, British soldiers were professional fighting men, patient in adversity, composed under stress, enthusiastic in action, proud of their units and remarkably loyal to them. In part this was due to their training. After traveling on the continent in 1765 to gather information for a military work he was contemplating, General Burgoyne observed that two systems divided the military disciplinarians of Europe: one, the

Prussian, consisted of "training men like spaniels," with the generous use of the cane; the other, practiced by the French, "substituted the point of honor in the place of severity." The Prussian school produced the most highly disciplined troops in Europe, the French school the worst. British training, Burgoyne believed, struck a happy medium between Prussian severity and French laxity. Because "an Englishman will not bear beating so well as the foreigners in question," he wrote in his *Code of Instructions* for the guidance of his officers, British soldiers had to "be treated as thinking beings." Although Burgoyne perhaps exaggerated the uniqueness of British training, it did succeed in producing a subordinate, disciplined, spirited soldiery, motivated neither by the mechanical valor which characterized the Prussian soldier nor by the "personal pique" and "private pride" which sometimes immobilized the French.[89]

The "publick spirit" often exhibited by British soldiers in battle was, to some extent, also due to the fact that the British army was composed of mature men of respectable family and occupational background, who were driven into the army by economic necessity. For many of them army life, though often dull, held out the possibility of excitement. Although army food was usually bad and the pay low and habitually late, the army provided what was for the times decent medical care and a primitive pension system, which combined to offer a relative degree of security. By contrast some European armies, such as the Prussian, still filled their ranks with, as Burgoyne scornfully observed, "strangers, deserters, prisoners and enemies of various countries, languages and religions. They cannot," he concluded, "therefore be actuated by any of the great moving principles which usually cause extraordinary superiority in armies." Because they had "no hopes of fortune, nor even prospect of comfortable old age to inspire them," neither did they have "national spirit nor attachment to their prince, nor enthusiasm."[90]

To be sure, not all British soldiers felt "national spirit" or "attachment to their prince." Some of them were actively discontented and caused chronic problems or else deserted at the first opportunity. The majority were, however, apparently satisfied with their lot, or else saw no practical alternative to it. These are among the principal factors that help to explain why most soldiers yielded to authority, endured exceptional hardships, and fought with extraordinary fervor in the American war. They are not, however, the only factors and they were not necessarily the primary ones.

6 BONDS AND BANNERS

THE ARMY WAS a brotherhood of men. The complete severance of accustomed social relations was compensated, at least in part, by the acquiring of comrades. The feeling of comradeship, of belonging together, was derived largely from the sharing of similar experiences and the development of a set of common understandings. It was deeply rooted in the experiences and traditions of each regiment. It was above all based on kinship, both actual and implied, which served as the great binding force. The group solidarity thus generated was the single most important source of emotional security under the physical and psychological stress of combat.

War is a bloody and destructive test of physical and moral strength. This was particularly true for line infantrymen in the eighteenth century. Tightly bunched together in ranks and files, with little opportunity for personal distinction, they marched to meet the enemy in cadenced step, deafened by the hammering sounds of battle: the rattling of grapeshot, the whistle of musketball, the whir of cannonball. Dimly through clouds of black smoke they sensed or saw comrades, mauled and battered by the hail of shot, die like cattle. Some were probably numb to the deliberate, purposive suffering they caused and experienced. Most, even seasoned veterans familiar with danger, must have felt the kind of corrosive fear that comes from exposure to violent and sudden death. Except for seasoned veterans, few if any fully appreciated the physical and psychic stress of combat until it was too late; then, when the will began to falter, deeply ingrained training and discipline, innate courage, or the will to survive probably took over. These factors alone, however, are not sufficient to explain what sustained the men when the effects of cumulative fatigue and accruing fear began to wear away resolution and break down acquired military habits. What sustained them is difficult to ascertain precisely, but certain factors, material and moral, apparently provided compensations for the bitter hardships they patiently endured.

Traditionally armies have relied on alcohol as a short-term reinforcement to allay anxieties aroused by the prospect of battle.

There was drinking in the ranks of the English and French armies before the Battle of Agincourt in 1415; soldiers drank spirits before and during the Battle of Waterloo in 1815. Strong Navy rum was issued to English troops before the Battle of the Somme in 1916, and throughout most of World War I.[1] During the American Revolution, however, the use of alcohol to induce a feeling of courage had at best no more than an indirect effect. Regimental memoirs of the Revolution make no direct reference to the distribution of spirits before or during battle, although there are oblique and isolated reports of soldiers being intoxicated in combat. A young soldier in the Bayreuth Regiment, Stephan Popp, for example, blamed the explosion of a powder magazine at Yorktown on English soldiers who had "drunk too much brandy."[2] Yorktown was of course under siege, a situation which many people, including soldiers, would find psychologically intolerable. While the absence of explicit mention of drinking in battle does not rule out the possibility absolutely, before major battles, including Saratoga and Guilford Court House, the English were either on short rations or had long since used up all supplies of rum.

Among material incentives perhaps the most important was the prospect of booty. As discussed in Chapter 4, the notion that soldiers had a legitimate right to share in the spoils of war still enjoyed wide currency among European armies in the eighteenth century. Although private looting was discouraged, money or property taken from the enemy in the course of military operations was sometimes given as a gratuity to officers and soldiers; since the bounty often exceeded in value the soldier's weekly or even monthly pay, it represented an important economic motive to fight. During military campaigns in New York and Pennsylvania beginning in the summer of 1776 and continuing through mid-1778, many officers and soldiers made modest fortunes in booty. Large sums of paper currency confiscated by Hessian troops during the Battle of Long Island were turned into English headquarters for division and distribution among the troops.[3] In operations around Philadelphia in the fall of 1777 the Hessian Jaeger corps seized a flour magazine of 4,000 tons, numerous iron implements and stores of commodities such as soap and candles. These and more than 2,000 broadaxes, horseshoes, and horseshoe nails were apportioned out to the regiments engaged.[4]

Sudden windfalls such as these were, however, limited and capricious. As often as not the impoverished soldiers' dreams of enrichment were disappointed. As a reward for the hardships suffered during the siege of Charleston in 1780, General Henry Clinton promised each soldier who participated a share in the spoils; since slaves belonging to rebel prisoners were originally

listed as booty along with captured ships and magazines, generous individual portions were anticipated. In a move aimed at
conciliating the inhabitants, however, the military command decided instead to restore the property of all citizens who swore
allegiance to Britain.[5]

Soldiers and sailors were promised a handsome share in the
richly successful military operations carried out in Virginia during the first six months of 1781. In January, Benedict Arnold led
an infantry regiment and fifty dragoons on a mission to seize or
destroy the salt and tobacco stores which were a major source of
foreign credit enabling Americans to buy war supplies abroad.
Striking at Richmond, Westover, Petersburg, Chesterfield Court
House, Manchester, and Warwich, Arnold's small force confiscated or burned stockpiles of tobacco, flour, leather, and war
materiel of every description, including brigantines, sloops, and
schooners loaded with goods, valued at £1,000,000,000 sterling
altogether. The eight thousand hogsheads of tobacco taken alone
were worth £300,000 sterling.[6] In the meantime, Banastre Tarleton proceeded with the legion cavalry and eighty mounted infantry on a mission to destroy stores at Albemarle Court House believed to be destined for the use of General Nathanael Greene's
army, and all tobacco supplies between the James and the Dan
rivers. Successful raids were carried out in Charlottesville, Prince
Edward Court House, and New London in Bedford County.[7]

Although a great deal of booty was destroyed, "tremendous
riches" remained. Profits from the sale of tobacco, war materiel,
and war vessels were designated as bounty for the navy; revenues
from the sale of grain and livestock were earmarked for the army.
Despite Adjutant General Major Baurmeister's optimistic predic-
tion that "everyone will enjoy his well-deserved and rightful share
of booty, which will not be small," bitter disagreement between
the services over the division of the spoils stopped the proceedings completely while the issue was remanded to the London
government for settlement.[8] Ultimately an Admiralty court ordered the confiscated materiel "condemned to the Crown" to be
disposed of according to the King's pleasure.[9] In the long interim
before a decision was made, the army retained a lawyer, Thomas
Charles Williams, to represent it; Williams argued that the navy
had "no share in the toil or danger" of the expedition and therefore was not entitled to any of the booty. He requested that the
army be awarded the share of prizes condemned to the Crown.
On this occasion at least the King was persuaded to decide in
favor of the army; in October 1782 orders were finally given that
one-eighth of all the proceeds from the sale of the prize goods
should be given to Arnold, the rest to be divided among the
officers and soldiers who had participated in the operation.[10]

Apart from the material factors, there were other equally important but less predictable incentives to fight. The endorsement of religion, for example, had long been used to strengthen the resolve of soldiers before battle. In primitive warfare the enactment of tribal rites was a means of corporate inspiration. In Christian armies of the high Middle Ages a religious service was one of the preliminaries to battle.[11] In the more secular world of the eighteenth century, religion continued to play a supportive role, although its influence was considerably diminished.

Theoretically, religious training was supposed to serve a dual function: to improve military discipline and to provide spiritual fortification for battle. Operating from the premise that "by making them better men you make them better soldiers,"[12] the army tried without much success to employ religious teaching to suppress vice and immorality and to encourage subordination. *The Soldier's Faithful Friend*, a handbook on morals which enjoyed wide circulation in the late eighteenth century, enjoined soldiers to remember that "The duty of a *peaceable* and quiet submission to commanders is more incumbent on you as a *soldier* than in any other contract for service." The moral obligation to submit to authority was threaded together with the concept of regimental honor and loyalty: "Whenever you act turbulently or unsoberly, you bring scandal on your corps, and possess people with prejudices against your profession. This ought to put you on your guard as a *good subject*, as well as a good *soldier* and a good *Christian*."[13]

More important, the army relied on religious precepts to provide moral consolation for the bloody work of war. The military obligation to destroy was reconciled with the Christian injunction to love by making service to the state synonymous with service to God. *The Soldier's Faithful Friend* reminded its readers that "To wield the sword in defense of your *king*, your *country*, *religion*, and *laws*, and drive away an enemy is the soldier's Christian duty."[14] The promise of life after death was the soldier's compensation for the imminent risk of death on the battlefield: ". . . we owe it to God and our country to inspire our soldiers with a sense of religion" because "he who loses sight of immortality abandons the strongest incentive to the noblest deeds."[15]

The articles of war cemented the relationship between church and state. Beginning with the rules of war of 1673 and continuing throughout the eighteenth century, all officers and soldiers "not having just impediment" were required to attend divine services.[16] A system of secular discipline was established for those who did not: commissioned officers were subject to a court martial and noncommissioned officers and enlisted men forfeited twelve pence from their pay for conviction on a first offense, to which was added the laying in irons for a second offense. Sutlers' tents, which dispensed alcohol and provided entertainment of sorts, were ordered closed on Sunday during the hours of divine service, on penalty of permanent loss of the sutling license.[17]

Until 1796 a chaplain was appointed as part of the establishment of every regiment. It was only when the regiment was in the field, however, that his presence was required; when the troops were in garrison or billeted over the countryside, a garrison chaplain or a local minister administered to their spiritual needs.[18] Enjoined to "improve the morals of the soldiers," the duties of regimental chaplains were defined in the broadest terms: to give prayers three times a week to the regiment and daily at the regimental hospital; to preach a sermon on Sunday "calculated for the understanding of the soldiers, and pointing at such vices as they have been most remarked in," and to discourage cursing, swearing, drunkenness, gambling, and sexual excesses by whatever means possible.[19]

There is little concrete evidence, however, that religion was a positive, directing force in the army. Although British chaplains were probably no worse than the *cadre religieux* of the French army,[20] the system which brought them into the service guaranteed that they would be no better. Appointments were made on the nomination of the regimental colonel, but in most cases chaplaincies were bought and sold like regular commissions. Ministers were considered part of the regular establishment and were entitled to pay and retirement benefits, but they were not eligible for preferment as officers of corps.[21] Neither the material advantages nor the limited opportunities for advancement were great enough to attract the most talented churchmen. Rather the modest security of pay and pension was more likely to bring into military service the unplaced of the church. Indeed the record of service of regimental chaplains suggests that the mission of salvation played an insignificant role in their choice of careers.

Although the articles of war provided that chaplains should not be absent from their regiments except for illness or excused leave, there was a high rate of absenteeism during the Revolution. It was common practice for a regimental chaplain to hire a deputy at a nominal sum to serve in his stead when the regiment was ordered on foreign service.[22] Early in the war General Thomas Gage complained to the War Office that of the four chaplains assigned to the four battalions of the Royal American Regiment, two were in England and two were in America: "Those in England sometimes had Deputy's to officiate for them, sometimes not. The two in America did duty occasionally in all, and none were properly fixed to any particular battalion, so that none knew who was their proper Chaplain."[23] A Mr. Leathes, chaplain to Sir John Scarbright's regiment, did not visit his regiment for over twenty years. In 1782 the chaplain of the 40th Regiment was ordered to begin holding weekly services for his regiment "which had not been done for years past."[24]

While cases of prolonged absence such as these were probably exceptional, it was not unusual for British regiments to be without the services of a chaplain for periods of a year or longer.[25] Moreover, although regimental memoirs make occasional reference to religious services, there is little evidence that the sabbath was observed on a regular basis. There are infrequent reports on the performance of divine service to celebrate a military victory, but there is no mention made of any religious preparation for battle, either corporate or private.[26]

Under these circumstances it is not surprising that religion impinged only marginally on the consciousness of British soldiers. Some were downright irreligious; most were at best indifferent. In commenting upon the "want of religion among our troops," Jonas Hanway noted the comparative piety of the German mercenaries, who he found to be "generally inclined to religion; they have or seem to have, this great and ruling principle of life stronger on *their* minds than we usually have on ours."[27] During a visit to a British encampment on Staten Island in the summer of 1776, Ambrose Serle, private secretary to Admiral Richard Howe, was impressed both by the irreligiosity of the British troops and the piety of the Germans: "It was pleasing," he said, "to hear the Hessians singing Psalms in the evening, with great solemnity; while to our shame, the British navy and army in general are wasting their time in imprecations or idleness."[28] The Germans also exhibited a greater desire for spiritual fortification before battle. At the troop landings at Kipp's Bay in New York in 1776 the young Lord Rawdon observed that "The Hessians, who were not used to this water business and who conceived that it must be exceedingly uncomfortable to be shot at whilst they were quite defenseless and jammed together so close, began to sing hymns immediately. Our men expressed their feelings as strongly, tho in a different manner, by damning themselves and the enemy indiscriminately with wonderful fervency." Later Rawdon wryly observed, "My grandmother will probably change sides when she hears the Hessians sing hymns as loud as Yankees."[29]

The ultimate and most important motivation to battle in the army was generated by regimental esprit. Although the thousands of young men who answered the recruiter's drum-call were of disparate social origins, once they signed enlistment papers they became part of what was in fact a reconstructed society. The eighteenth-century soldier, separated from his family and usually unmarried, lived in relative isolation from the civilian community. For purely military reasons the army exploited that fact and in the process revived a kind of primitive tribalism whose central focus was the regiment.

Eighteenth-century military practice in general and English military practice in particular was to rely on the long service of both officers and soldiers as the principal means of developing regimental esprit. Mature veterans were thought to be more reliable soldiers. Because they had a home and friends in the regiment, they were less likely to desert than new recruits. Long years of training and experience in complex infantry tactics gave them superiority of performance in combat situations. As discussed in Chapter 2, over half of the privates in infantry regiments and nearly half of the members of elite regiments in the British army in the late eighteenth century were thirty years of age or over. The average foot soldier had better than ten years of service, while the average dragoon or grenadier, who represented the elite manpower of the army, had almost nine years.[30] The permanence of personnel made the development of group loyalties both necessary and inevitable. Friendships were bound to develop between men who lived and worked together, who cooked and ate their meals together, who trained and fought together for years on end.

Military society in the eighteenth century was above all founded on comradeship. The British army consciously created groups of friends, tenuously bound by links of kinship and friendship. The British officer corps was in a sense an exclusive club, or brotherhood, whose members were bound together not only by shared values but by family ties as well.[31] The laws of primogeniture, which cut younger sons off from inherited property, forced many young aristocrats to earn a living in government service, business, or the professions. The relative security they found in the military frequently induced all male members of the same family to follow the example of their father in choosing an army career. Many British officers who served in the American Revolution had close relatives in the service. Lieutenant General Archibald Robertson of the Royal Engineers, a member of an old Scottish family, had a brother who served for a time as deputy barrack master with the British army in Philadelphia.[32] Captain Alexander McDonald of the Royal Highland Emigrants had two sons in the army.[33] Three of the four sons of Major William Hughes, a thirty-year veteran, served in the British armed forces. Thomas left Eton at age fifteen to purchase an ensigncy in the 53d Regiment, in which his father held a commission. In April 1776, father and son sailed on the same transport for service in the American Revolution. Thomas Hughes's eldest brother, Ensign John Hughes of the 33d Regiment, served in America from 1781 to 1785 and was wounded in the battle of Guilford Court House. A third brother, Philip, was a captain in the East India Company fleet.[34] The war, moreover, provided greater access to the commissioned ranks for many younger sons; death, promotions, and augmentations created numerous vacancies, which were eagerly sought by ranking officers for their sons, nephews, and close family friends.[35]

The effects of tradition, or more precisely family inheritance, were apparently widespread among the men in the ranks as well. Having a father who was a career soldier was for many young men a decisive influence. Indeed, most male children born in the army remained in the army as professional soldiers. As an example, one contemporary account reports that of thirty males born into one regiment, twenty-five eventually became soldiers in the same regiment.[36] Usually such men, attracted by the personal experience of military life, made good soldiers; some of them became noncommissioned officers. John Stewart, for example, was born in the Royal Highland Emigrant Regiment in which his father served. The young Stewart started out as a drummer, went into the ranks, and gradually advanced to corporal.[37] Charles Atkinson was born and raised in the 47th Regiment. As a young man he joined the light company of the regiment, was promoted to corporal and then to sergeant, in which capacity he served for sixteen years.[38] Having brothers, uncles, cousins, or other relatives in the army also attracted men to the service. Robert Jenkinson of the 57th Regiment had a brother in the 54th Regiment; John Sutherland of the 64th Regiment had a brother in the grenadiers.[39] Sometimes, of course, strong family ties worked to the detriment of the service, as brothers who joined together deserted together, or deserted to be with relatives in other regiments.[40]

Contrary to the practice in modern armies of separating brothers in different military units, the British army made a concerted effort to unite brothers, relatives, and friends in the same company, employed even at the same work, as "nothing binds them more strongly to the service."[41] Some regiments limited recruiting to a particular county in order to exploit the desire of village boys "to enlist into a corps where they are certain of meeting many countrymen and perhaps relations." Sometimes recruiting teams included former members of the community who had enjoyed relative success in the army. Local men and boys, eager to rise above their ordinary expectations, volunteered after seeing "some of their friends, who probably enlisted only a few years before, return among them in the character of non commissioned officers, or sometimes in a higher station."[42] Since many soldiers had neither relatives nor friends in the regiment, the army tried to give new recruits "an early liking for the corps" by pairing each with "a good old Soldier appointed for his comrade."[43]

The fact that many men discovered kinsmen and friends among their fellow soldiers facilitated the transference of sentimental attachment from relatives and friends in a given locality to friends and relations in a particular regiment. So too did the designation of the regimental officer as head or father of the regimental family. Despite the exaggerated distinctions in rank in the eighteenth-century British army,[44] the moral authority of regimental officers was at least ideally based on affectionate, parental leadership. Training manuals urged young officers to treat their troops with "respect and good nature," to lead by example, and "never to drink or game with them," to practice restraint in discipline and "never presume to strike them, when [you] can possibly confine them." Affection without intimacy, respect without familiarity, firmness without severity would lead the men "to look on [the officer] as their father."[45]

Although these were ideals which the army only approximated, officers paid at least rhetorical respect to the general principles. A letter written by Captain Alexander McDonald to young Ensign James Robertson repeats the official canon:

> Justice leaning rather toward mercy than to severity with affability and attention to the men are the only necessary points—Do all you can to supply their wants reasonably— when they apply to you, answer them kindly and without harshness. When you must refuse their demands do it with apparent regret and take opportunity of giving satisfactory reasons for it, do not be too ready to punish them unless for crimes that will be allowed at all hands—when it becomes necessary to pass over their faults rather do not seem to know them—when you must punish them do it with regret— accompanied with advice and instruction. In short let them love and fear you as they would a kind parent.[46]

Whatever else can be said about the British officer corps, there were many decent men among them, who cared for the men in the ranks and tried to improve the conditions under which they lived and fought. Moreover, during war they were, of necessity, forced to share the same hardships and dangers endured by the men, which produced a kind of rough camaraderie upon which loyalty was built. In an age still bound by strong social ties, the long familiarity of officers and men made it possible for the officers to bring peer group sanctions to bear in the development of regimental esprit. Thomas Simes, whose work on military matters ranked among the best written in English,[47] considered this to be the most essential unifying element: "The praises and reproaches which each man has to expect from witnesses with whom he is to pass his life, are powerful inducements to those of the battalion to follow their example; they dread having reason to blush at their conduct before a comrade, and in some measure it is this salutary dread that constitutes what we term the spirit of corps, which preserves and cherishes the courage of a soldier."[48]

The same theme recurs in Samuel Bever's *The Cadet*, published in 1772: "It is certain," Bever wrote, "that officers and soldiers who belong to the same company, and who are thoroughly acquainted with one another, have an emulation and an obligation of doing their duty, lest their comrades should reproach them for the contrary."[49]

The wish to stand high in the opinion of comrades, coupled with the innate human desire for glory, was in fact turned to practical account by the army. Recruiting teams represented military service as an opportunity for healthy, active men to exchange monotonous work and grinding poverty for a life of excitement and adventure in the company of men associated in brotherly union. The recruiter's appeal set forth in one contemporary manual was probably imitated in a general way: "To all aspiring heroes bold, who have spirits above slavery and trade, and inclinations to become gentlemen, by bearing arms in His Majesty's ———— regiment, commanded by the magnanimous ————, let them repair to the drum-head where each gentleman volunteer shall be kindly and honourably entertained and enter into present pay and good quarters."[50]

The crafty Sergeant Kite in Farquhar's stock Restoration comedy, *The Recruiting Officer*, charmed and cajoled the young men of Shropshire into the Queen's Grenadiers by promising them an escape from all the mundane routines of daily living. As he leads potential recruits to sign the listing papers, Kite sings:

Our prentice Tom may now refuse
To wipe his scoundrel master's shoes
For now he's free to sing and play,
Over the hills and far away.
We shall all lead more happy lives
By getting rid of brats and wives,
That scold and brawl both night and day,
Over the hills and far away.[51]

The feeling of belonging to a group, united by emotional bonds, was also fostered by the use of various group distinguishing marks, each of which was emblematic of the solidary interests of the group. Although the military uniform has an obvious functional purpose, it has a symbolic one as well, that being to signify group unity and to symbolize the spirit of the regiment. Most

regiments wore scarlet jackets, but each regiment was distinguished by different color facings and cuffs, waistcoats and
breeches. Each regiment had its own distinctive pattern of lace, its
own design for the lapels, loops, and arrangements of the buttons
of the waistcoat.[52]

Regimental colors, large silk flags fixed on half pikes, were
equally important as a symbolic source of inspiration. Each regiment carried two, one displaying the king's colors, the other the
regimental facing color.[53] Despite the mechanical nature of infantry tactics, the battlefield was often a confusing scene. The many
separate actions that characterized eighteenth-century battle—
charges, bayonet assaults, cavalry attacks—were carried out in the
midst of a sound and smoke storm. The sheer volume of noise
produced by music, by the roaring of cannon, and by the whis-
tling of bullets from hundreds of rifle pieces drowned out the
commands shouted by officers. Dense smoke from artillery and
infantry balls, made of a basic composition of powder, sulphur,
and saltpetre, severely limited visibility.[54] Under these circumstances the colorful banner, six feet square on a pike nine feet ten
inches tall, acted as a rallying point around which the units engaged could coalesce. Although their weight and hazardous position in the center of the first rank exposed the color-bearers to
great danger, to carry the colors was considered an honor. Ordinarily only ensigns were ordered to the colors, but at the battle
of Camden Sergeant Lamb was permitted to carry one standard
of the 23d Regiment, a fact which he proudly noted in his
journal.[55]

A traditional ritual of consecration which followed the formation of a regiment invested the colors with special meaning and
character. When the newly raised units of the Royal Highland
Emigrant Corps were finally united in Halifax in the summer of
1777, a solemn ceremony was held to mark the occasion. Before
the troops were reviewed by Lieutenant Colonel Francis McLean,
their colors were consecrated in a formal religious service. After a
sermon "suitable to the occasion" was preached, each soldier was
individually administered a loyalty oath, by which he pledged
himself to honor and defend the colors. To close out the ceremony, the commanding officer delivered a speech to the troops,
explicitly emphasizing the almost mystic quality of the regimental
colors:

> Though we do not worship the colours, yet the awful cere-
> mony of this day sufficiently evinces, that they are with us, as
> in ancient times, the object of peculiar veneration; they hold
> forth to us the ideas of the prince whose service we have
> undertaken, of our country's cause which we are never to

forsake, and of military honor which we are ever to preserve. The colours, in short, represent everything that is dear to a soldier; at the sight of them all the powers of his soul are to rouse, they are a post to which he must repair through fire and sword, and which he must defend while life remains; to this he is bound, besides every other consideration, by the acceptance of a most solemn oath: to desert them is the blackest perjury and eternal infamy: to lose them by such an accident, even as one might otherwise judge unavoidable, is not to be excused, because to lose them, no matter how, is to lose everything; and when they are in danger, or lost, officers and soldiers have nothing for it but to recover them or die.[56]

To abandon or to lose the colors was the worst disgrace that could befall a soldier or his regiment, as Hanway's *The Soldier's Faithful Friend* grimly reminded its readers: "He who deserts his *colours*, or acts like a coward, is the vilest of all wretches"—except, added Hanway in a thinly veiled reference to the American rebels, "him who turns his arms against the breast of his own friends and countrymen."[57] As punishment for their humiliating defeat at Trenton, the Landgrave of Hesse took the colors of all of the Hessian regiments involved in that engagement and refused to restore them until they should "distinguish themselves in the future."[58] In order to prevent their being taken by the enemy as war trophies, the 3,500 survivors of Burgoyne's army burned their regimental colors before the final parade at Saratoga. Four years later Cornwallis's troops repeated the ceremony in similar circumstances.[59]

The bonds of unity formed by emotional ties and material objects were for the most part unarticulated and unconscious. It was regimental officers who inspired their men with the kind of corporate consciousness which in eighteenth-century armies substituted for patriotism. The aristocratic officer cadre, sworn to personal fealty to the Crown, were charged with the responsibility "to make [the men] fond of *their King, their country,* and *their corps*."[60] The moral authority for this kind of leadership stemmed from several disparate sources.

In the first place it was based on custom, tradition, and, most important of all, the officer's social position. Contemporary English society was, above all, hierarchical. Its broad base was formed by the working classes; the middle ranks were occupied by those who had either skills or property, and at the apex stood the nobility and gentry. It was an extremely status-conscious society in which each individual had a place which was generally accepted without question and without overt resentment toward those who enjoyed higher rank and greater privilege. For the great majority of people, habits of obedience were ingrained.[61] Military society closely approximated that old society, the rank and file being drawn from the base and from the lower middle classes, the officer corps composed almost entirely of gentlemen soldiers.[62] Conditioned to subordination by experience and upbringing, most soldiers readily accepted the ascribed authority of the officer class.[63] By contrast, the highly individualistic American soldiers, drawn from a relatively fluid society, showed great reluctance to accept authoritarian domination.[64]

In the second place the officers' moral authority was derived from the economic power entrusted to them by the state to pay and equip the troops.[65] Unlike the self-equipped yeoman warrior of ancient times, the eighteenth-century British soldier was paid and equipped by the state acting through its designated agent, the regimental colonel. Procedures established by Parliament provided for the pay appropriated for each regiment to be divided into subsistence and arrears. Subsistence money was paid out on a weekly or monthly basis by the Paymaster General to an agent appointed by each regimental officer; the agent paid the regimental paymaster, who then paid the company. Arrears, the difference between the full pay and subsistence of each man, was paid once a year by the agent.[66]

The system for clothing the troops operated in a similar fashion. The first regulations governing the issuance of clothing were adopted in the seventeenth century, when James II directed that clothing and equipment for the army, excepting ordnance, be purchased by the regimental colonel from a fixed sum of money known as "off reckonings." Any balance remaining after payment was made to the clothing contractors represented personal profit to the regimental officer. The first complete code of clothing regulations, adopted in 1707, retained the essential features of the system, which in fact was continued in use until 1855.[67] In contrast to the freedom and independence once enjoyed by the occasional soldier, the regular soldier was thus directly dependent on the regimental officer for his income, clothing, and equipment. Such an arrangement strengthened the authority of the officer corps.

Above all, the leadership of the British officer was founded upon attributes peculiar to officer cadres of the eighteenth century. The aristocratic British officer corps was a cohesive brotherhood with its own rigid code of honor which specified how all members were to behave. Gentlemanly conduct, personal fealty to Crown and country, intense group loyalty, and the pursuit of glory were the basic components of military honor.[68] Unlike military-manager leaders of a later period, who directed battlefield events from a distance, eighteenth-century officers willingly exposed themselves to great personal danger, almost in fact equalizing the risks of warfare between themselves and the rank and file. A typical example of the conspicuous heroism dictated by the military code is that of a sixteen-year-old officer, Lieutenant Stephen Harvey of the 62d Regiment, at the Battle of Saratoga. Although wounded several times during the engagement of the nineteenth of September, young Harvey refused to leave the battlefield. Finally, once again struck by a ball in the leg, he was mortally wounded while being carried from the field. His dying words, "Tell my uncle [the adjutant general by the same name] I died like a soldier," epitomize the feudal notions of glory that still operated among officers.[69]

Traditional conceptions of military honor, moreover, demanded that even general and field officers be prepared to directly suffer the consequences of their orders. Indeed, as one contemporary military manual reminded officers, "The more exalted the station, the more requisite the example to inspire the irresolute with firmness and the timorous with fortitude."[70] Frequently this meant personal participation at the height of the fighting. At the battle of Guilford Court House, for example, Lieutenant Colonel James Webster of the 23d Regiment ordered his brigade to charge the enemy across open ground. The brigade quickly formed and advanced at a rapid run until it approached within forty yards of the enemy line; seeing the American force, with arms presented and resting on a fence rail, the troops halted in confusion. Webster rode to the front of the line and, with a flamboyance typical of his profession, cried out, "Come on, my brave Fusiliers," and led the charge into enemy fire. He later died of wounds sustained in the charge.[71] Brigadier General Charles O'Hara was wounded twice in the action at Guilford Court House, but he remained in the field as long as the action lasted.[72] Although he was not wounded, Cornwallis himself had two horses shot from under him during the action.[73]

The consequences of officers' willingness to share with their men the risks of front-line fighting were twofold. First, the British army suffered a high rate of officer battle casualties. Nineteen officers were killed at Bunker Hill in contrast to 207 rank and file; 70 officers were wounded, along with 758 enlisted men. In the Battle of Long Island, 2 lieutenant colonels and 6 captains were among the 400 casualties. At Germantown, 4 officers, including Brigadier General James Agnew, Colonel of the 44th Regiment of Foot, and Lieutenant Colonel James Bird of the 15th Regiment of Foot, were killed. Thirty, including Lieutenant Colonel William Walcott of the 5th Regiment of Foot, were wounded.

At Camden 2 officers were killed and 8 wounded, along with 64 rank and file killed and 213 wounded. At Guilford Court House Cornwallis lost 5 officers killed and 21 wounded as compared to 75 enlisted men killed and 369 wounded. Cornwallis and General Alexander Leslie were in fact the only general officers of the British army who were not wounded. At Cowpens, South Carolina, Daniel Morgan's marksmen picked off British officers early in the action, a fact which Sir John Fortescue claims accounted for Morgan's ultimate victory. There were 66 officer casualties in that contest. At Eutaw Springs the British suffered the highest percentage of losses by either side during the entire war; out of a force of 1,800 the British lost 20 officers and 664 men killed, wounded, and taken prisoner.[74]

Second, by exposing themselves to risks, by accepting the possibility of death or disablement, officers not only met the criteria of honor but also enhanced their effective authority over the troops. Their legitimate authority established by traditions, social custom, and inspiration, they served as the co-ordinating organs of regimental esprit. The mechanisms they used to develop corporate spirit were principally coercion and manipulation.

There is no concrete evidence of direct and personal coercion of common soldiers during combat in Revolutionary records, such as the flogging forward of soldiers by their officers that occurred at Waterloo.[75] Although European officer corps still counted among the prerogatives of leadership the right to use violence, British officers seldom resorted to arbitrary and extreme force to develop fighting spirit. To be sure, the personal consequences of defeat were harsh enough incentives for most soldiers to perform honorably. Captivity by the enemy meant separation from family and friends in the regiment and, in the Revolutionary era, usually severe deprivation in enemy prison camps.[76] Moreover, as discussed in Chapter 4, the military code of law permitted drastic sanctions for those who ran away or refused to fight.

Fear of punishment certainly made some men remain soldiers; it did not necessarily make them good soldiers. In the psychodynamics of esprit, the ability of the officer corps to inculcate the values of the military code weighed far more heavily. Except for the gentleman concept, which was not operative where ordinary soldiers were concerned,[77] all of the components of military honor—fealty, brotherhood, and especially the pursuit of glory— were passed on by officers to the men in the ranks. Since officers were seldom directly and personally involved with the training of their men and since familiarity with common soldiers was considered a breach of behavior,[78] the battlefield was the place where soldiers were taught the code, primarily by example but also by exhortation.

Shortly before the troops were brought to action it was customary for regimental officers to address the men of their command. Most speeches were probably given extemporaneously, but
a few survive, at least in substance; these are significant indices to
the realities of military life. The speech made by General Eyre
Massey to the men of the Royal Highland Emigrants in June 1777
was probably representative of the genre. In his opening remarks
Massey assigned to the military profession a higher status than
most contemporaries conceded to it: "While inferior professions
hold out sordid views as a spur to emulation, the object of the
military is of the most sublime nature, viz. to perform gallant
actions, that shall gain the approbation of their sovereign and
superior officers, the esteem even of the enemy, the gratitude of
fellow subjects and the admiration of posterity." Time and time
again Massey challenged the troops to devote all of their energies
to the pursuit of glory: "It is in the strongest manner recommended to the soldiers, to cherish in their breasts this natural and
laudable passion for true glory." For it "the greatest men that ever
existed did not think it too much to sacrifice interests, ease and
even life." Despite the harsh realities of battle there were personal satisfactions for those who tried to distinguish themselves:
"Who then does not feel the influence of that divine spark, which
prompts us to rise above the common level? Who has not ambitions to transmit his name with applause to posterity? Who does
not wish and pant for the opportunity to signalize himself?" Besides being able to transcend the narrow confines of the world in
which they were forced to live, bravery and courage on the part
of the soldier would produce more conventional compensations
as well: "The approbation of their officers will follow, and from
thence many indulgences."[79]
     Although the language and the style of delivery of these pre-
action speeches probably varied widely, they had apparently a
common content which exploited two basic human needs: the
need to experience feelings of self-worth and the need to win the
approval of others. A contemporary military handbook offered to
its readers what the author described as a typical pre-action
speech; addressed to "Brother soldiers," it promised respect and
recognition to the brave, censure and disgrace to the cowardly:
"It is likely you may soon be brought to the test, when, if you
perform like brave men against the enemy, I shall applaud, esteem and respect you; if otherwise, you may rest assured of meeting with the disgrace and punishment due to your cowardly
behaviour."[80]

     Because there were only a very limited number of social roles
open to them, because heroism in battle provided at least an
opportunity for recognition if not for glory, and because soldiers

were conditioned by training and experience to accept personal responsibility for "the credit and reputation of the regiment," they accepted those precepts and tried to emulate the behavior of their officers in battle. During the American Revolution, British troops fought with a revolutionary ardor. Commenting in the early stages of the war on the quality of the troops, Francis, Lord Rawdon, observed, "I never saw better stuff, and they are as keen for action as ever men were."[81] Anxious to avenge their Pyrrhic victory at Bunker Hill, British troops, according to Ambrose Serle, were "actuated by one spirit, and impatiently wait for the arrival of the Hessians and other troops." High spirits persisted through the summer; as he watched the battle for Long Island from the poop deck of the British flagship *Eagle*, Serle wrote with admiration of the British troops that "nothing could exceed their spirit and intrepidity in attacking the enemy." With tongue in cheek Serle complained that the infantry failed only in one respect—they could not outrun the fleeing Americans.[82]

The fire and spirit which distinguished these early actions persisted. At Bedford, the light infantry, who were the first engaged, "dashed in as fast as foot could carry." Retreating rebels were met by the grenadiers "who behaved with the most astonishing coolness and intrepidity."[83] Earl Percy, leading the elite Guards, praised "their readiness and willingness to do whatever they were desired [which] has gained them the esteem and approbation of the whole army." In short, Percy rhapsodized, "they are not only the finest body of men that ever was seen, but it seems to be the study of every officer and man among them to be as distinguished for discipline, spirit and conduct. Nothing is a hardship, nothing is a difficulty with them. Whatever they are directed to do, they do with chearfulness and pleasure."[84]

Successive British victories increased the army's confidence and buoyed its spirits. During the siege of Quebec the beleaguered redcoats displayed such courage and perseverance as to reflect honor on both officers and privates. When the siege failed, the British pursued the remnants of the Montgomery-Arnold force in the direction of Crown Point, their spirits rising in proportion to the difficulties they had to encounter. Throughout the campaigns of 1777 headquarters repeatedly commended the "animated and spirited good will" of the troops.[85] On the long and difficult march to their destiny at Saratoga, Burgoyne's men remained in "highest spirits, admirably disciplined," prompting the general to report that their behavior was "as uniformly good in the camp as in action."[86] After the arduous campaign that ended at Guilford Court House, Cornwallis reported to Secretary of State Germain:

The conduct and actions of the officers and soldiers that compose this little army will do more justice to their merit than I can by words. Their persevering intrepidity in action, their invincible patience in the hardships and fatigues of a march of above 600 miles in which they have forded several large rivers and numberless creeks, many of which would be reckoned large rivers in any other country in the world, without tents or covering against the climate, and often without provisions, will sufficiently manifest their ardent zeal for the honour and interests of their sovereign and their country.[87]

There is no reason to believe that men who fought so well after enduring so much did so because they were artificially aroused by a tot of rum or a crack of the whip. Alcohol and discipline imposed from above were at best of limited use in getting men to fight. Indeed the fact that so many deserters and prisoners of war eventually escaped and voluntarily returned to their regiments, often at great personal risk, precludes the traditional assumption that they were motivated exclusively by fear. Unlike the captured American seamen studied by Jesse Lemisch, who engaged in active resistance rather than defect,[88] many British prisoners defected in order to betray the enemy; their conduct reveals a good deal about their loyalties.

Although battle casualties were comparatively low in eighteenth-century wars, armies were heavy consumers of manpower. To offset the losses suffered by desertion and disease, belligerents tried to lure men from the ranks of the adversary into their own. During the American Revolution the Continental Army enlisted German and—often to the Americans' acute distress—British defectors. Because they were mercenaries, the German troops were more likely than the British to desert. In recognition of that fact the American Congress launched what proved to be a very successful propaganda campaign, beginning with the Hessian troops encamped on Long Island. Christopher Ludwig, a German-American baker, was engaged to circulate inflammatory literature, which stressed the involuntary nature of their service. Copies of British treaties with the six foreign princes were printed and distributed in order to expose the "slavish" character of the contracts. To excite disaffection the mercenaries were offered citizenship and a fifty-acre freehold in the new republic.[89] Similar material was circulated later in the war among troops in the South. A handbill addressed to "My dear brother soldiers" and signed with the mark of Henry Humphrey, an illiterate British deserter, urged the soldiers to desert "from the bondage of tyranny to liberty and happiness" and promised those who did two

hundred acres of land, "a sow and two breeding swine."[90] Either
in response to Humphrey's message or because they had, as General Alexander Leslie warned General Clinton, formed "too many
connections," large numbers of Hessians deserted.[91]

Because of their special vulnerability, particular attention was
given to German war prisoners. Prisoners from the Convention
Army were released to live and work in nearby German-American communities. Those taken later at Yorktown were separated
from the Scottish and English troops and quartered in towns such
as Winchester and Fredericksburg, with heavy concentrations of
German-Americans, in order that they might see at first hand "in
what a comfortable manner their countrymen live."[92] In most
cases the townspeople were extremely hospitable to them; so too
was the American Congress, which offered land and jobs to all
those who switched sides: those who agreed to enlist in the American army were promised an eight dollar bounty and one hundred acres of land at the end of the war; those who took an oath
of allegiance to the United States and paid an eighty dollar assessment for their maintenance as prisoners of war were given certificates of discharge and citizenship in the United States; those who
were willing to take the oath but were unable to pay the eighty
dollars for their keep were allowed to sign three-year work contracts with local farmers, who paid the charge in exchange for
their labor.[93] At the end of the war several German officers protested to Commander in Chief Guy Carleton that many of the
Germans who indented as servants or enlisted in the rebel army
did so under compulsion.[94] A subsequent investigation conducted
by Major Carl Leopold Baurmeister, Adjutant General of the
Hessian forces, revealed, however, that the majority had voluntarily defected and that "very few showed any desire to return."[95]

By contrast, the deep attachment most British soldiers felt for
their regiments led many of them, prisoners and even deserters,
to attempt to return to their regiments. As mentioned in Chapter
4, many of those who deserted from the Convention Army while
it was in captivity in Virginia and Pennsylvania first notified their
officers of their intention to escape in order to join Clinton's
forces in New York; they requested and received certificates enti-
tling them to arrears in clothing and payment. One group of 20
such deserters organized themselves into a small company, appointed a sergeant to command them and, prior to their escape,
drew up a set of rules modeled on the articles of war, swore to
abide by them, and prescribed penalties, ranging from instant
death by hanging at the first tree to cutting off of the ears of any
man who broke the rules.[96] These and 230 others eventually
made their way to New York, where most of them were drafted
into regiments stationed there.[97]

Although there was not as yet any formal system of rewards, the army was slowly beginning to appreciate the value of such loyalty and to publicly recognize it. In 1774 Robert Begent, a private in the 43d Regiment of Foot, was singled out by Earl Percy for his "fidelity and attention to his duty" in apprehending a would-be deserter. Percy thanked Begent in the general orders and promised to "take care that he is properly rewarded."[98] Later three captured soldiers belonging to the Royal Welch Fusileers and twelve marines were commended by the commander in chief because they had "nobly despised the offers, and defied the threats of the rebels, who have tried to seduce them to take arms against their king and fight against their brother soldiers." The general ordered that money be brought to them in the Worcester jail so as "to prevent such bravespirited soldiers from suffering."[99]

Substantial numbers of British soldiers did, of course, desert to rebel service, but even among these there were many who deserted again at the first opportunity to rejoin their old regiments. It was in fact so common an occurrence that American military leaders soon became highly skeptical about enlisting British deserters. In a report to the American Congress, Timothy Pickering, Adjutant General of the Continental Army, observed that "the fidelity of the Hessians may be relied on without scruple," but he continued, "We have been cautious in letting out the British unless recommended as trusty men."[100] As commander in chief of the Continental Army, General Washington's personal experience with British deserters convinced him too that the average British soldier had a "treacherous disposition." Although he proposed raising a corps composed entirely of German-Americans and German deserters,[101] Washington adamantly opposed the enlistment of British soldiers.[102] Indeed, he objected, "Mr. Burgoyne could hardly, if he were consulted, suggest a more effectual plan for plundering us of so much money, reinforcing Mr. Howe with so many men, and preventing us from recruiting a certain number of regiments, to say nothing of the additional losses which may be dreaded, in desertions among the native soldiers, from the contagion of ill example and seduction."[103]

Several factors were at work in influencing so many deserters to return to British service. One of them was certainly the fear of being apprehended as a deserter. Despite greater leniency in military discipline, desertion was still a capital crime. In the event of conviction the best one could hope for, short of severe corporal punishment, was to be permanently exiled to service at some remote post in a hostile environment, such as Africa or the West Indies,[104] where mortality rates were exceptionally high even by the standards of the day.[105] Disillusionment with life in the rebel ranks probably caused some deserters to have a change of heart.

In his account of his own escape from Yorktown, Sergeant Lamb recalled meeting a man who had deserted from the Royal Welch Fusileers two years earlier. As he roamed about the countryside looking for work, he was surprised at "finding himself universally despised by the Americans." [106]

Fear and disillusionment were not, however, the only factors, and they were certainly not the most important ones. The life of a soldier in the British army was not by any standards, either then or now, good. Still, there were sufficient compensations to attract some men to it and to keep most of them in it. It provided security: a job, however hazardous; income, however inadequate; and for some a pension, however stingy. It provided adventure, however grim at times, and recognition, however remote for the line infantryman. Above all, it provided a sense of belonging.

By its very nature the military style of life tended to produce a cohesive community. The historical continuity of regiments and the social isolation of the army helped to develop distinctive values and heroic traditions. For years on end the same soldiers lived and worked in the same regiments in the closest physical proximity. Over time they made lasting friendships and developed that sense of fraternity which was the very essence of regimental esprit. Although most did not aspire to the hero's role, there were few who did not want to stand high in the opinion of friends; it was for this that they sometimes acted beyond their personal capacities. In a sense the negative sanctions for cowardice as well as the positive benefits for bravery merely encouraged soldiers to act the way they wanted to anyway. As they participated in battle, sharing terrible defeat and great victory, they became convinced that they had experienced an extraordinary event. A brotherhood of veterans now, they came to identify with the historical achievements of their regiments. Elaborate rituals and ceremonies, such as the consecration of the colors, enhanced the feeling of self-esteem and the sense of group solidarity. The effect was to produce a powerful sense of loyalty to the regiment which in the eighteenth century substituted for patriotism. It was that loyalty to the regiment which was the primary psychological motive that made soldiers endure patiently the rigors of campaigning or of captivity and made them fight bravely in battle. Fear was, of course, a component, but not in the way usually suggested. Fear often made men desert; loyalty frequently brought them back.

Conclusion

The British army in the late eighteenth century was a small organization of officers and men more or less isolated from the civilian society which gave it grudging support. Like most armies then and now it possessed institutional characteristics some of which contrasted sharply with those of the civilian life around it. It was an authoritarian organization which demanded exact obedience. It was a rigidly stratified social system with a hierarchy of command established and maintained by formal rules and regulations, infractions of which were subject to severe punishment. It was a self-contained society, which provided for all of the physical and most of the psychological needs of its members. It was a society with deeply rooted traditions or ways of doing things which prized conformity and discouraged initiative among its members.

Although some of the same characteristics were shared by other eighteenth-century institutions, they existed in the army in exaggerated form; as a consequence the young men who signed listing papers were forced to radically alter many of the values by which they had lived and to adjust to a new and different set of values. The new world of the army loosed them from previous social controls but forced them to accept other kinds of constraints imposed by the military organization and discipline. In the process they were changed in many ways.

Without the testimony of the soldiers themselves, no profound conclusions can be reached. It is, however, possible to abstract the essence of group personality by examining the characteristics of military life to which individual soldiers had to respond and adjust. In fact a wide range of institutional factors contributed to the development of a basic personality pattern: the hierarchy of officers supported by authority and rigid discipline, the paternalistic nature of army life, and group solidarity based upon common experiences, intimate coexistence, and kinship.[1]

To a considerable degree British soldiers were culturally conditioned to accept certain values distinctive of military life. They, for example, accepted the hierarchy of officers because they were accustomed to a definite hierarchical placement in the general civilian society. Traditional patterns of social interaction conditioned them to accept the idea of rank and to accept or at least to play the role of subordinate. In the eighteenth-century army high civilian status automatically converted to officer rank. The status of officers was maintained by rigid social distance and enforced symbolic deferential behavior and by a system of social privileges.[2]

Rituals of deference exacted from all common soldiers clearly established and defined their relationship with those of higher rank. Manners and behavior were highly stylized to conform to the great law of subordination. In the presence of an officer soldiers were obliged to display "a humble, decent and proper mode of behaviour."[3] They were not permitted to wear hats in the company of an officer because to do so implied an unacceptable degree of familiarity. When addressed by an officer, they were supposed to remove their hats and take care that "their countenance should be open, calm and attentive; and that they give mild and submissive answers to all questions."[4] When saluting an officer, a signal both of greeting and of recognition of those of higher station, soldiers were forbidden to smile, since "that carries with it too great an air of freedom, which must never be taken or admitted with a superior."[5]

Distinctions in dress were also a conspicuous mark of rank in the army, as they were in civilian society. Although regimental uniforms of officers and noncommissioned officers were similar in design to those worn by the rank and file, they were of superior quality materials and were more elaborately embellished. The lace-trimmed cocked hat, silk or velvet stocks, and linen gaiters with horn buttons, the tops lined with white leather edged in red and supported by inch-wide garters and silver buckles, emblematically clarified the institutional social structure and the role of the individual in it.[6]

In order to preserve the social distance suggested by rituals and by ceremonial dress, fraternization by officers with the rank and file was treated as a breach of behavior. Defined as an honor crime, it was punishable by forfeiture of rank. Relatively few such cases ever came to trial, however, probably because of rigid self-enforcement by the class-conscious Englishmen.[7] Those which did are illustrative of the formalized interpersonal relations which existed in the army. In one such case Ensign John Miller was court martialed for keeping company with soldiers: he was allowed to resign from the service. In another, Lieutenant John Cummings was accused of fraternization with common soldiers because he drank with them; although it was acceptable for a soldier to drink to an officer, officers were forbidden to drink with soldiers since to do so would convey an impression of equality or companionship.[8]

Preferential treatment and the lion's share of material goods also emphasized the presumed superiority of officers over men in the ranks. Officers were exempt from degrading tasks and from corporal punishment, no matter what the crime.[9] They were entitled to more and better food and drink, to the best lodgings available, and to a variety of fringe benefits ranging from lodging money to "furniture money" and "utensil and bed money" when their living quarters were not furnished. Bat and forage money was paid to them when they took the field. In the event they suffered a disabling wound, or lost an eye or a limb, they were allowed to collect benefits up to a full year's pay plus medical costs. Survivors' benefits ranging from sixteen to fifty pounds per annum were paid to the widows of officers killed in battle. Upon retirement from the service officers were eligible for a pension of half pay for life.[10]

In addition to legal pay and pensions, there were extralegal perquisites incidental to rank. It was, for example, considered the officer's prerogative to pocket the pay of all battle casualties, which frequently involved substantial amounts of money. On one occasion during the American Revolution, an officer realized £800 profit by such means. By estimate of the War Office in 1783, the average regimental colonel of dragoons earned about £2,177 a year during peace and £2,653 during war, while the income of the average infantry colonel ranged from £800 in peace to £1,200 in war.[11]

Perhaps the key to effective control of the rank and file was the Oedipal situation which characterized relations between officers and soldiers. As father-surrogates, officers were the source of all necessaries, privileges, and gifts. As such they loomed large as great benefactors. They simultaneously figured as great oppressors, however, in the exercise of the paternal functions of authority, discipline, and justice.[12] From all indications soldiers accepted both the principle and the practice of authority by their officers. Although the principles underlying military authority were rarely explicitly explained to them, they were nonetheless impressed upon them in the experiences they had to undergo as soldiers.

The regimentation of army life accustomed soldiers to rigid discipline and submission. Their daily chores were prescribed in detailed orders; aspects of their daily lives normally considered to be within the realm of private discretion, such as the hours of sleep, eating, and bathing or the selection of social acquaintances, were all controlled by the army. The incessant repetition of the martial routine, such as marching in cadence in files or columns, or loading and firing muskets in battalion, conditioned them to act without question and to do as they were told. Failure to obey the rules led to punishment or to personal humiliation. Their lives organized both overtly and covertly, soldiers became dependent upon institutional routines. Their initiative inhibited or destroyed, they looked to the institution to make all decisions and to give all directions.

Feelings of dependence were also fostered and maintained by the paternalistic nature of the organization, which provided its members with virtually all of their biological and psychological needs. As members of the military community, soldiers were assured of food, clothing, shelter, and medical care. Protections such as these provided them with a kind of security for which there was no civilian counterpart. In civilian life, each man was responsible for his own maintenance. He must forage for himself, provide his own shelter, clothing, and health services. The army, by contrast, was a protected environment, which provided a fair degree of security, notwithstanding great deprivations.[13] Compared with civilians of similar age and status, soldiers had relatively few outside concerns.[14] Such security, however, could be gained only by conformity and dependency.

Although there was variety in behavior, soldiers were in general submissive and obedient. A study of military court records and of personal memoirs of officers reveals no widespread insubordination or intransigence. There was, to be sure, a considerable amount of delinquent behavior. For the most part, however, it was individual rather than collective. It was usually prompted by some personal and immediate problem instead of being organized, premeditated action. It was in many cases produced by the incentives to delinquent behavior found within the army itself. Although the army officially frowned upon excessive drinking, the issuance of rum as part of the daily ration and as a special reward for cooperative behavior or for extra work, was an institutional routine which in fact encouraged if it did not promote habitual alcoholism. The policy of a single soldiery and the enforced isolation of the army from the civilian community had multiple consequences. Limited sexual opportunities produced sexual frustrations and gave an exaggerated value to sexuality. Sexual anxieties in turn contributed directly to restlessness, boredom, alcoholism, and sexual promiscuity.[15] The ultimate purpose of the army to destroy the human and material resources of the enemy tended to alter among soldiers the traditional civilian attitude toward the rights of private property and as a consequence encouraged widespread looting.[16]

Army life was a succession of deprivations and frustrations. It was dangerous and uncomfortable. It encouraged dependency and demanded conformity. It thwarted spontaneity and undermined initiative. It impeded the normal maturation of personality and, to some extent, constricted and standardized it.[17] Despite these destructive features, there were constructive and compensatory aspects of military life. It gave soldiers an opportunity for change and excitement. It freed them from multiple civilian problems. Most of all it fostered in them a feeling of fraternity. The development of group solidarity is characteristic of all militaries, no matter how primitive or how modern. In modern armies the dynamic binding force is identification with cause or country. In the eighteenth-century British army, it was identification with the regiment. The impregnable solidarity of the regiment was based upon several institutional influences.

In the first place, it was based upon the peculiar occupational fact that the purpose of the army was the destruction of the enemy and the protection of itself. The fact that the welfare of the individual was inextricably bound with that of the group magnified and intensified collective thinking. Group consciousness was also implanted through traditions, themselves derived from the intimate nature of army living and from the historical achievements of the regiment. Soldiers developed a sense of belonging together because they were together constantly. They cooked and ate their meals together; they slept together in the same barracks, even in the same beds; they suffered together the incessant repetition of drill; they survived together the dangers and discomforts of war: the mud and vermin, the hunger and thirst, the fatigue and fear.

Above all, group consciousness was based upon feelings of kinship. Denied the personal security that comes from participation in a stable family life and prevented from forming new attachments by the frequency of army moves, soldiers came to identify with their comrades in a special way. In the peculiar social environment of the army they absorbed feelings of solidarity not only with their blood relations and friends but also with other men in the regiment, no matter who they were or where they came from. The image of solidarity linked them together and distinguished them from civilians, from their German allies, and from any other group. It was a source of emotional security under the stress of combat or the exigencies of daily life. It was the sustaining force for morale.

The reactions of soldiers to the conditions imposed in the military situation were by no means uniform. Some soldiers were obedient, submissive, and loyal all of the time; others were obedient, submissive, and loyal some of the time; a few were rebellious, intractable, and maladjusted most of the time. Most men after all entered the service with well-developed personalities and with a set of cultural values that were not always compatible with the objectives of the organization. The majority of soldiers, however, successfully adjusted to army life: they abandoned their old daily living habits and acquired new ones; they accepted the authoritarian structure of the army and their own subordinate role in it; they submitted to the constraints imposed by army life and rejected many of the social restraints which governed civilian behavior; they surrendered their egos to the group and relegated individual initiative and responsibility to the organization. They did what was required of them, and as a consequence they became converted to the institutional view of themselves: obedient, submissive, loyal, and good soldiers.

Appendix
Parliamentary Debate on Responsibility for the British Loss in America

The humiliating defeat of Burgoyne's army at Saratoga and four years later the surrender of Cornwallis at Yorktown each produced bitter debate over responsibility for British military failures. Members of Parliament blamed ministers; ministers blamed generals; generals blamed each other, ministers, and admirals. Significantly, no one blamed the performance of British soldiers. It was the nature rather than the extent of Burgoyne's defeat that first stirred debate. Rumors of Burgoyne's surrender reached England on 2 December 1777. Three days later a prolonged and often vitriolic debate began in the House of Lords. The anarchy of groups and individuals that generally characterized Parliamentary politics up to 1812 had for the time being divided into two loose groups: those who formulated or supported government policy in America and those in open opposition to it. Although there was a Parliamentary majority in favor of the war, the opposition, including the brilliant William Pitt, Earl of Chatham, the eloquent Charles James Fox, and other lesser figures held together by family ties, personal ambitions, and general agreement on the great issues raised by the American war, eventually brought down the government and all attempts to recover the American colonies.[1]

On 5 December 1777, before the news of Burgoyne's surrender was official, Pitt called for a Parliamentary inquiry into "that melancholy disaster." In a lengthy speech he attacked the policies of Lord George Germain's government, dwelling principally upon the impossibility of reconquering America and upon the incompetence of ministers in waging the war. Burgoyne and his army were, he said, obliged "to surrender themselves prisoners of war to the provincials" because of the "ignorance, temerity and incapacity of ministers." The invasion of Canada was, he said, "a mad project" and the decision to employ Indians in it a "bloody, barbarous and ferocious" one. If he ignored the army and its leaders it was because he was totally convinced that neither was at fault.[2] Three weeks earlier, in a speech that lashed out at the government, he had praised the troops' performance in America: "No man," he said, "thinks more highly of them than I do; I love and honour the English troops. I know their virtue and their valor. I know they can achieve anything except impossibilities and I know that the conquest of English America is an impossibility."[3]

The debate that began in the House of Lords was continued by the opposition in the House of Commons, when Colonel Isaac Barré called on Lord Germain to reveal to the House "what has become of General Burgoyne and his brave troops." Germain confirmed the "unfortunate affair" but begged the Commons "not [to] be over anxious in condemna-

tion either of ministers or generals." Far from anxious to condemn the
generals, Barré, joined by James Luttrell and Edmund Burke, vehe-
mently denounced the ministry. "With the general and his troops," Burke
spoke for the opposition, "there was no fault to be found."[1]

Burgoyne arrived in England on 13 May and requested an audience
with the King, but the one-time court favorite was told that he should
wait until a board of general officers had inquired into his conduct. After
the board decided that no inquiry could take place because Burgoyne
was a prisoner of war, on parole to the Congress, the general requested a
court martial, which was refused on the same grounds. On 26 May, he
appeared before the House of Commons to defend himself and his conduct of the expedition. In an impassioned speech he denied all responsibility for the invasion plan and for its failure. As a general, he
contended, he had simply followed "the principle, the spirit and the
letter of his order," as it was given by the American minister, Lord Germain. For his troops Burgoyne had only praise:

> . . . Whatever fate may attend the general who led the army
> to Saratoga, their behaviour at that memorable spot must entitle
> them to the thanks of their country—Sir, it was a calamitous, it was
> an awful but it was an honourable hour. During the suspence of the
> answer from the general of the enemy to the refusal made by me of
> complying with the ignominious conditions he had proposed, the
> countenance of the troops beggars description; a patient fortitude, a
> sort of stern resignation that no pencil or language can reach. . . .
> I am confident every breast was prepared to devote its last drop of
> blood rather than suffer precedent to stand upon the British annals
> of an ignoble surrender.[5]

The vituperative debate that followed Burgoyne's speech produced one
of the most emotional scenes the Commons ever witnessed, when Lord
Germain, taunted by Temple Luttrell for his conduct at the Battle of
Minden in 1759, which had cost Germain his rank and reputation, challenged Luttrell to a duel.[6]

In the fall of 1778 the ministry tried to prevent Burgoyne from
taking his seat in the House of Commons by ordering him to rejoin his
troops in America. The general, however, pleaded that frequent visits to
Bath were essential to his health and was granted a respite. Henceforth,
he voted consistently with the opposition, believing as he said on 14 December 1778, that the war "would never be terminated with success on
our side." In frequent, long, and often tedious speeches, he reiterated his
grievances and censured the incompetence of the administration. At almost every session he reproached the government for its treatment of his
troops. What steps, he asked in November, had been taken "to release
those brave men who so gallantly fought and bled in the service of their
country?" In December, in the course of a debate on army estimates, he
lashed out again at the government. "The soldiers at Boston," he told the
Commons, "deserved the utmost grateful treatment from their country;
for however criminal their general might have been, they had done
everything that could be performed by men." Instead of showing con-
cern for their plight as prisoners of war, the government had "totally
forgotten and neglected them."[7]

At last, in May 1779, an inquiry was opened into the failure of his expedition. Burgoyne himself began the proceedings with a long speech, full of the arguments he had used repeatedly.[8] He then took the lead in examining witnesses. Through it all Lord Germain maintained a discreet silence, but Richard Rigby, a supporter of government policies in America, in a frankly factious speech, insisted that it was not the policy, but only its execution that was at fault. He repeatedly attacked Burgoyne, accusing him of leading "one of the best disciplined and appointed armies that was ever sent from this country . . . into terms of ignominious captivity by ordering them to pile up their arms in the face of a despicable enemy, an undisciplined militia," and of then abandoning them to suffer "every species of indignity and mortification" while he indulged himself "in all the amusements and pleasures of the first metropolis on the globe."[9]

In his reply, Burgoyne accused Rigby of disregarding the facts. The catastrophe at Saratoga was the result of government policies, he said, not of military leadership. His troops Burgoyne completely exonerated, recalling again that they had "been seven days and nights fighting, marching in the most severe weather, watching, famishing, without an hour's repose but with arms in their hands, and then exposed to the enemy's fire in every spot of ground they possessed." Even then, he concluded in a storm of emotion, "they offered themselves to death rather than accept dishonourable terms."[10] Although he was not disposed to assume any of the responsibility for the failure of the expedition, Lord Germain concurred with Burgoyne in his assessment of the troops, "who were at this day," he said to the Commons, "perhaps the bravest in the world, and had in the present war performed services unequalled in the history of empires."[11]

On 31 May, after hearing Burgoyne's narrative of the campaign, supported by ministers' dispatches and other documentary evidence, together with the testimony of Sir Guy Carleton and all the principal officers who had served under Burgoyne's command, the inquiry ended without adopting a single resolution regarding anything.[12] Because of the imperfect publication of Parliamentary debates, Burgoyne published a full account of his campaign and of his dealings with the administration. *A State of the Expedition from Canada* was dedicated to the officers of the army he had commanded.

The surrender of Cornwallis at Yorktown, which virtually involved the conclusion of peace, ironically occurred almost four years to the day from Burgoyne's surrender at Saratoga. The news forced a hasty revision of the King's speech scheduled for the opening of Parliament on 27 October—which had predicted a speedy end to the war.[13] Debate on the latest military catastrophe was initiated by the Duke of Chandos, who demanded an inquiry into the causes of Cornwallis's defeat.[14] Three weeks later a resolution, which lost by only one vote, was moved against continuing the war.[15] On 6 March the Duke of Chandos again took the floor to strike the keynote that would be repeated many times before the controversy had ended. Defending the military, Chandos argued that they had "discharged their duty with an integrity becoming their characters." The loss was due not to army failures, but to the absence of an adequate naval force to cover and protect Cornwallis's army.[16] Although

Chandos attacked the administration only by insinuation, other M.P.'s were loud in their denunciation of government. Edward Smith Stanley, the Earl of Derby, until then a strong supporter of British rights in America, directly charged that the "Administration had ruined this country."[17] Charles Lennox, the Duke of Richmond, spoke in a similar vein, accusing the ministry of "ignorance, incapacity, want of exertion."[18]

Rallying to the thinning phalanx of the ministerial forces, John Montagu, the Earl of Sandwich, who voted regularly with the government, gamely denied all charges of neglect on the part of either the administration or the Admiralty. However his argument that the defeat was due to "an unhappy combination of circumstances" coupled with the fact that "the hand of Providence did not seem to favor us" failed to convince the skeptical M.P.'s, and on 8 March 1782 a motion by Lord John Cavendish to censure the government for its conduct of the war lost by only ten votes.[19] A similar motion on 15 March by Sir John Rous, a self-proclaimed independent, lost by only nine votes, indicating the rapid erosion of support for government policies.[20] Germain, disliked by the King, the ministers, and the generals, remained in office, however, but on the condition that the war be pursued with greater vigor. Because his policy found favor with few besides the King, Germain was finally forced to resign in February 1782; he was subsequently elevated to the peerage. On 27 March, King George grudgingly ordered Lord North to form a new government.

Although the government was broken by the blow, the controversy over responsibility continued to rage among the military commanders involved in the Virginia campaign. Each, hoping to clear himself of responsibility, wrote a detailed account recapitulating the events that led to the surrender and vindicating his own decisions. Sir Henry Clinton, commander in chief, wrote a memoir of his view of the events leading up to the surrender in which he attributed Cornwallis's defeat to his having entered Virginia contrary to orders and then having forced operations there at an unseasonable time of the year; to the American minister's having overruled Clinton's strategy in favor of Cornwallis's; and to the lack of adequate naval support promised by the American minister but never delivered by Sir George Rodney.[21] Never during his often rambling and repetitive analysis of the factors that brought about Britain's final defeat did Clinton ever fault the soldiers' performance.

Instead he repeatedly found occasion to praise their courage and patience during the whole of the arduous Southern Campaign. In his account of the preliminaries to the battle of Guilford, Clinton commended Cornwallis's leadership, but he reserved his highest praise for the troops: "Nor can too much be said in commendation of the firm alacrity with which the troops under him bore up against and surmounted difficulties not frequently the lot of a superior army—being often without provisions and ever without covering, or even rum, to comfort them under the hardships of a long, fatiguing march through all the inclemencies of a cold and rainy winter."[22] Although he did not agree with General Nathanael Greene that the British victory at Guilford was due solely to the superior discipline of the King's troops, he was quick to commend their performance: "It is, however, but justice to say that nothing could possibly have been more honourable to the British arms than the spirited and judicious exertions of both officers and men on this day."[23] Clinton believed not only in the superiority of the British soldier as a fighter, but in his greater loyalty as a citizen as well. Earlier, in writing about the revolt of the Pennsylvania line on 1 January 1781, over arrears in pay and clothing and the refusal of Congress to discharge them at the expiration of their enlistment terms, Clinton compared the Continentals to British regulars: "I should have scarcely taken the trouble of noticing the transaction," he wrote, "had it not been for the opportunity it gives me of mentioning, to their honour, with how much alacrity and zeal the King's troops exposed themselves on this occasion [Southern Expedition] to all the severities of a very rigorous season, though most of them had enlisted on much the same terms with the revolters (for three years or during the war), but had very properly and zealously submitted to the opinion of the Commander in Chief that the option lay in the King."[24]

Cornwallis left no memoir, but his defense of his operations in the Chesapeake in the summer and fall of 1781 are contained in *An Answer to that Part of the Narrative of Lt. General Sir Henry Clinton, K.B., Which Relates to the Conduct of Lt. General Earl Cornwallis during the Campaign in North America in the Year 1781*. Published in 1783, Cornwallis's narrative argued that the march into Virginia was undertaken "for urgent reasons"; that he occupied the posts at Yorktown and Gloucester by order and was induced to remain in them by the repeated assurance of relief given him by the commander in chief; that from his arrival at Portsmouth to that of the French fleet in the Chesapeake, his corps was completely at the disposal of Clinton, to be either withdrawn or employed in the Upper Chesapeake, or sent back to the Carolinas.[25]

Throughout the campaign, to its bitter end at Yorktown, Cornwallis praised his troops. From his camp near Wilmington he reported to Clinton on their performance at Guilford: they "showed the most persevering intrepidity in action," he wrote, and "underwent with cheerfulness such fatigues and hardships as have seldom been experienced by a British army."[26] From North Carolina Cornwallis led his exhausted army by a meandering route to Cross Creek on the Cape Fear River and there made the fateful decision to advance into Virginia. After a month of inconclusive campaigning, he arrived in Williamsburg on 25 June, and from there he moved to Yorktown.

The hot month of August was spent fortifying Yorktown and Gloucester. In September, although they had endured long and tedious marches, casualties which thinned their ranks, the absence of opportunities for plunder, and the exhausting work of transporting soil and building parapets and ramparts for the defense of the works, the troops remained high-spirited. "There was," Cornwallis wrote to Clinton, "but one wish throughout the whole army, which was that the enemy would advance."[27] But after waiting in vain for the promised relief, and badly outnumbered by the allied force, Cornwallis surrendered his army on 19 October 1781. The following day he sent a long dispatch to the commander in chief, recapitulating the events that led to his surrender. In it he left no doubt as to the conduct of his gallant troops.

Despite the disparity in numbers, he had, Cornwallis reported, considered an attack against General Washington's army upon their arrival in open field, "where it might have been just possible that fortune would have favored the gallantry of the handful of troops under my command." But because he expected relief, he withdrew within the works at Yorktown on the evening of 29 September, "hoping by the labor and firmness of the soldiers" to protract the defense until reinforcements arrived. Instead, the ranks of his army depleted by incessant enemy fire and disease and exhausted by the fatigue of constant duty, Cornwallis decided to surrender. "I thought," he explained, "it would have been wanton and inhuman to the last degree to sacrifice the lives of this small body of gallant soldiers who have ever behaved with so much fidelity and courage, by exposing them to an assault, which from the numbers and precautions of the enemy, could not fail to succeed." Despite the tragedy of the surrender, Cornwallis concluded, "the patience of the soldiers in bearing the greatest fatigues and their firmness and intrepidity under a persevering fire of shot and shells, that I believe has not often been exceeded, deserves the highest admiration and praise." [28]

A few Cornwallis subordinates, among them Banastre Tarleton, also published works relating to the Southern Campaign. In *A History of the Campaigns of 1780 and 1781*, Tarleton defended his actions, sometimes at the expense of accuracy. In pleading his case, he attempted to clear himself of blame by assigning all of it to others—with the significant exception of the soldiers. After Guilford, Tarleton praised the "steadiness and composure" of the British troops, and their "disciplined perseverance." On the long march to Virginia, he noted with satisfaction, they "surmounted almost incredible difficulties without murmuring or desertion." Once the decision was made to occupy Yorktown, they "worked with great industry" to complete the works. When at last, despite the "tried powers and superior qualities" of his army, Cornwallis was forced to surrender, he gave up what was in Tarleton's view "the flower of the King's troops." [29]

The books, pamphlets, and Parliamentary debates inspired by the controversies among disappointed ministers and commanders suggest that the blame for British military failures in America rests to some extent with the home government, in particular with Lord Germain, who tried to direct events from a great distance in an age of slow communication; it rests in part in the strategy of the generals, which created the crises; and it rests as well in the mutual friction that existed between individual commanders and between military and naval leaders. [30] The same sources suggest quite powerfully that neither officers, ministers, nor M.P.'s held the troops accountable for British military failures in America. On the contrary, the high command and the administration—able to agree on little else—were unanimous in the view that the soldiers' performance in the American war was exemplary.

Notes

ABBREVIATIONS USED IN NOTES

Add. Mss.   Additional Manuscripts, British Museum, London.
B.H.P.   British Headquarters (Sir Guy Carleton) Papers, Howard-Tilton Library, Tulane University, New Orleans (microfilm). Originals are in the Public Record Office, London (P.R.O. 30/55).
Clements Library.   William L. Clements Library, Ann Arbor, Mich.
Clinton Papers.   Sir Henry Clinton, 1731?–1795, Papers, 1750–1812, Clements Library.
C.O.   Colonial Office papers, P.R.O.
Coote Papers.   Order Books, Letter Books, Journals, Letters, and Other Documents of Lt. Gen. Sir Eyre Coote . . . , 1775–1782, 6912/14, Nos. 31–50, National Army Museum, London.
Cornwallis Papers.   Charles Cornwallis (1738–1805), second Earl Cornwallis and first Marquis Cornwallis, Papers, 1614–1854, P.R.O. 30/11.
Gage Papers.   Thomas Gage, 1721–1787, Papers, 1754–1783, Clements Library.
Germain Papers.   George Sackville Germain, 1st Viscount Sackville, 1716–1785, Papers, 1683–1785, Clements Library.
H.O.   Home Office papers, P.R.O.
L.C.   Library of Congress, Washington, D.C.
Leslie Papers.   Leven and Melville Muniments, Papers of General Alexander Leslie and Captain William Leslie, G.D. 26/9/512–523, S.R.O.
Mackenzie Papers.   Frederick Mackenzie Papers, 1755–1783, Clements Library.
MacLaine Papers.   MacLaine of Lochbuie Muniments, Papers of Captain Murdock MacLaine of the 84th or Royal Highland Emigrants, 1775–1784, G.D. 174/34, S.R.O.
Peebles Diary.   Journal of Lt. John Peebles of the 42d or Royal Highland Regiment during the War of Independence, in Cunningham or Thorntoun Papers, 1746–1782, 1876–1883, G.D. 21, S.R.O.
P.R.O.   Public Record Office, London.
S.P.   State Papers, P.R.O.
S.R.O.   Scottish Record Office, Edinburgh.
Vaughan Papers.   Sir John Vaughan, 1738?–1795, Papers, 1779–1781, Clements Library.
W.O.   War Office papers, P.R.O.
Wray Papers.   George Wray Papers, 1770–1793, Clements Library.

INTRODUCTION

1. John W. Fortescue, *A History of the British Army*, deals primarily with operations but also notes changes in administration. Originally published in 1899–1930, it is still the best general work on campaigns. Charles M. Clode, *Military Forces of the Crown*, shows the evolution in administration, discipline, and arms. John Shy, *Toward Lexington: The Role of the British Army in the Coming of the American Revolution*, focuses on the British army in America during and after the Seven Years War. Peter Paret, *Yorck and the Era of Prussian Reform, 1807–1815*, compares military practice in Britain and on the Continent during the eighteenth century.. Stanley Pargellis, *Lord Loudoun in North America*, is an extensive study of Loudoun's command in the Seven Years War. For the period of the American Revolution, Edward E. Curtis, *The Organization of the British Army in the American Revolution*, is a standard study. There are numerous studies, both contemporary and recent, of eighteenth-century tactics. The records of the Judge Advocate General are very useful in regard to procedures of the eighteenth-century court martial. Stephen Payne Adye, *A Treatise on Courts-Martial with an Essay on Military Punishment and Rewards*, is a detailed treatment of court procedures. See also Sylvia R. Frey, "Courts and Cats: British Military Justice in the Eighteenth Century," *Military Affairs*, 43, No. 7 (1979): 5–11. Sir John Pringle, *Observations on the Diseases of the Army*, is the best contemporary statement of military medicine. A recent work is Sir Neil Cantlie, *A History of the Army Medical Department*. Biographies of prominent officers include Winston Churchill, *Marlborough: His Life and Times*; William T. Waugh, *James Wolfe, Man and Soldier*; Rex Whitworth, *Field Marshal Lord Ligonier: A Study of the British Army, 1702–1770*; Sir George Forrest, *Life of Lord Clive*; John Alden, *General Gage in America*; Franklin and Mary Wickwire, *Cornwallis: The American Adventure*. Numerous figures remain to be studied, including Sir Jeffrey Amherst.

2. Shy, *Toward Lexington*, p. 345, briefly discusses the stereotype. For examples in recent historiography see Eric Robson, "The Armed Forces and the Art of War," in *The New Cambridge Modern History*, vol. 7, *The Old Regime, 1713–1763*, ed. J. O. Lindsay, pp. 175–190; Wickwire and Wickwire, *Cornwallis*, pp. 52–55. One notable exception is Richard A. Preston and Sydney F. Wise, *Men in Arms*, p. 138, which correctly suggests that ". . . the mass of the soldiery was recruited by voluntary enlistment from peasant and urban unemployed."

1. VOLUNTEERS AND CONSCRIPTS

1. For the German army see Fritz Redlich, *The German Military Enterpriser and His Work Force: A Study in European Economic and Social History*. For the French army see André Corvisier, *L'Armée française de la fin du XVIIe siecle au ministère de Choiseul: Le Soldat*.

2. "Beating up" was the term used for signing volunteers. Although recruiting parties varied in size, they usually included a captain, three subalterns, four sergeants, four corporals, and four drummers. Each

party carried "beating orders," signed by the King, which the officer in command delivered to the chief magistrate of the town or village where the search was concentrated. Because of the chronic manpower shortage there was vigorous competition, and recruiters sometimes tried to outbid one another in their efforts to fill their quotas and collect the five guineas to which they were entitled for each man attested; see Order from the War Office, 6 February 1766, W. O. 4/1044.

3. In "raising men for rank," gentlemen or noblemen usually filled the company or regiment by trading off commissions in exchange for a specified number of men mustered; the Earl of Seaforth, for example, conditioned a captaincy in the 78th Regiment on the raising of fifty volunteers, a lieutenancy on twenty-five volunteers, an ensigncy on twenty; see Letters and Papers relating to the raising of the 78th Regiment of Foot or Seaforth's Highlanders, Add. Mss. 42,071. Lieutenant Archibald MacLaine of the first battalion of the 84th Regiment agreed to raise a quota of forty-five men to serve in the 42d or Royal Highland Regiment. He was required to deposit £450 with Mansfield Ramsay and Company of Edinburgh; upon approval of the forty-five recruits, MacLaine secured a captaincy in the 42d Regiment. See MacLaine Papers, G.D. 174/34.

4. George Germain to William Howe, 18 February 1778, and Germain to Sir Henry Clinton, 8 March 1778, Germain Papers; William Wildman, Lord Barrington, to Alexander Leslie, 17 January 1778, Leslie Papers, G.D. 26/9/517; Barrington to William Howe, 3 February 1778, Barrington to Howe, 27 February 1778, and Barrington to Howe, 28 April 1778, B.H.P.

5. William Cobbett, ed., *The Parliamentary History of England from the Earliest Period to the Year 1803*, 19: 626, 631, 644.

6. Statistics on the number of recruits can be found in Recruits raised in Britain, 4 March 1771, W.O. 26/28. The regiment receiving drafted men compensated the regiment losing them at the rate of £5 per man transferred; drafted men were each allowed a guinea and a half. See S.P. 41/27; Peebles Diary, 29 January 1781. See also Edward E. Curtis, "The Recruiting of the British Army in the American Revolution," American Historical Association *Annual Report*, 1 (1922): 320.

7. Redlich, *German Military Enterpriser*, 2: 173.

8. Commissioners of the land were appointed to serve in the counties, shires, ridings, cities, and boroughs to enforce a parliamentary act termed "An act for granting an aid to his Majesty by a land tax, to be raised in Great Britain, for the service of the year 1775."

9. Various Papers relating to the Army in North America, 1768–1783, Add. Mss. 38,343; Operations of the press act to raise men for the army, W.O. 4/965. Bills of Mortality were weekly reports, issued by the parish clerks, showing the number of deaths from plague or other causes as well as a list of parishes that were free from plague.

10. Barrington to the sheriff for the shire of Ayr, 25 June 1778, W. O. 4/965; for War Office instructions regarding implementation of the act, see also S.P. 41/27.

11. Redlich, *German Military Enterpriser*, 2: 179.

12. Arthur N. Gilbert, "Army Impressment during the War of the

Spanish Succession," *The Historian*, 36 (August 1976): 689–708, points out that popular opposition, the lack of cooperation by local authorities, and the minimal legal protection offered by the courts made it difficult to execute the press acts. British army impressment reached its peak in the War of the Spanish Succession and was finally brought to an end in 1780.

13. The statistics cited are from Secretary-at-War Charles Jenkinson's report on the press act of 1779 in W.O. 4/966.

14. Thomas Barston to the Secretary-at-War, 1 December 1778, W.O. 1/995; G. Christie to Charles Jenkinson, 18 May 1780, W.O. 1/51; Jenkinson to Sir John Fielding, 21 February 1779, W.O. 4/965.

15. Redlich, *German Military Enterpriser*, 2: 187–188.

16. Dale Williams, "The English Bread Riots in 1766," M.A. thesis, Tulane University, 1972.

17. J. L. and Barbara Hammond, *The Skilled Laborer, 1760–1832*, pp. 137–142.

18. G. E. Mingay, "The Agricultural Revolution in English History: A Reconsideration," in W. E. Minchinton, ed., *Essays in Agrarian History*, 2: 25; J. D. Chambers and G. E. Mingay, *The Agricultural Revolution 1750–1880*, pp. 34–35.

19. William Marshall, *The Rural Economy of the West of England*, pp. 21, 27; idem, *The Rural Economy of the Midland Counties*, 2d ed., 1: 82–83.

20. Chambers and Mingay, *Agricultural Revolution*, pp. 34–35.

21. For the controversy on English population changes see H. J. H. Habakkuk, "English Population in the Eighteenth Century," *Economic History Review*, 2d ser., 6, No. 2 (1953): 117–133; Thomas McKeown and R. G. Brown, "Medical Evidence Related to English Population Changes in the Eighteenth Century," *Population Studies*, 9 (July 1955): 119–141.

22. Asa Briggs, *The Age of Improvement, 1783–1867*, pp. 50–55, 59; Phyllis Deane, *The First Industrial Revolution*, pp. 145–146.

23. T. S. Ashton, *An Economic History of England: The Eighteenth Century*, pp. 15, 202–203.

24. Deane, *First Industrial Revolution*, pp. 36–37, 43–46, 138–143; Briggs, *Age of Improvement*, pp. 61–62.

25. Curtis, *Organization of the British Army*, pp. 1–2.

26. Corvisier, *L'Armée française*, 2: 373–374.

27. Ibid., pp. 374–375.

28. The conclusions which follow are in large measure based upon my analysis of the following records: Return of a British Brigade of Foot Guards, March 1776–December 1779, Preliminary Inventory No. 144 (Revised), Entry 23, National Archives, Washington, D.C.; Records of the 58th Regiment of Foot, 1756–ca. 1800, W.O. 25/435. The Coldstream Guards is one of the oldest regiments in the history of the British army. Embodied in 1669, the regiment served under Oliver Cromwell in the Parliamentary army and was then known as Monck's Regiment. The 58th or Rutlandshire Regiment was formerly Colonel Anstruther's Company, a supplementary company which had been added to the existing battalion in 1755. In 1756 ten new regiments were formed and numbered consecutively the 50th to the 59th. Anstruther's Company was incorporated into the 58th, which served under James Wolfe in the French and Indian War during the reduction of Quebec. My analysis is thus based on

one of the oldest regiments as well as a newly raised regiment. For the origins of each, see Fortescue, *History of the British Army*, 1: 240; 2: 288–289, 361.

29. Less comprehensive records which indicate the social origins of the men in the ranks include: Captain Walter Home, Officer's Memorandum Book, George Chalmers Collection, Peter Force Papers, L.C.; Return of Recruits raised for the First Battalion Royal Highland Regiment, Head Quarters Records, America, W.O. 28/4; Register of British Deserters, Munn Collection, Fordham University Library, New York; Description of British Recruits for the 71st Regiment, Gage Papers.

30. Arthur N. Gilbert, "An Analysis of Some Eighteenth Century Army Recruiting Records," *Journal of the Society for Army Historical Research*, 54 (Spring 1976): 38–47.

31. Steven Watson, *The Reign of George III, 1760–1818*, p. 10, n. 1.

32. Gilbert, "Army Recruiting Records," p. 45.

33. Peter N. Stearns, *European Society in Upheaval: Social History since 1800*, pp. 38–43.

34. Hammond and Hammond, *The Skilled Laborer*, pp. 137–142.

35. David Montgomery, "The Working Classes of the Pre-Industrial American City, 1780–1830," *Labor History*, 9, No. 1 (1968): 3–22.

36. E. P. Thompson, *The Making of the English Working Class*, pp. 269–313.

37. Of the 161 men who enlisted between 20 August and 28 August 1759 (19.25 percent of whom were ex-weavers), 54.6 percent were over 30 years of age; see Gilbert, "Army Recruiting Records," p. 41.

38. Ibid., pp. 41, 46.

39. Stearns, *European Society in Upheaval*, pp. 38–42.

40. Gilbert, "Army Recruiting Records," pp. 41, 46.

41. Adam Smith, *An Inquiry into the Nature and Causes of the Wealth of Nations*, ed. James E. Thorold Rogers, 2d ed., 2: 337–341.

42. T. S. Ashton, *Economic Fluctudtions in England, 1700–1800*, pp. 1–5.

43. Stearns, *European Society in Upheaval*, pp. 36–37.

44. Smith, *Wealth of Nations*, 1: 75–76.

45. Ashton, *Economic History*, pp. 15, 202–203.

46. Marshall, *Rural Economy of the West*, pp. 21, 27; idem, *Rural Economy of the Midland Counties*, 1: 82–83.

47. See Harold Perkin, *The Origins of Modern English Society, 1780–1880*, p. 31, for a discussion of industrial workers.

48. Deane, *First Industrial Revolution*, pp. 100–114.

49. Theodore Ropp, *War in the Modern World*, p. 37; Lee Kennett, *The French Armies in the Seven Years War: A Study in Military Organization and Administration*, pp. 74, 76.

50. Redlich, *German Military Enterpriser*, 2: 201.

51. The percentages are derived from regimental records for nine elite regiments for the year 1775 and for the same regiments for the year 1779; 1st (King's) Regiment Dragoon Guards, 1st (Royal Regiment) Dragoons, 3d (Prince of Wales's) Dragoons, 4th Regiment Dragoons, 7th (Queen's Regiment) Dragoons, 10th Regiment Dragoons, 11th Regiment Dragoons, King's (15th) Regiment Light Dragoons, Royal Regiment of

Horse Guards, Queen's (2d) Dragoon Guards, all in W.O. 27/33 and W.O. 27/42. Percentages for the infantry regiments are based on figures given for nine regiments of foot, two in 1775 (32d Regiment of Foot and 36th Regiment of Foot), which averaged 28 percent foreign troops; six in 1782 (29th Regiment of Foot, 31st Regiment of Foot, 44th Regiment of Foot, 53d Regiment of Foot, 84th Regiment of Foot, King's [8th] Regiment of Foot); and one in 1783 (29th Regiment of Foot), all in W.O. 27/34 and W.O. 28/10.

52. Stephen F. Gradish, "The German Mercenaries in North America during the American Revolution: A Case Study," *Canadian Journal of History*, 4 (March 1969): 25–27, 31. Copies of the treaties signed with the German princes can be found in Correspondence and Papers of the Foreign Office, H.O. 32/1.

53. See Redlich, *German Military Enterpriser*, 2: 171–190 for details both on recruiting methods and on the social composition of the army.

54. Information from analysis of 417 German mercenaries listed in the following sources: Register of British Deserters, Munn Collection, Fordham University Library, New York; William S. Stryker, *The Battles of Trenton and Princeton*, p. 196; Letters of the engineers department and general hospital returns, Head Quarters Records, America, W.O. 28/6.

55. Thomas Anburey, *Travels through the Interior Parts of America by an Officer*, 2: 441–442.

56. J. G. Seume, "Memoirs of a Hessian Conscript: J. G. Seume's Reluctant Voyage to America," trans. Margaret Woeffel, *William and Mary Quarterly*, 3d ser., 5 (October 1948): 553–559; "Journal of Lieutenant John Charles Philip von Krafft . . . ," in New-York Historical Society, *Collections* 15 (1882): 122; Stephan Popp, "Popp's Journal 1777–1783," ed. Joseph G. Rosengarten, *Pennsylvania Magazine of History and Biography*, 26, Nos. 1–2 (1902): 26–27.

57. Archibald Campbell to Lord George Germain, 16 January 1776, Germain Papers.

58. John Murray, Lord Dunmore, to Germain, 1 March 1775, Dunmore to Germain, 20 February 1776, and Dunmore to Germain, 30 March 1776, C.O. 5/1573. For secondary literature on the subject see Benjamin Quarles, "Lord Dunmore as Liberator," *William and Mary Quarterly*, 3d ser., 15 (October 1958): 494–507.

59. *Virginia Gazette*, 11 May 1775, 6 April 1775, 9 November 1776.

60. Proclamation, 30 June 1779, B.H.P.

61. Clinton to Cornwallis, 30 August 1781, Clinton Papers.

62. Lieutenant General Alexander Leslie to General Henry Clinton, 12 March 1782, B.H.P.

63. Greene to Marion, 15 April 1782, in R. W. Gibbs, ed., *Documentary History of the American Revolution*, 2: 164; James Weymss to John André, 27 February 1780, and Weymss to André, 29 February 1780, Clinton Papers.

64. Benjamin Quarles, *The Negro and the American Revolution*, stresses the need for labor and the difficulty of controlling armed blacks; Sylvia R. Frey, "The British and the Black: A New Perspective," *The Historian*, 39 (Feburary 1976), stresses racial prejudice as an important formative factor.

65. David B. Davis, *The Problem of Slavery in Western Culture*, p. 59.
66. John Cruden, Commissioner of Sequestered Estates, Narrative, 1 June 1781, Cornwallis Papers, P.R.O. 30/11/110.
67. Return of Negroes employed in the service of the Royal Artillery, 28 April 1780, Clinton Papers; Return of Negroes employed as artificers, laborers and servants in the Royal Artillery Department, Wray Papers.
68. John McNamara Hayes, Memorandum for the General Hospital, 29 February 1780, Clinton Papers; 24 October 1781, Peebles Diary; Orderly Books, Regimental Order Book, British Army, Siege of Savannah, 2 July–2 October 1779, L.C.; Benjamin Thompson to George Germain, 6 August 1782, Germain Papers; Colonel George Corbin to Colonel William Davis, 18 August 1781, in William L. Palmer et al., eds., *Calendar of Virginia State Papers and Other Manuscripts* . . . , 2: 340; Petition of Sundry Persons Residing on the Rappahannock River to the Governor of Virginia, 8 September 1781, in ibid., 2: 404–405; Patrick Lockhart to Governor Nelson, 6 November 1781, in ibid., 2: 604–605; Francis Triplett to the Governor, 2 July 1781, in ibid., 5: 333–334.
69. 22 March 1778, British General Orders, Cornwallis in Virginia, Orderly Books of Lt. Gen. William Howe, Clements Library; Order Books of the 43d Regiment at Yorktown, 1781, Add. Mss. 42,449; Order Book, America, 1780, Coote Papers, no. 42; G. Christie, Memorandum, 30 March 1780, St. Leger to Patrick Ferguson, 29 August 1780, and George B. Rodney to John Vaughan, 2 July 1780, Vaughan Papers; Cornwallis to Brigadier General Charles O'Hara, 4 August 1781, Cornwallis Papers, P.R.O. 30/11/89.
70. Lord Cornwallis' Regulations respecting the number of Negroes and Horses, May, 1781, Orderly Books, British General and Brigade Orders, Lord Cornwallis, Virginia and Yorktown, 23 May–22 October 1781, L.C.; Report of the Commissioners of Claims, in Georgia Historical Society, *Collections*, 3: 297–300; Order Books, 43d Regiment, Add. Mss. 42,449.
71. Governor James Wright to George Germain, 5 November 1779, in Georgia Historical Society, *Collections*, 3: 260–262; Wright to Germain, 27 October 1780, in ibid., 3: 321–322; Account of the Siege of Savannah, in ibid., 5: 129–139.
72. Walter Hart Blumenthal, *Women Camp Followers of the American Revolution*, p. 42, estimates there were approximately 5,000 British camp followers, with the feminine ratio doubling by "wayside accretion" during the course of the war.
73. Elisha Bostwick, "A Connecticut Soldier under Washington: Elisha Bostwick's Memoirs of the First Years of the Revolution," ed. William S. Powell, *William and Mary Quarterly*, 3d. ser., 6 (January 1949): 104; John André, *Major André's Journal: Operations of the British Army under Lieutenant Generals Sir William Howe and Sir Henry Clinton*, p. 30; Roger Lamb, *An Original and Authentic Journal of Occurrences during the Late American War*, p. 143; Johann Conrad Doehla, "The Doehla Journal," trans. Robert J. Tilden, *William and Mary Quarterly*, 2d ser., 22 (July 1942): 274.
74. Krafft, "Journal," p. 148; John Graves Simcoe, *Simcoe's Military Journal: A History of the Operations of a Partisan Corps, called the Queen's Rangers* . . . , p. 217.

75. Thomas Sullivan, "The Common British Soldier," ed. S. Sydney Bradford, *Maryland Historical Magazine*, 62 (September 1967): 234.

76. Amelia Taylor to General Guy Carleton, 24 April 1783, and Elizabeth Hurley account with General Carleton, 16 August 1783 to 16 November 1783, B.H.P.

2. DISEASES AND DOCTORS

1. Thomas Simes, *A Military Course for the Government and Conduct of a Battalion* . . . , p. 158.

2. Barrington to Howe, 18 May 1778, B.H.P., notes that every recruit was supposed to be examined by a field officer and a surgeon before embarkation, but the Secretary-at-War acknowledged that "many of the men were sent off as soon as enlisted."

3. Regimental records giving age and size of the troops are uncommonly complete. My analysis of the age and size structure is based on data for four marching regiments: the 29th, 31st, 44th, and King's (8th) Regiment in Head Quarters Records, America, 1746–1901, W.O. 28/10; and for four elite regiments: the 1st (King's) Regiment Dragoon Guards, 1st (Royal) Regiment Dragoons, 4th Regiment Dragoons, and 7th (Queen's) Regiment Dragoons, in Inspection Returns, W.O. 27/33. Willard R. Fann, "On the Infantryman's Age in Eighteenth Century Prussia," *Military Affairs*, 41, No. 4 (December 1977): 165–170, found a similar preference for mature men in the Prussian army, which suggests that it was a general tendency.

4. Quoted in Fann, "Infantryman's Age," p. 168.

5. Barrington to Gage, 4 January 1775, W.O. 4/273.

6. Bennett Cuthbertson, *A System for the Compleat Interior Management and Oeconomy of a Battalion of Infantry*, p. 68.

7. Instructions for recruiting His Majesty's Regiments of Foot in North America to the Establishment voted by Parliament for the Year 1771, Army in Ireland and North America, Papers, 1751–1771, Peter Force Papers. L.C. In Jenkinson to Captain Bolton Power, 6 March 1779, W.O. 4/965, the Secretary-at-War advised Power to accept able-bodied recruits "although [they] should not be precisely of the Size and Age required by the act." In Jenkinson to Clerk to the Commissioners of Doncaster, 12 March 1779, W.O. 4/965, he repeated that officers need "not always insist upon a strict adherence to the directions of the Act respecting the size of the recruits."

8. Instructions for recruiting, cited above, give the legal height requirements. The statistical basis for the size structure is provided by analysis of the data for the same eight regiments for which age calculations are given (see note 3).

9. The comparison of British soldiers to other European recruits is based on figures quoted in Eric J. Hobsbawm, *The Age of Revolution*, p. 8.

10. Simes, *Military Course*, p. 68.

11. Jenkinson to Sir John Fielding, 21 February 1779, W.O. 4/965; Jenkinson to Lieutenant Colonel Fraser, 28 August 1789, W.O. 4/966; in both letters Jenkinson uses the same phrase.

12. Abstract of Reports on New Corps, 28 April 1781, Add. Mss. 38,344.

13. John Hunter to Robert Adair, 9 July 1782, W.O. 7/96.

14. Lieutenant Governor Archibald Campbell to Carleton, 13 August 1782, B.H.P.

15. Major General James Paterson to Carleton, 8 October 1782, B.H.P.

16. Only four feet in length, including the stock, the carbine was used by all horse and by the light infantry; see George Smith, *An Universal Military Dictionary*, p. 50.

17. To Captain Congreve, 27 September 1779, and to Captain Chapman, 27 September 1779, in "Official Letters of Major General James Pattison," in New-York Historical Society, *Collections*, 8 (1875): 122, 124.

18. Robert Hamilton, *The Duties of a Regimental Surgeon Considered*, 2: 262 (Dr. Hamilton was a member of the Royal College of Physicians of London and an army doctor); Richard Brocklesby, *Oeconomical and Medical Observations from the Year 1758 to the Year 1763*, p. 200 (Brocklesby was also an army physician and a fellow of the College of Physicians and of the Royal Society of London).

19. Various Papers relating to the Army in North America, 1768–1783, Add. Mss. 38,375, folios 51, 74; the figure is incomplete since it does not include the fatalities in Clinton's army in 1780.

20. The statistics on the weapon's accuracy are from H. C. B. Rogers, *Weapons of the British Soldier*, pp. 94, 110–114; the figure for the percentage of operational weapons is from Richard Lambart, 6th Earl of Cavan, *A New System of Military Discipline Founded upon Principle*, p. 23. The author, Richard Lambart, the 6th Earl of Cavan, had a son by the same name who became the 7th Earl of Cavan. In 1779, the son was appointed to the Coldstream Guards; however, his name is not on the roll of officers of his regiment who served in America.

21. McKeown and Brown, "Medical Evidence," pp. 139–140.

22. Stearns, *European Society in Upheaval*, p. 44; Dorothy George, *London Life in the Eighteenth Century*, pp. 196–200, 204–205.

23. Richard H. Shryock, *Medicine and Society in America: 1660–1860*, pp. 90–91.

24. Pringle, *Observations*, first used the term to identify those diseases which had the highest incidence in the army. Pringle was an army physician, president of the Royal Society of Physicians, and later physician to the royal family.

25. Walter L. Dorn, "The Prussian Bureaucracy in the Eighteenth Century," *Political Science Quarterly*, 46 (September 1931): 403–423; 47 (March 1932): 75–94, 259–273.

26. By 1770 a civil service had been created in Prussia which provided for special training and examinations as prerequisites for holding public office; see ibid., 46: 405. In Britain influence rather than merit filled government jobs in the post office, the customs, the army and navy, and the whole civil administration with the single exception of the War Office, which, under the capable direction of Lord Barrington and then Charles Jenkinson, was remarkably free of jobbery. In Prussia uniformity of bureaucratic procedures had been achieved through detailed written

instructions which established invariable rules. In England the exercise of authority was more or less discretionary and to a large degree depended upon the talent and personality of the office holder. It was in the conduct of international politics that the shortcomings of the administrative system were most keenly felt. Until the Crimean War, military administration was without a single executive head. Whatever coordination there was, was accomplished by the Secretary at War, whose authority over the other independent departments was based primarily on persuasion; see Olive Gee, "The British War Office in the Later Years of the American War of Independence," *Journal of Modern History*, 26 (June 1954): 123–136.

27. R. Arthur Bowler, *Logistics and the Failure of the British Army in America, 1775–1783*, deals with the whole problem of supply.

28. Redlich, *German Military Enterpriser*, 2: 192.

29. For a typical food contract, see Articles of Agreement Made by the Lords Commissioners of the Treasury and Arnold Nesbitt, Adam Drummond, and Moses Franks, 2 April 1776, and John Robinson to Henry Clinton, 6 October 1779, B.H.P.

30. Redlich, *German Military Enterpriser*, 2: 193.

31. Extracts of orders, New York and Boston, 10 June 1773–6 January 1776, American Rebellion, Entry Books, W.O. 37/1, pp. 138, 140.

32. Carl Leopold Baurmeister, *The Revolution in America: Confidential Letters and Journals, 1776–1784, of Adjutant General Major Baurmeister of the Hessian Forces*, trans. Bernhard A. Uhlendorf, p. 265; Abstract of Disbursements in the Quarter Master General's Department for the Hire of Gardeners and Laborers for Raising Vegetables for the Use of the Army and Navy at New York, 7 March 1779, Clinton Papers.

33. Mure, Son, and Atkinson to Guy Carleton, 28 September 1776, Miscellaneous Papers, Regimental Returns, Orders, 1756–1776, Add. Mss. 21,687. Shipments included seed for "winter sallad seed," to be sown on wet blankets or in water.

34. "General Orders by Major General The Honourable William Howe," in New-York Historical Society, *Collections*, 16 (1883): 293, 299, 303, 309; for healthy troops this quantity may have been adequate, but scurvy victims required considerably more, and the rate for them was usually three pounds per man per week.

35. Humphrey Bland, *A Treatise of Military Discipline . . .* , p. 189; the rule was enforced; see entries in Order Book of the 37th Regiment kept by Charles Allen Buckeridge, National Army Museum, London; American Rebellion, Entry Books, W.O. 36/1, pp. 54, 139, 151; Sir William Howe, *General Sir William Howe's Orderly Book at Charleston, Boston and Halifax*, ed. Benjamin Franklin Stevens, pp. 38, 94, 120.

36. Frederick Mackenzie, *A British Fusilier in Revolutionary Boston*, ed. Allen French, pp. 17–18.

37. Johann David Schoepff, *The Climate and Diseases of America during the Revolution*, trans. James Read Chadwick, pp. 13–18 (Schoepff was surgeon of the Anspach-Bayreuth troops in America); James M. Hadden, *Journal and Orderly Books: A Journal Kept in Canada and upon Burgoyne's Campaign*, p. 54; Baurmeister, *Revolution in America*, pp. 90, 152, 463, 478; Frederick Mackenzie, *Diary of Frederick Mackenzie: Giving a Daily*

Narrative of His Military Service as an Officer of the Regiment of Royal Welch Fusiliers during the Years 1775–1781, ed. A. French, 2: 586; Anburey, *Travels*, 1: 139; Sullivan, "The Common British Soldier," p. 236.

38. M. C. Buer, *Health, Wealth and Population in the Early Days of the Industrial Revolution*, p. 158.

39. John Duffy, "The Passage to the Colonies," *Mississippi Valley Historical Review*, 38 (June 1951–March 1952): 31, 38.

40. Donald Monro, M.D., *An Account of the Diseases which were most Frequent in the British Military Hospitals in Germany from January 1761 to . . . March 1763*, pp. 326–329, 330–331. Monro was an army physician and physician to St. George's Hospital.

41. Popp, "Journal," pp. 32–33.

42. *The Montresor Journals*, ed. G. D. Scull, New-York Historical Society, *Collections*, 14 (1881): 495; an average of 41,000 soldiers, followers of the army, and refugees were fed daily; see Abstract of the Advices Received from Daniel Wier of the Number of Rations Daily Consumed, John Robinson to William Howe, 22 September 1775, B.H.P.

43. John André, On Plundering (1779?), Proposed Plan for bringing the army under strict discipline with regard to marauding, by Patrick Ferguson, November 1779, Clinton Papers. During the War of the Spanish Succession, Marlborough maintained exceptional discipline on his Danube march and as a result won the good will of the German people. He restrained excesses by demanding rigorous levies and he paid for all supplies; see R. E. Scouller, *The Armies of Queen Anne*, p. 287.

44. Major General Augustine Prevost to Clinton, 16 April 1779, B.H.P.

45. W. O. 36/1, p. 11.

46. Augustine Prevost to Clinton, 16 April 1779, B.H.P.; General G. Christie to Vaughan, 17 April 1780, Vaughan Papers. See also General Return of the State of Camp Equipage, New York, 26 March 1783, B.H.P., which shows that, for nearly twenty regiments listed, there were only 269 camp kettles in good condition, with 13 needing repair. The army was lacking 1,151 kettles needed for cooking.

47. W. O. 36/1, p. 11. Zweibach, burned or toasted biscuit, was popular with the German mercenaries; see Georg Pausch, *Journal of Captain Pausch of the Hanau Artillery during the Burgoyne Campaign*, trans. William L. Stone, pp. 79, 86, 87.

48. Mackenzie, *A British Fusilier*, p. 19.

49. Margaret Wheeler Willard, ed., *Letters on the American Revolution, 1774–1776*, pp. 132–133; W. Glanville Evelyn, *Memoir and Letters of Captain W. Glanville Evelyn, of the 4th Regiment, from North America, 1774–1776*, pp. 55, 67; John Barker, "A British Officer in Boston in 1775," *Magazine of History*, 18 (January 1914): 8–9; Sullivan, "The Common British Soldier," p. 239.

50. Williard, ed., *Letters*, p. 205.

51. James Murray, *Letters from America, 1773–1780*, ed. Eric Robson, p. 30; Prevost to Germain, 10 January 1779, Promiscuous Military Correspondence, Letters of Officers of Lesser Rank, C.O. 5/182.

52. Baurmeister, *Revolution in America*, p. 215, records that 6,000 sheep were brought to Rhode Island by a foraging expedition led by General Charles Grey.

53. Mackenzie, *Diary*, 1: 137, 141, 144, 270, 281; 2: 394–395, 404, 432–433, 437, 549, 599; Popp, "Journal," pp. 32–33; Baurmeister, *Revolution in Ameirca*, p. 215.

54. Baurmeister, *Revolution in America*, pp. 247–248; Krafft, "Journal," p. 59, notes that in August 1778 the Jaegers almost mutinied because they were without provisions for three days. In December the shortage of flour forced the army to bake bread out of oat-grits, three measures of grits to one of cornmeal. Krafft complained that "it weighed very heavy and with the same weight it lay in our stomachs." The half-baked bread caused "terrible stomach aches" and "great as our delight had been to get it, equally great were our pains and curses after eating it" (pp. 76–79).

55. "Journals of Lieut.-Col. Stephen Kemble," in New-York Historical Society, *Collections*, 16 (1883): 23, 25, 58.

56. Survey of Provisions at New York and Jamaica, Long Island, 13 July 1782, B.H.P.

57. Carleton to George Washington, 23 November 1782, B.H.P.; Clothing Regulations for Marching Regiments, by Order of George III, 27 July 1768, W.O. 26/28.

58. Clode, *Military Forces*, 1: 109; 2: 568–569.

59. The experience of the Revolution helped to demonstrate the feasibility of adapting the uniform to the service; in the following decade the coat was closed all the way down to the waist, the tails were shortened, and tight-fitting pantaloons replaced breeches; see W. Y. Carman, *British Military Uniforms*, p. 93.

60. Cavan, *A New System*, pp. 11, 14.

61. *Montresor Journals*, pp. 511–512; Krafft, "Journal," pp. 48–49; Lamb, *Journal*, p. 244.

62. Shryock, *Medicine and Society*, pp. 90–91.

63. Order Book, New York, 1781, 6912/14, No. 45, Coote Papers.

64. Pringle, *Observations*, pp. 341–342; Monro, *Account of the Diseases*, pp. 265–267.

65. Curtis, *Organization of the British Army*, pp. 33, 50; Smith, *Universal Military Dictionary*, p. 218. The staff officer in charge of the soldiers' clothing, quarters, bread, ammunition, etc., was called the quartermaster.

66. Redlich, *German Military Enterpriser*, 2: 196.

67. Clothing Regulations for Marching Regiments, W.O. 26/28; Scouller, *Armies of Queen Anne*, pp. 150–157.

68. *Orderly Book of the Three Battalions of Loyalists Commanded by Brigadier General Oliver De Lancey*, p. 47; John Johnson, *Orderly Book of Sir John Johnson during the Oriskany Campaign, 1776–1777*, pp. 36, 41; A. R. Newsome, ed., "A British Orderly Book, 1780–1781," *North Carolina Historical Review*, 9 (January 1932): 177, 179.

69. "Letter-Book of Captain Alexander McDonald of the Royal Highland Emigrants, 1775–1779," in New-York Historical Society, *Collections*, 15 (1882): 227, 228, 231, 235, 237–238, 242, 253, 295–296. The next renewal shipment was apparently also delayed, since Brigadier General McLean complained to Clinton in September 1780 that it had been nearly thirty months since his regiment had received new clothing; see Francis McLean to Clinton, 14 September 1780, B.H.P.

70. Pattison, "Official Letters," pp. 1, 26, 37, 39.

71. Kemble, "Journals," p. 227.

72. The 1776 clothing replacements for the Northern Army had not yet arrived in April 1777; see Anburey, *Travels*, 1: 198; in the waning stages of the war the problem remained unsolved; the movement of Cornwallis's army from Wilmington in the spring of 1781 was delayed because the cavalry and infantry were "in need of everything"; Cornwallis to Clinton, 23 April 1781, Cornwallis Papers, P.R.O. 30/11/5, folio nos. 249–250.

73. McDonald, "Letter Book," p. 257, reports that a number of men in the Royal Highland Emigrants suffered from frostbite.

74. Captain John Polson, in command of the expedition to the Spanish Main, warned Colonel Kemble that a better system of supply must be found "or the men will be ruined"; Kemble, "Journals," p. 227.

75. "Orders by Major-General Daniel Jones," in New-York Historical Society, *Collections*, 16 (1883): 612.

76. Redlich, *German Military Enterpriser*, 2: 197.

77. Johnson, *Orderly Book*, pp. 29–30; *Orderly Book of . . . De Lancey*, pp. 41, 62.

78. Monro, *Account of the Diseases*, pp. 323–324; Dr. Monro urged that special care be taken with men "picked up in the streets," or "taken out of the Savoy or other jails." He recommended that they be isolated and that their "dirty rags" be burned.

79. For conditions on board military transports, see Sullivan, "The Common British Soldier," pp. 225–226; "Diary of a Voyage from Stade in Hanover to Quebec in America of the 2d Division of Ducal Brunswick Mercenaries," *Quarterly Journal of the New York State Historical Association*, 8 (October 1927): 324, 334.

80. When the weather permitted, the hatches were opened and fires were lighted in iron kettles and then sprinkled with rosin or bits of rope dipped in tar in order to fumigate the air. Berths were sprinkled with vinegar and sleeping mats were aired on deck; see Mackenzie, *A British Fusilier*, p. 14.

81. An account of the number of troops sent to the West Indies for the years 1775–1782, Add. Mss. 38,345; see also Add. Mss. 38,344, which shows an average loss of 6.25 percent for the 1,170 troops embarked for the Leeward Islands.

82. Schoepff, *Climate and Diseases*, p. 22; Mackenzie, *Diary*, 2: 554; William Digby, *The British Invasion from the North*, p. 188.

83. See reports entitled "State of His Majesty's Land Forces in North America and the West Indies at the end of the year 1779," Add. Mss. 38,344; "An account of men lost and disabled in His Majesty's Land Service in North America and the West Indies from 1 November 1774," Add. Mss. 38,378.

84. Cornwallis to Germain, 20 August 1780, Germain Papers; Clinton to Germain, 21 August 1779, and John McNamara Hayes to Clinton, 24 May 1780, Clinton Papers; To John Powell, secretary Chelsea Hospital, 14 December 1781, W.O. 7/96.

85. Norman Baker, *Government and Contractors: The British Treasury and War Supplies, 1775–1783*, p. 4, notes that in 1780–1781 there were

92,000 troops in America, including the Floridas and the West Indies.
    86. John Barker, *The British in Boston*, p. 5. Barker was a lieutenant in
the King's Own Regiment; Evelyn, *Memoir*, pp. 34, 39, 41.
    87. Baurmeister, *Revolution in America*, p. 140; September 26, 1777,
Peebles Diary.
    88. Ewald Gustav Schaukirk, "Occupation of New York City by the
British," *Pennsylvania Magazine of History and Biography*, 10, no. 1 (1886):
422, 437.
    89. Mackenzie, *Diary*, 1: 125–127; Pattison, "Official Letters," p.
290, Leonard Lispenard to Carleton, 24 August 1783, B.H.P.; Ambrose
Serle, *The American Journal of Ambrose Serle, Secretary to Lord Howe,
1776–1778*, ed. Edward H. Tatum, Jr., p. 109.
    90. Baurmeister, *Revolution in America*, p. 231; *Montresor Journals*, pp.
483, 487, 534–541. Most of the timber was used for fuel and for the
construction of the extensive defense works that encircled garrison
towns. See also *Proceedings of a Board of General Officers of the British Army
at New York, 1781*, in New-York Historical Society, *Collections*, 49 (1916):
60–61.
    91. Smith, *Universal Military Dictionary*, p. 20. The Barrack Master
was responsible for quartering the troops. His duties included the inspection of bedding, furniture and utensils and the supply of fuel and candles; see Rules and Directions Relating to His Majesty's Barracks in
North America, Add. Mss. 21,684.
    92. Papers Relating to the Barrack Masters Department in Canada,
Add. Mss. 21,850; Correspondence of Haldimand and Dr. Hugh Alexander Kennedy, Add. Mss. 21,857.
    93. Richard L. Blanco, "Henry Marshall (1775–1851) and the
Health of the British Army," *Medical History*, 14, No. 3 (July 1970): 270,
n. 53.
    94. Archibald Robertson, *Archibald Robertson, Lieutenant General,
Royal Engineers: His Diaries and Sketches in America, 1762–1780*, ed. Harry
Miller Lydenberg, p. 70.
    95. Mackenzie, *Diary*, 2: 555; Pausch, *Journal*, p. 92.
    96. Mackenzie, *Diary*, 1: 179, 206, 217.
    97. Ibid., 2: 555, John Robinson to William Howe, 25 September
1775, B.H.P.; Howe, *General Sir William Howe's Orderly Book*, p. 213. Wel-
lington finally abolished the rule that two soldiers share a bed; Blanco,
"Henry Marshall," p. 264, n. 22. The dimensions for berths can be found
in Papers Relating to the Barrack Masters Department in Canada, Add.
Mss. 21,850.
    98. *Proceedings of a Board of General Officers*, pp. 98, 100, 102;
McDonald, "Letter-Book," p. 310.
    99. Mackenzie, *Diary*, 2: 555.
    100. Bowler, *Logistics*, pp. 61–62, points out that the old French
mines at Spanish River on Cape Breton Island barely produced enough
to supply the garrison at Halifax.
    101. "General Orders by Major General The Honourable William
Howe," in New-York Historical Society, *Collections*, 16 (1883): 276, 297;
Proceedings of a Board of General Officers, p. 97.
    102. *Proceedings of a Board of General Officers*, p. 98.

103. Proclamation, 1 November 1777, Philadelphia, B.H.P.
104. Mackenzie, *Diary*, 1: 129, 130, 170–171, 185, 190, 210, 221, 222, 228, 238, 240; 2: 428, 429, 435.
105. Pattison, "Official Letters," pp. 302, 304, 318, 334, 336–337, 340, 348, 364; *Proceedings of a Board of General Officers*, pp. 99–100; Thomas Jones, *History of New York during the Revolutionary War*, 1: 316–317.
106. Baurmeister, *Revolution in America*, p. 341; see also Popp, "Journal," p. 34. Frederika Charlotte Luise, Baroness von Riedesel, *Letters and Journals Relating to the War of the American Revolution*, trans. William L. Stone, p. 173, notes that the poor were forced to burn fat to keep themselves warm and to cook their meals. Barracks at outposts suffered most from lack of repairs: in 1778 the Royal Barracks at Quebec, built for 368 men, needed all new berths, the Dauphine Barracks were reported to be uninhabitable; those at Montreal needed new flooring and a new roof; those at Oswegatchie were "scarcely habitable"; see Return of the State and Condition of the Different Barracks in the Province of Quebec and Frontiers, 30 April 1778, Add. Mss. 21,850. A major problem in maintaining barracks at outposts was the difficulty of bringing in supplies; to house a regiment at Sorel it was estimated that it would take twenty-four days with forty horses drawing twenty carriages just to haul the timber; see William Tuiss England to Haldimand, 27 September 1778, Add. Mss. 21,814.
107. Smith, *Universal Military Dictionary*, p. 243.
108. General Return of the State of Camp Equipage, B.H.P., shows that of 1,521 privates' tents only 413 were in good condition; 255 needed repairs and 853 needed to be replaced.
109. The military command did, however, recognize the problem and tried to introduce sanitary practices; soldiers, for example, were ordered to dig trenches around each tent to drain off the moisture, and boards from barracks floors and berths were sometimes placed under the paillasses to ward off the dampness; see 11 September 1777, Orderly Book for King's American Regiment, 1776–1777, Item 106, Clements Library; Mackenzie, *Diary*, 1: 31; Howe, *General Sir William Howe's Orderly Book*, pp. 11, 131.
110. General Orders by Carleton and Haldimand. May 1776–July 1783, Add. Mss. 21,743. Two thirty-six pound trusses of straw were allowed each tent for the first bedding; the paillasses were supposed to be "refreshed" weekly with one truss and fresh straw issued every three weeks; Letters from the Secretary-at-War, S.P. 41/27; Orders of British Generals Who Commanded at Rhode Island, December 1776–October 1779, W.O. 36/2.
111. See 2 November 1778, 9 November 1778, 2 December 1778, 10 June 1779, 13 August 1779, 3 November 1779, 10 December 1779, 15 February 1780, 16 October 1780, 3 December 1780, and 18 June 1781, Peebles Diary; Journals and Diaries, Major Richard Augustus Wyvill, of the British Army, L.C., p. 18; Jethro Summer to Hortio Gates, 1 October 1780, Jethro Summer Papers, Clements Library.
112. The statistic on deaths attributed to "fevers" in the eighteenth century is from Lester S. King, *The Medical World of the Eighteenth Century*,

p. 123; see also Brocklesby, *Oeconomical and Medical Observations*, p. 200.
    113. Duffy, "Passage," pp. 27–28.
    114. Pringle, *Observations*, pp. 64–65, 84–85; John Robinson to Howe, 9 September 1775, B.H.P.
    115. Brocklesby, *Oeconomical and Medical Observations*, p. 173.
    116. Shryock, *Medicine and Society*, pp. 85–88; Wyndham Blanton, *Medicine in Virginia in the Eighteenth Century*, p. 259; John Duffy, *Epidemics in Colonial America*, pp. 206–208.
    117. Pringle, *Observations*, pp. 223–226; Duffy, *Epidemics*, pp. 215–218.
    118. Shryock, *Medicine and Society*, p. 91.
    119. Baurmeister, *Revolution in America*, p. 307.
    120. Minutes of a hospital board held at New York, 27 September 1779, Clinton Papers; Krafft, "Journal," pp. 92, 93, 95, 97; Pattison, "Official Letters," pp. 120–121, 192; 31 August 1779, 1, 4, 5, 6, 14, 27 September 1779, 1, 24 October 1779, 6, 16 November 1779, 8 July 1780, and 12, 18, 20, 22, 29, 30 September 1780, Peebles Diary.
    121. Cantlie, *History of the Army Medical Department*, 1: 150–151.
    122. Cornwallis to Germain, 20 August 1780, Germain Papers; Wemyss to Cornwallis, 4 August 1780, and Cruger to Cornwallis, 28 November 1780, Cornwallis Papers.
    123. Cornwallis to Clinton, 10 April 1781, Clinton Papers.
    124. Rawdon to Cornwallis, 1 August 1780, Wemyss to Cornwallis, 3 September 1780, and Cornwallis to Balfour, 5 August 1780, Cornwallis Papers.
    125. Kemble, "Journals," pp. 14–15, 29, 36. The Vaughan Papers contain numerous reports of the ravages of disease in the West Indies; see for example Joseph Ferguson to Vaughan, 27 August 1780, St. Leger to Vaughan, 19 November 1780, L. Tottenham to Vaughan, 8 May 1780, and Governor W. Mathew Burt to Vaughan, 31 May 1780, Vaughan Papers.
    126. Brocklesby, *Oeconomical and Medical Observations*, p. 232.
    127. Hugh Thursfield, "Smallpox in the American War of Independence," *Annals of Medical History*, 3d ser., 2 (July 1940): 312–318.
    128. Willard, ed., *Letters*, pp. 57–58.
    129. W.O. 36/1, p. 165.
    130. George Turnbull to Cornwallis, 2 October 1780, Cornwallis Papers; 4 May 1780, Peebles Diary.
    131. Robert Hamilton, *Thoughts Submitted to the Consideration of the Officers in the Army*, pp. 29, 32–35.
    132. Brocklesby, *Oeconomical and Medical Observations*, p. 291.
    133. Sullivan, "The Common British Soldier," pp. 234–236.
    134. Digby, *British Invasion*, pp. 213, 219–220.
    135. Lamb, *Journal*, p. 143.
    136. Digby, *British Invasion*, p. 274.
    137. Lamb, *Journal*, p. 357; Cornwallis to Germain, 17 March 1781, B.H.P.
    138. Monro, *Account of the Diseases*, pp. 64–65, 361; Brocklesby, *Oeconomical and Medical Observations*, p. 52. In New York the British used a building of King's College, the Brick Meeting House, the Poor House,

and the Quaker Meeting House. In Philadelphia they took over the Pennsylvania Meeting House, the oldest in the United States, and made emergency use of two Presbyterian meeting houses, the State House, a Seceder Meeting House, and the Play House; Robert Morton, "The Diary of Robert Morton," *Pennsylvania Magazine of History and Biography*, I, No. 1 (1877): 17–18.

139. Monro, *Account of the Diseases*, p. 361; Pringle, *Observations*, pp. 108–110.

140. Monro, *Account of the Diseases*, p. 366; Simes, *Military Course*, p. 231.

141. Daniel Chamier to Gage, 24 April 1775, Gage Papers; Observations by Benjamin Thompson, 4 November 1775, Germain Papers; John McNamara Hayes to John André, 9 March 1780, 18 July 1780, Clinton Papers; Robert Adair to Charles Jenkinson, 20 September 1780, Vaughan Papers; Pattison, "Official Letters," pp. 264, 309.

142. Monro, *Account of the Diseases*, pp. 364–365.

143. Gerard Freiherr van Swietan, *The Diseases Incident to Armies, with the Method of Cure*, pp. 119, 121, 126, 129–130.

144. Sullivan, "The Common British Soldier," p. 237.

145. "Camp Life in 1776: The Siege of Boston," *Historical Magazine*, 8 (1864): 329.

146. Riedesel, *Letters and Journals*, pp. 129, 130.

147. That ruthless act was recorded by a Mr. Grant, surgeon at the military hospital in Boston; see Willard, ed., *Letters*, p. 141.

148. Morton, "Diary," p. 17. Morton, a young man of sixteen or seventeen, reported watching Dr. John Foulke, lecturer on human anatomy in the Medical College of Philadelphia, remove an American soldier's leg in twenty minutes; the same procedure, he noted, took forty minutes at the military hospital. As late as 1874, mortality following all forms of amputation was between 35 and 50 percent, and following certain forms as high as 90 percent; McKeown and Brown, "Medical Evidence," p. 120.

149. Hamilton, *Duties of a Regimental Surgeon*, 2: 226, 232.

150. It was not until 1786 that the necessity of a large dosage was demonstrated; McKeown and Brown, "Medical Evidence," p. 124.

151. Observations by Benjamin Thompson, Germain Papers; George B. Griffenhagen, *Drug Supplies in the American Revolution*, p. 169.

152. Kennett, *French Armies*, pp. 131–132.

153. Hamilton, *Duties of a Regimental Surgeon*, 1: 4, 42.

154. Brocklesby, *Oeconomical and Medical Observations*, pp. 30–31.

155. The position was first offered to John Napier, who turned it down. It was then offered to John Adair, who also declined. John Mervin Nooth was finally appointed; see Barrington to Howe, 3 February 1778, Barrington to Clinton, 30 November 1778, and Return of the General Hospital Staff, 15 January 1783, B.H.P.

156. Barrington to Howe, 3 April 1776, W.O. 4/273.

157. A. Peterkin and William Johnston, eds., *Commissioned Officers in the Medical Services of the British Army, 1660–1960*, p. xxxviii.

158. Hamilton, *Duties of a Regimental Surgeon*, 2: 264–265.

159. Act of 18 George II c. 15, required the College of Surgeons to

examine, without pay, all army and navy surgeons and mates. They were also obliged to offer free lectures on practical surgery to military surgeons.

160. Robert Adair to Charles Jenkinson, 11 September 1781, Jenkinson to Clinton, 1 October 1781, and Jenkinson to Clinton, 2 July 1781, B.H.P. The sale of surgeoncies was apparently carried on clandestinely, however. James Latham offered his surgeoncy for £340, "£60 less than the usual price"; James Latham to Gage, 5 December 1774, Gage Papers. Charles Blake Garrison purchased the surgeoncy of the 34th Regiment, Memorial of Charles Blake Garrison, Add. Mss. 21,873.

161. Peterkin and Johnston, eds., *Commissioned Officers*. Mates' duties included such functions as filling prescriptions, dressing wounds, and bleeding patients.

162. Brocklesby, *Medical Observations*, p. 37.

163. For a discussion of their status see Richard L. Blanco, "The Prestige of British Army Surgeons," *Societas: A Review of Social History*, 2 (Autumn 1972): 333–351.

164. Jenkinson to Clinton, 2 May 1781, B.H.P.

165. *Advice to the Officers of the British Army; with the Addition of Some Hints to the Drummer and Private Soldier*, pp. 58–59, 61.

166. William Barr to Haldimand, 8 September 1780, Add. Mss. 21,857.

167. Hamilton, *Duties of a Regimental Surgeon*, 1: 6, 148–150; 2: 170.

168. Monro, *Account of the Diseases*, pp. 394, 397–398.

169. Hamilton, *Duties of a Regimental Surgeon*, 2: 151, 156–157. Hospital mates were largely ignored by the government in other ways: they were denied all fringe benefits for which surgeons and soldiers were eligible and, like that of private soldiers, their pay was often months in arrears; see John McNamara Hayes to John André, 13 April 1780, Clinton Papers; G. Christie to Adjutant General Major Ferguson, 16 August 1780, Vaughan Papers.

170. Hayes to André, 9 March 1780, Hayes to Clinton, 25 April 1780, Hayes to André, 18 May 1780, Hayes to Clinton, 20 May 1780, and Nooth to André, 21 June 1780, Clinton Papers; J. Stewart to V. Barbaton, 5 December 1780, Vaughan Papers.

171. Nooth to Clinton, 14 November 1779, Clinton Papers.

172. Matthew Powell to Governor Dalling, 6 September 1779, W.O. 1/683.

173. Buer, *Health, Wealth, and Population*, pp. 118–120.

174. Simes, *Military Course*, p. 162; see also Cuthbertson, *System*, p. 133.

175. 20–21 July 1777, Orderly Book for King's American Regiment, Clements Library; 23 July 1776, Kennedy Orderly Book, 33d Regiment, Coote Papers; 30 September 1779, Regimental Order Book, British Army, Siege of Savannah, L.C.; 16 June 1781 and 23 June 1781, Order Book of the 43d Regiment at Yorktown, 1781, Add. Mss. 42,449; 12 August 1781, Lord Cornwallis, Orderly Books, British General and Brigade Orders, Virginia and Yorktown; General Orders by Carleton and Haldimand, Add. Mss. 21,743.

176. Cantlie, *History of the Army Medical Department*, 1: 156, 163.

177. For hospital mortality rates, see Shryock, *Medicine and Society*, pp. 22–23. At St. Thomas and St. Bartholomew's hospitals in London, death rates averaged about 600 a year, or approximately one in thirteen; at the Hôtel-Dieu in Paris one out of five patients died; see *The Surgical Works of the Late John Jones, M.D.*, pp. 151–153; Jones was professor of surgery at the college of New York.

178. Florence Nightingale, Army Sanitary Reform under the late Lord Sidney Herbert, 1862, Add. Mss. 43,395, F. 321.

3. REWARDS AND RECREATION

1. Redlich, *German Military Enterpriser*, 2: 265, makes this point.

2. Beginning in 1685 and continuing throughout the eighteenth century, the rules of war permitted captains, acting with the approval of their regimental colonels, to discharge any noncommissioned officer or private "when they find cause"; see *Rules and Articles for the Better Government of His Majesty's Land-Forces in Pay during This Present Rebellion* (1685), p. 24. Successive rules of war of 1718, 1722, 1753, 1786, 1789, 1790, and 1791 reserved that power for officers.

3. See Peter Mathias, "The Social Structure in the Eighteenth Century: A Calculation by Joseph Massie," *Economic History Review*, 2d ser., 10 (1957–1958): 42–43.

4. Smith, *Wealth of Nations*, 1: 133.

5. The distribution of pay through the army was made by the Paymaster General after the authorized number of officers and men in each regiment was certified by the Commissary General of Musters. The gross amount owed each regiment was then subject to various deductions, which were the responsibility of regimental colonels. The actual disbursement of pay to the men was done through regimental agents hired by each regimental colonel and answerable to him; see Clifford Walton, *History of the British Standing Army, A.D. 1660–1700*, pp. 640, 644–645.

6. Barrington to Howe, 10 January 1777, B.H.P.

7. "Rules and Directions Relating to His Majesty's Barracks in North America," Add. Mss. 21,684.

8. Report of the Director of Clothing for the Year 1882–1883, W.O. 33/51.

9. Barrington to Howe, 10 January 1777, and Howe to Barrington, 27 March 1778, B.H.P.

10. Warrant for deducting twelve pence in the pound, 16 October 1761, and similar warrants dated 27 February 1762, 24 October 1763, 7 January 1767, 2 November 1769, 17 September 1770, 19 September 1771, 18 November 1772, 23 December 1773, and 23 December 1774, all requiring the twelve pence deduction, are in America, British Colonies, Two Folio Volumes of Documents Relating to the Equipment of the British Forces in America, 1728–1792, L.C.

11. Regimental pay books show that after all deductions were made for provisions, articles of clothing, soap, laundry services, etc., debits and credits usually balanced out, leaving the soldier in fact with no surplus

money; see Regimental Pay Books of the 84th Regiment of Foot, Mac-Laine Papers.

12. Maurice Morgann to Post Master General J. Foxcroft, 19 March 1783, B.H.P.

13. *Rules and Articles for the Better Government of Our Horse and Foot-Guards and All Other Our Land-Forces in Our Kingdoms of Great-Britain and Ireland, and Dominions beyond the Seas* (1722), p. 18. Successive rules of war of 1753, 1786, 1789, 1790, and 1791 repeat this provision.

14. Orders, Whitehall, 26 June 1778, W.O. 34/188. Payment for this kind of work was usually made on a daily basis; otherwise "the works would go but slowly on." The pay scale actually ranged from three pence for making a fascine and picket to one shilling four pence for making a gabion—a dirt-filled basket used between embrasures to protect the gunners from enemy fire; see Bland, *Treatise of Military Discipline*, pp. 256–258.

15. General Orders, Gage, Maitland, and Robertson, Add. Mss. 21,683.

16. Private Evan Evans of the 52d Regiment of Foot, a shoemaker by trade, worked in a hovel near camp; so did John McKie of the 23d Regiment; W.O. 71/84, pp. 51, 334.

17. Ashton, *Economic History*, p. 218.

18. Quoted in ibid., pp. 210–212.

19. Campbell Dalrymple, *A Military Essay: Containing Reflections on the Raising, Arming, Cloathing and Discipline of the British Infantry and Cavalry*, p. 146n.

20. The problem was common to all European armies; see Redlich, *German Military Enterpriser*, 2: 254.

21. Ibid., 2: 259–260.

22. 35 Elizabeth, c. 4; 39 Elizabeth, c. 21; 43 Elizabeth, c. 3; 1 James I, c. 25; 21 James I, c. 28; 3 Charles I, c. 5.

23. 43 George III, c. 61; this act revised 32 George III, c. 45, which had declared begging "highly improper" and designated begging soldiers as "rogues and vagabonds" subject to penalties of the law.

24. 46 George III, c. 69; Section III of the act read "that every soldier who shall from and after the passing of this act become entitled to his discharge, by reason of the expiration of any period of service fixed in any orders and regulations made by his Majesty in that behalf, or shall have been discharged by reason of being an invalid, or disabled, or having been wounded, shall thereupon become legally entitled to receive such pension, allowance or relief."

25. Blanco, "Henry Marshall," pp. 264–265.

26. Redlich, *German Military Enterpriser*, 2: 261.

27. Walton, *History of the British Standing Army*, pp. 595–597, 603. Hospitals for sailors were established at Hasler, Plymouth, and Greenwich; 33 George II, c. 18.

28. Admission Books, Royal Hospital, Chelsea, 1715–1882, W.O. 116/1.

29. In 1684 the Kilmainham Hospital accommodated only ten officers and one hundred soldiers; Walton, *History of the British Standing Army*, pp. 596–597, 603–604.

30. Barrington to Howe, 1 May 1778, and William Yonge, Secretary of War, to Carleton, 5 February 1783, B.H.P.

31. Barrington to Howe, 18 February 1777, Barrington to Clinton, 29 June 1778, Clinton to Cornwallis, 5 March 1781, and Oliver De Lancey to Lt. Col. Humphreys (79th Regiment), 12 November 1782, B.H.P. The case of Thomas Willis was typical: a veteran of twenty-nine years, most of them in the 63d Regiment of Foot, Willis was wounded in the shoulder in the Battle of Bunker Hill, in the head at the Battle of Bedford, and in the arm at the Battle of Trenton. Because the soldier's pension was too small "to maintain a helpless man without trade or calling," Willis requested assignment to an independent company of invalids; see Memorial of Thomas Willis, B.H.P.

32. Walton, *History of the British Standing Army*, p. 604.

33. 26 George III, c. 10.

34. 29 George III, c. 2.

35. The right was finally legalized in 1792 in 43 George III, c. 61.

36. W.O. 36/1, p. 87.

37. The widow of any officer killed in action was entitled to a yearly pension, ranging from £20 for the widow of a lieutenant to £50 for the widow of a colonel; Pensions to Officers' Widows, W.O. 24/825, W.O. 24/826, W.O. 24/827; these volumes cover the years 1778, 1779, and 1780 respectively. In fact, in 1759, 33 George II, c. 8, allowed all regiments to carry "fictitious names" instead of private soldiers, "in order to raise and settle a fund for the maintenance of such widows of officers, as are or shall be entitled to His Royal Bounty."

38. The widow of Private Zachariah Linton, killed in America after fourteen years' service, is a typical case. Left with four children to raise, Mrs. Linton begged for temporary state relief; Petition of Mary Linton, H.O. 42/2. For other examples, see Petition of John McKinzie and Petition of Mary Driskill, B.H.P.

39. Compassionate Lists, W.O. 24/771 and W.O. 24/772, cover the years 1779 and 1780, giving the names and sums awarded "in consideration of their, or their near relations' long and faithful services in our army."

40. Jonas Hanway, *The Soldier's Faithful Friend: Being Moral and Religious Advice to Soldiers*, p. 69.

41. Pattison, "Official Letters," pp. 311–312.

42. Carleton to Governor John Pan, 23 August 1783, B.H.P.

43. J. R. Western, *The English Militia in the Eighteenth Century: The Study of a Political Issue, 1660–1802*, p. 269.

44. Hanway, *Soldier's Faithful Friend*, pp. iii, 4; the last edition was printed in 1777.

45. William Bamford, "Bamford's Diary: The Revolutionary Diary of a British Officer," *Maryland Historical Magazine*, 27 (December 1932): 258.

46. Howe to George Danberry, Esq., 29 May 1776, B.H.P.

47. Howe to John Smith, Treasurer of the Committee for the Relief of the Soldiers, Their Widows and Orphans, 18 May 1776, Howe to Smith, 5 June 1777, and Howe to Smith, 24 October 1777, B.H.P.

48. G.O. by Haldimand and Carleton, Add. Mss. 21,743.

49. Nathaniel Day to John Robinson, 22 August 1777, T 64/103.
50. Robert Mackenzie to Lt. Col. Clerk, 1 March 1778, B.H.P.
51. *New York Gazette and Weekly Mercury*, 6–27 January 1777.
52. *Royal Gazette*, 10 October 1778; 20 January 1779. Theatre Royal was located in the old John Street theatre on Broadway.
53. Hamilton, *Thoughts*, p. 16, implies that only noncommissioned officers were financially able to do this, but Secretary-at-War Jenkinson to the Commanding Officer 43d Regiment, 8 January 1782, W.O. 4/275, requests a death certificate for a private soldier because the steward "of a society to which he belonged refuses to pay the sum due from the said Society to his Widow and six Children, who are in great Distress."
54. Peter Laslett, ed., *Household and Family in Past Time*, pp. 46, 156. See also J. Hajnal, "European Marriage Patterns in Perspective," in D. V. Glass and D. E. C. Eversley, eds., *Population in History*, pp. 101–143; Hajnal has discovered a distinction within the European marriage patterns. Western Europeans married very much later than others, and far more of them remained permanently single.
55. Redlich, *German Military Enterpriser*, 2: 208.
56. Walton, *History of the British Standing Army*, p. 491.
57. Cuthbertson, *System*, pp. 192–194.
58. 12 November 1777, Orderly Book for King's American Regiment, Clements Library; 5 December 1780, Order Book, New York, 1780, 6912/14, No. 43, Coote Papers.
59. A penurious gentleman, Laurence's father, Roger Sterne, held the lowest rank of ensign; he married the daughter of a camp sutler and the family made their home in a succession of Irish barracks. See Laurence Sterne, *Letters of the Late Rev. Mr. Laurence Sterne . . .* , 1: 11.
60. Thomas Simes, *The Military Guide for Young Officers*, 2: 212.
61. W.O. 36/1, p. 98.
62. Hamilton, *Thoughts*, p. 14.
63. Laslett, ed., *Household and Family*, pp. 134, 139, 167; mean household size refers to the husband, wife, children, servants, and relatives living in the same dwelling. There is considerable controversy over Laslett's thesis that the nuclear family has dominated throughout history. The leader of the revisionists is Lutz Berkner, "The Use and Misuse of Census Data for the Historical Analysis of Family Structure," *Journal of Interdisciplinary History*, 5, No. 4 (Spring 1975): 721–738.
64. Clode, *Military Forces*, 2: 379.
65. Hanway, *Soldier's Faithful Friend*, pp. 68, 71.
66. Cantlie, *History of the Army Medical Department*, 1: 156; the size of the army of course varied considerably over time.
67. Hanway, *Soldier's Faithful Friend*, p. 68. Hanway's broad experience gave him special insight into the problem of infant mortality, in both the civilian and the military sectors. He worked actively on behalf of the infant parish poor in England, and tried to call public attention to the excessive mortality of infants by visiting slum areas. He was, moreover, commissioner of the Victualling Office in 1762; see *Dictionary of National Biography*, ed. Leslie Stephen and Sidney Lee, 24 (1890): 312–313.
68. Sterne, *Letters*, 1: 8, 9, 13.
69. Hanway, *Soldier's Faithful Friend*, p. 47. Redlich, *German Military*

Enterpriser, 2: 209, notes the same tendency in the Prussian army.
70. Pausch, *Journal*, p. 33.
71. Krafft, "Journal," p. 140.
72. W.O. 71/33, p. 108; W.O. 71/80, pp. 446, 451; W.O. 71/85, pp. 290–307; W.O. 71/90, pp. 87, 88.
73. Thomas Simes, *The Military Medley*, p. 79.
74. Blumenthal, *Women Camp Followers*, pp. 19, 42.
75. "Patrick M'Roberts' Tour through Parts of the North Provinces of America, 1774–1775," ed. Carl Bridenbaugh, *Pennsylvania Magazine of History and Biography*, 59, No. 2 (1935): 142; 1 January 1778, Peebles Diary.
76. Hanway, *Soldier's Faithful Friend*, p. 68.
77. Krafft, "Journal," pp. 139–140.
78. George Farquhar, *The Recruiting Officer*, ed. Michael Shugrue, pp. 14–15.
79. Hamilton, *Thoughts*, p. 20.
80. J. H. Plumb, "The Commercialization of Leisure in Eighteenth Century England," paper presented at Conference of Anglo-American Historians, London, 1972.
81. George, *London Life*, pp. 287, 289, 300.
82. Kemble, "Journals," p. 69; Howe, *General Sir William Howe's Orderly Book*, pp. 27, 53. See also Bowler, *Logistics*, pp. 171–172.
83. Ibid., p. 174; Mackenzie, *Diary*, 1: 31.
84. The actual consumption was 5,000 puncheons. The capacity of a puncheon varied from 72 to 120 gallons; I have used the more conservative figure. See *Proceedings of a Board of General Officers*, pp. 10, 81, 83.
85. W.O. 36/1, p. 53. The appointment of sutlers was made by commanding officers of regiments.
86. W.O. 36/1, p. 70; Hadden, *Journal*, p. 278; Barker, *British in Boston*, p. 44.
87. Thomas Simes, *The Regulator, or Instructions to Form the Officer and Complete the Soldier*, p. 4.
88. The rum consumed in America was purchased under government contract in the following proportions: a quarter from Jamaica, a quarter from Barbados, a quarter from the Leeward Islands, and a quarter from the Ceded Islands. All contracts stipulated proof and quality, but an inferior grade was so often substituted that on the recommendation of General Clinton, the Treasury Board appointed Henry White as inspector; see John Robinson to Howe, 1 May 1776, Rum Contract, 1776, and Clinton to Robinson, 5 July 1779, B.H.P.; Clinton to H. White, 28 May 1779, Vaughan Papers; H. White to Clinton, 21 December 1779, Clinton Papers.
89. In the West Indies, where rum was especially valued for medicinal purposes, it was frequently found to be "of so pernicious a quality" that soldiers became ill soon after drinking it; see Christie to Vaughan, 14 July 1780, Vaughan Papers. Mackenzie, *Diary*, 1: 6, reported that two soldiers died in one evening; the same incident was recorded in W.O. 36/1, p. 70, which attributed the deaths to "poisonous liquor" on which "the men get intoxicated in a very extraordinary manner."

90. 17 March 1781, Peebles Diary; Kemble, "Journals," pp. 146, 149; 13 June 1780, 22 August 1780, and 11 October 1780, Orderly Book Royal Artillery, Wray Papers; 1 November 1775, 14 December 1775, and 11 January 1776, Thomas Ainslie, Orderly Book, 1775–1781, Peter Force Papers, Ser. 8A [George Chalmers], No. 58, L.C.

91. 24 May 1778, Journal of Christopher French, a British Army Officer, 1756–1764, 1776–1778, L.C.

92. June 1780, 15 July 1780, Orderly Book Royal Artillery, Wray Papers; Barker, *British in Boston*, p. 449; Pattison, "Official Letters," pp. 287, 307; "General Orders by Major General The Honourable William Howe," pp. 315, 316, 317, 318, 319, 322.

93. Benjamin Rush, *Directions for Preserving the Health of Soldiers*, p. 5; in 1778 the Board of War ordered the pamphlet reprinted for wider circulation.

94. Swietan, *Diseases Incident to Armies*, pp. 154, 158.

95. Blanco, "Henry Marshall," p. 266.

96. George, *London Life*, pp. 286–287, 316–317.

97. Barker, *British in Boston*, p. 19; *The Detail and Conduct of the American War under Generals Gage, Howe, Burgoyne, and Vice Admiral Lord Howe*, p. 42.

98. Howe, *General Sir William Howe's Orderly Book*, p. 37.

99. *Detail and Conduct of the American War*, p. 42.

100. Baurmeister, *Revolution in America*, p. 312.

101. Anburey, *Travels*, 2: 221–222, 453.

102. Eric Robson, "Purchase and Promotion in the British Army in the Eighteenth Century," *History*, 36 (February 1951): 60. The French Revolution brought about the gradual end of aristocratic dominance in the French army, but in England purchase of rank continued until 1871; Samuel P. Huntington, *The Soldier and the State: The Theory and Politics of Civil-Military Relations*, pp. 20–23, 43–47. See also James Hayes, "The Social and Professional Backgrounds of the Officers of the British Army, 1714–1763" (M.A. Thesis, University of London, 1956), especially Chapter 3.

103. Anne Hulton, *Letters of a Loyalist Lady* (Cambridge, Mass., 1927), pp. 19, 43, 45; Barker, *British in Boston*, p. 8.

104. *Royal Gazette*, 24 January 1778, 25 November 1778; Hadden, *Journal*, p. 35.

105. The *Virginia Gazette*, ed. Dixon and Hunter, 20 January 1776, carried a report of British plans to open a new theatre in Boston with the production of a farce called *The Blockade of Boston*; but the report concluded prophetically, "it is more probable before that time, the poor wretches will be presented with a tragedy called the Bombardment of Boston." For another account of the Boston theatre, see Lord Rawdon to the 10th Earl of Huntington, 5 October 1775, in Historical Manuscripts Commission, *Report on the Manuscripts of Reginald Rawdon-Hastings*, 3: 160.

106. *New York Gazette and Weekly Mercury*, 6–27 January 1777.

107. Theatre Broadsides, 19 January 1778, 26 January 1778, 16 February 1778, 2 March 1778, 9 March 1778, 16 March 1778, 25 March 1778, 12 April 1778, 24 April 1778, 1 May 1778, and 6 May 1778, Library Company of Philadelphia, Philadelphia, Pennsylvania.

108. *Royal Georgia Gazette*, 20 September–29 November 1781;
Evelyn, *Memoir*, p. 79.
109. Ray W. Pettengill, ed. and trans., *Letters from America,
1776–1779: Being Letters of Brunswick, Hessian and Waldeck Officers with the
British Armies During the Revolution*, pp. 150–151.
110. *Royal Gazette*, 10 October 1778, 3 January 1779; *New York Gazette
and Weekly Mercury*, 5 January–20 April 1778.
111. Ibid.
112. Pettengill, ed., *Letters from America*, pp. 150–151.
113. Ibid.
114. Thomas Hughes, *A Journal by Thomas Hughes, 1778–1789*, p.
110.
115. *Royal Gazette*, 10 October 1778, 3 January 1779; *New York Gazette
and Weekly Mercury*, 5 January–20 April 1778.
116. The American Company of Comedians played the seaboard
cities until the eve of the Revolution; when in 1774 the Congress adopted
a resolution calling for an end "to every species of extravagance and
dissipation," the company withdrew from America; see Hugh F. Rankin,
The Theater in Colonial America, pp. 19, 70–71.
117. Kenneth Lockridge, *Literacy in Colonial New England*, p. 87.
118. Depositions of British Soldiers, C.O. 5/88; Regimental Pay
Book (84th Regiment), MacLaine Papers; Account of the Money Delivered to the Men of the 71st Regiment, G.D. 153, H48c, Gilchrist of
Opisdale Muniments, S.R.O.
119. Michael Sanderson, "Literacy and Social Mobility in the Industrial Revolution in England," *Past and Present*, 56 (August 1972): 89.
120. Sullivan, "The Common British Soldier," p. 248. Thomas Sullivan entered the army as a volunteer in Dublin at the age of twenty; he
was promoted to corporal and eventually made sergeant. In 1776 he was
named "clerk to the regiment and was writing all the time." General and
regimental orders, letters from the War Office, monthly returns, and
records of courts martial were kept by the regiments in large folio volumes. For additional evidence of the promotion of privates to n.c.o.'s, see
Captain John Stanton to Lt. Gen. William Koppel, 10 June 1775, W.O.
4/273.
121. Sterne, *Letters*, p. 11; Sterne's biographer, Arthur Cash, *Laurence Sterne: The Early and Middle Years*, contends that the young Sterne
was probably taught by a regimental chaplain.
122. Cuthbertson, *System*, p. 10; Simes, *Military Course*, p. 230.
123. Lewis Lochée, *An Essay on Military Education*, pp. 65–66.
124. Simes, *Military Course*, p. 230.
125. Blanco, "Henry Marshall," pp. 271, 273.

4. CRIMES AND COURTS

Parts of this chapter are reprinted from MILITARY AFFAIRS,
February 1979, pp. 5–11, with permission. Copyright 1979 by the American Military Institute. No additional copies may be made without the

express permission of the author and of the editor of MILITARY
AFFAIRS.

1. Redlich, *German Military Enterpriser*, 2: 213. Washington's Continental Army had an overall desertion rate of 18.2 percent; Hugh F. Rankin, *The North Carolina Continentals*, p. 393.

2. An Account of Men Lost and Disabled in His Majesty's Land Service . . . in North America and the West Indies from 1 November 1774, War Office, January 1783, Add. Mss. 38,375.

3. Baker, *Government and Contractors*, p. 4.

4. W.O. 71/15, pp. 1, 145–146; W.O. 71/17, p. 152; W.O. 71/18, pp. 39, 41, 77–78, 79–80; W.O. 71/34, p. 220; W.O. 71/35, p. 217; W.O. 71/36, pp. 203, 305, 320–321. Some soldiers used aliases to enlist with different officers of the same regiment; see W.O. 71/34, p. 220.

5. W.O. 71/16, p. 5; W.O. 71/34, pp. 140, 254; W.O. 71/71, pp. 107, 245, 246; W.O. 71/83, p. 57; W.O. 71/89, p. 248; W.O. 71/90, p. 409.

6. W.O. 71/15, pp. 6, 73–74; W.O. 71/16, pp. 23, 29; W.O. 71/17, p. 136; W.O. 71/34, pp. 114, 131; W.O. 71/67, p. 9; W.O. 71/93, p. 200.

7. W.O. 71/17, pp. 43, 50, 125, 164; W.O. 71/18, p. 342; W.O. 71/19, pp. 171–172; W.O. 71/34, pp. 160, 266, 332, 339, 352, 409, 414; W.O. 71/35, pp. 14, 26, 27, 39, 40, 203, 250–256; W.O. 71/38, pp. 2–4, 194–197; W.O. 71/69, pp. 243–246; W.O. 71/67, pp. 155, 156, 216, 265, 272; W.O. 71/71, p. 104; W.O. 71/73, pp. 144, 267, 270; W.O. 71/75, p. 224; W.O. 71/80, p. 374; W.O. 71/85, pp. 217–223; W.O. 71/87, p. 182; W.O. 71/88, p. 48; W.O. 71/90, p. 8.

8. Secretary-at-War Charles Jenkinson's Report on the Press Act of 1779, W.O. 4/966.

9. Pettengill, ed. and trans., *Letters from America*, pp. 120–130, 145–146, 150–151. Conditions in prison camps on both sides were abominable; see Elias Boudinot, Commissary General of Prisoners, to the Commissary of Prisoners in the British Army in Philadelphia, 12 November 1777, Washington to Howe, 14 November 1777, Mr. Boudinot's Report, 13 November 1777, and W. Phillips to Clinton, 12 July 1780, B.H.P.

10. Anburey, *Travels*, 2: 438.

11. German and British prisoners taken at Yorktown were also allowed freedom to live and work in the area; see Evelyn, *Memoir*, p. 52; Willard, ed., *Letters*, pp. 36–37, 51–52, 60–61; Doehla, "Journal," p. 272; Anburey, *Travels*, 2: 309; Lamb, *Journal*, p. 398. The German mercenaries were particularly susceptible to American overtures. All told, between five and six thousand remained in America; see Lyman H. Butterfield, "Psychological Warfare in 1776: The Jefferson-Franklin Plan to Cause Hessian Desertions," American Philosophical Society, *Proceedings*, 94, No. 3 (June 1950): 234–235.

12. Samuel Graham, "An English Officer's Account of His Services in America, 1779–1781," *Historical Magazine*, 9 (August–September 1865): 304; John Burgoyne, *The Substance of General Burgoyne's Speeches, on Mr. Vyner's Motions, on the 26th of May; and upon Mr. Hartley's Motion on the 28th of May*, pp. 14–15.

13. Anburey, *Travels*, 2: 438–439, claims that many of the British deserters "communicated to their officers their intentions, previous to their desertion, requesting a certificate" (regarding payment and clothing

due them). Upon arriving in New York, the deserters then filed claims for payment and clothing; see 28 January 1781, Order Book of the 43d Regiment, 8 July 1780–17 February 1781, B.H.P. A Board of Inquiry was set up to investigate their claims; the board acknowledged the claims of all those who "used their utmost efforts to escape from the enemy" and rejected the claims of those who had continued in rebel service or had worked at their trades "for some time before re-joining their regiments." See Abstract of Bounty Money Paid by Order of His Excellency Sir Guy Carleton to Soldiers Who Have Made Their Escape from the Rebels between 20 July and 3 September 1782, Abstract of Bounty Money Paid by Order of His Excellency Sir Guy Carleton to Soldiers Who Made Their Escape from the Rebels between 10 September and 12 November 1782, and Abstract of Bounty Money Paid by Order of His Excellency Sir Guy Carleton to Soldiers Who Made Their Escape from the Rebels between 26 February and 26 March 1783, Proceedings of a Board of Inquiry held at New York on 20 January 1783, B.H.P.

14. Scouller, *Armies of Queen Anne*, pp. 267–282. Mutiny was endemic in American armies during the Revolution. Minor outbreaks occurred regularly in 1777, especially among the New York militia; Enoch Poor's brigade of New Englanders mutinied in November. The army at Providence mutinied four times during the winter and spring of 1778–1779 over pay and provisions. Mutinies over food shortages occurred in 1779 in Charlottesville and at West Point. Risings took place among the Massachusetts troops and among troops at Lancaster and Fort Schuyler in 1780. In 1781, Moses Hazen's Regiment rebelled, as did the New York Regiment and the Virginia militia. The Connecticut line under Washington's command mutinied in 1780, claiming neglect by the state of Connecticut. Pennsylvania troops mutinied in 1782, as did Marylanders. The most serious mutinies were those of the Pennsylvania and New Jersey lines in 1781 and 1783; see Allen Bowman, *The Morale of the American Revolutionary Army*, pp. 32–38.

15. The mutineers claimed that some regiments had waited three years for clothing replacements and that £800 sterling was owed the men of the 24th Regiment; W.O. 71/87, pp. 29–51.

16. Copy of the Conditions Entered Into by the General Officers in Scotland with the Mutineers of the Earl of Seaforth's Regiment, September 1778, Add. Mss. 42,071.

17. Andrew Marshall to General Alexander Leslie, 12 February 1783, and Marshall to Leslie, 13 March 1783, Leslie Papers, G.D. 26/9/520.

18. Sir George Clark, *War and Society in the Seventeenth Century*, pp. 79, 84–85.

19. Redlich, *German Military Enterpriser*, 2: 221.

20. Bowler, *Logistics*, pp. 41–56.

21. From headquarters at Halifax, Howe admonished those who "imagine that the crime of stealing is lessened because the goods were the property of persons ill affected to government"; "General Orders by Major General Howe," p. 381.

22. Barker, "A British Officer in Boston," p. 8; Sullivan, "The Common British Soldier," p. 241.

23. "General Orders by Major General Howe," pp. 257, 285, 315.

24. André, *Journal*, pp. 37–38, 47; "General Orders by Major General Howe," pp. 481, 504.

25. Kemble, "Journals," pp. 91, 98.

26. Serle, *American Journal*, pp. 77, 86–87.

27. Ibid., p. 120.

28. Seume, "Memoirs of a Hessian Conscript," pp. 555–559.

29. Krafft, "Journal," pp. 60, 61; Kemble, "Journals," p. 91.

30. *Detail and Conduct of the American War*, p. 43.

31. "Proposed Plan for bringing the army under strict discipline with regard to marauding," by Patrick Ferguson, November 1779, Clinton Papers.

32. "Gen. Sir Henry Clinton's Orders," in New-York Historical Society, *Collections*, 16 (1883): 595; A. R. Newsome, ed., "A British Orderly Book, 1780–1781," *North Carolina Historical Review*, 9 (January 1932): 180–183, 378–379, 386.

33. Newsome, ed., "A British Orderly Book," pp. 177, 276, 296–297, 370–371.

34. George Ferguson to Vaughan, 24 March 1780, St. Leger to Ferguson, 14 June 1780, and Prescott to Vaughan, 7 July 1780, Vaughan Papers.

35. See Michael Mullin, "British Caribbean and North American Slaves in an Era of War and Revolution, 1775–1807," in Jeffrey J. Crow and Larry E. Tise, eds., *The Southern Experience in the American Revolution*, pp. 235–263, for an analysis of why no collective resort to arms by blacks occurred in the American South during the Revolution. See also Jeffrey J. Crow, "Slave Rebelliousness and Social Conflict in North Carolina, 1775–1802," *William and Mary Quarterly*, 3d ser., 37 (January 1980): 79–102.

36. This was apparently generally true of eighteenth-century England as well; the great majority of crimes were offenses against property rather than persons; see Leon Radzinowicz, *A History of English Criminal Law and Its Administration from 1750*, pp. 150–151, 155–156. It is of course possible that soldiers accused of murder, especially of civilians, were proceeded against by the ordinary courts of law. For example, when Henry Worswick of the 31st Regiment was charged with murder in Lancashire, Secretary at War Barrington ordered Worswick sent home for the trial; see Barrington to Carleton, 10 August 1776, W.O. 4/273.

37. W.O. 71/82, pp. 377–388; W.O. 71/83, pp. 108, 219; W.O. 71/84, p. 342; W.O. 71/85, pp. 164–166; W.O. 71/86, pp. 190–196, 219–230; W.O. 71/87, pp. 256–263; W.O. 71/92, pp. 217–222; W.O. 71/93, pp. 185, 198, 213.

38. See for example W.O. 71/83, p. 219; W.O. 71/93, p. 195; in both cases cited, all of the convicted soldiers were hanged; in one case the court ordered the bodies of the convicted men "Afterwards to be hanged in chains, or delivered to the surgeon for dissection, according to the will of the commander in chief."

39. W.O. 71/82, pp. 377–388; W.O. 71/93, p. 185; W.O. 71/93, p. 198; W.O. 71/92, pp. 217–222; W.O. 71/86, pp. 190–196; W.O. 71/87, pp. 256–263.

40. William Howe, *The Narrative of Lieutenant General William Howe, in a Committee of the House of Commons, on the 29th of April, 1779,* pp. 58–60.

41. Lord Rawdon to the 10th Earl of Huntingdon, 5 August 1776, in Historical Manuscripts Commission, *Manuscripts of Rawdon-Hastings,* 3: 179.

42. Frank Moore, ed., *Diary of the American Revolution: From Newspapers and Original Documents,* 1: 419–422.

43. *Orderly Book of . . . De Lancey,* pp. 86, 93–94; W.O. 71/86, pp. 200–206.

44. Simcoe, *Military Journal,* p. 212; Simcoe to Cornwallis, 2 June 1781, Cornwallis Papers.

45. W.O. 71/88, p. 528; Captain Peebles refers to the execution in his diary on 6 June 1779, Peebles Diary.

46. W.O. 71/85, pp. 290–307; "General Orders by Major General Howe," pp. 556, 560; W.O. 71/73, p. 108; W.O. 71/80, pp. 446, 451; W.O. 71/90, p. 87; W.O. 71/80, p. 421.

47. Cuthbertson, *System,* p. 144.

48. W.O. 71/71, pp. 246, 247; W.O. 71/81, pp. 61–78; W.O. 71/84, p. 243; W.O. 71/86, pp. 216–218; W.O. 71/88, p. 57; W.O. 71/92, pp. 163–171.

49. W.O. 71/80, p. 57; W.O. 71/89, p. 248.

50. W.O. 71/90, pp. 409–410.

51. W.O. 71/83, p. 57.

52. Paret, *Yorck,* pp. 18–19; Redlich, *German Military Enterpriser,* 2: 203.

53. Simes, *Regulator,* p. 158.

54. Simes, *Military Guide,* p. 169.

55. Insubordination was apparently a serious disciplinary problem throughout the century; see W.O. 71/15, pp. 3–4, 22–24, 24–31, 32–33; W.O. 71/35, n.p.; W.O. 71/36, pp. 328–329; W.O. 71/37, p. 156; W.O. 71/71, p. 307; W.O. 71/73, p. 223; W.O. 71/75, pp. 26–31; W.O. 71/80, pp. 106, 355; W.O. 71/82, pp. 37–52; W.O. 71/84, p. 298; W.O. 71/85, pp. 137–141; W.O. 71/86, pp. 99–105, 239–250, for cases involving insubordination to an officer; for those involving NCO's and privates, see W.O. 71/15, pp. 168–169, 186–187; W.O. 71/17, pp. 65, 62–67, 122, 126; W.O. 71/34, pp. 125, 153–55; W.O. 71/65, pp. 284–287, 287–289; W.O. 71/69, pp. 119 125, 290; W.O. 71/71, p. 283; W.O. 71/82, pp. 275–279; W.O. 71/86, pp. 1–6; W.O. 71/88, p. 323.

56. It has been incorrectly assumed that discipline under the medieval ordinances of war was enforced by the Court of Chivalry; see for examples Adye, *Treatise on Courts-Martial,* pp. 2–4. Captain Stephen Payne Adye's *Treatise* was the first book written in English on military law since *An Abridgement of the English Military Discipline,* published in 1686; *A Treatise* went through eight editions, including publication in America, and helped to standardize court procedures. Although Hector Theophilus Cramahé was Judge-Advocate of the North American establishment, Adye, who was a captain in the Royal Artillery, served as Deputy Judge-Advocate and in fact did the actual work of Judge-Advocate from 1775 through 1783; see Frederick Bernays Wiener, *Civilians under Mili-*

tary Justice: The British Practice since 1689 Especially in North America, pp. 182–183. Wiener also offers a brief discussion of the distinction between the Court of Chivalry and the courts-martial, pp. 165–166. See also G. D. Squibb, *The High Court of Chivalry: A Study of the Civil Law in England*, pp. 1–8; Squibb argues convincingly that there were in fact two different forms of jurisdiction, the first exercised under the Statutes and Ordinances and the second that of the Court of Chivalry.

57. *Rules and Articles* (1685).

58. Arthur N. Gilbert, "The Regimental Courts Martial in the Eighteenth Century British Army," *Albion*, 8, No. 1 (Spring 1976): 50–66, is the best article on the subject.

59. Edward Hughes to Henry Pelham, 31 October 1729, W.O. 71/17, p. 5.

60. *Rules and Articles* (1685), p. 30.

61. Hughes to Pelham, 31 October 1729, W.O. 71/17, p. 5.

62. Lieutenant A. Tullekers to E. Hughes, 22 February 1724, W.O. 81/2, p. 46.

63. Ibid., p. 47.

64. Directive of Adjutant General E. Hughes, W.O. 71/34, p. 378.

65. Hughes to George Treby, Secretary at War, 3 March 1722/3, W.O. 81/2, p. 17.

66. Cuthbertson, *System*, p. 173.

67. Hughes to Treby, 3 March 1722/3, W.O. 71/15, p. 69; Hughes to Treby, 4 August 1722, W.O. 81/2, p. 17.

68. Hughes to Treby, 3 March 1722/3, W.O. 71/15, p. 69.

69. Hughes to Pelham, 31 October 1729, W.O. 71/17, p. 5.

70. Hughes to Pelham, 29 August 1728, W.O. 81/2, p. 102.

71. See Of the Wooden Horse, W.O. 93/6.

72. In 1679, for example, three prisoners were confined "for some time" without being charged with any crime; W.O. 89/2, pp. 64–65; two privates were held from 12 January 1720 to 18 June 1720 before being brought to trial; W.O. 71/34, p. 332; in 1740 one private was held and confined in irons for twenty-two weeks; W.O. 71/37, p. 47.

73. *Rules and Articles for the Better Government of His Majesty's Horse and Foot-Guards, and All Other His Majesty's Forces in Great-Britain and Ireland, Dominions beyond the Seas and Foreign Parts* (1753), pp. 56, 57.

74. See for example W.O. 71/94, n.p.; W.O. 71/38, pp. 91–99, 99–100, 100–102, 103–105, 105–107.

75. Adye, *Treatise on Courts-Martial*, pp. 33, 35.

76. D. P. O'Connell, "The Nature of British Military Law," *Military Law Review*, No. 19 (January 1963): 153–154. For biographical sketches of Judge Advocates General and their deputies from the post-Restoration through the end of the Eighteenth Century, see Wiener, *Civilians under Military Justice*, pp. 165–188.

77. On the method of proceeding against criminals and other offenders in the French Armie, W.O. 93/6.

78. Adye, *Treatise on Courts-Martial*, p. 82.

79. *Rules and Articles for the Better Government of Our Horse and Foot-Guards and All Other Our Land-Forces in Our Kingdoms of Great-Britain and Ireland, Dominions Beyond the Seas* (1718), p. 16.

80. On the method of proceeding against criminals, W.O. 93/6; for the text of the oath administered to English general courts, see Smith, *Universal Military Dictionary*, p. 68.

81. The first case I discovered was in 1774; see W.O. 71/83, p. 181; in 1779 a general court meeting in New York granted the defendant's request for a delay of trial in order to allow him to prepare his defense; W.O. 71/88, p. 336.

82. Trial records for 1774 show a prisoner being asked by the court if he had any objections to any member of the court; W.O. 71/83, p. 176.

83. W.O. 71/90, p. 426.

84. See, for example, the trial of Pvt. William Richards of the 79th Regiment of Foot, 14 July 1779, W.O. 71/90, p. 23.

85. *An Act for Punishing Mutiny and Desertion and for the Better Payment of the Army and their Quarters, George II* (1753).

86. Hughes to William Pulteney, Secretary at War, 6 January 1716/17, W.O. 81/1.

87. Hughes to William Berkeley, Deputy Adjutant General with Major General Pepper's Regiment of Dragoons, 29 December 1716, W.O. 81/1.

88. Instructions to Deputy Judge-Advocates from Judge-Advocate Hughes, 15 June 1734, W.O. 71/17, pp. 73–74.

89. To commanding officer of Sir Charles Hotham's Regiment, 20 February 1715/16, and To Lt. Col. Norcliffe, 8 March 1715/16, W.O. 81/1; in 1723 Hughes declared the proceeding of a general court, which had sentenced a prisoner to death, illegal on the grounds that the court included one captain, a lieutenant, and three corporals instead of thirteen commissioned officers as required by law; he ruled that unless the requisite number of commissioned officers were available, military prisoners must be sent to England for trial; Hughes to Treby, 17 June 1723, W.O. 81/2, pp. 32–33.

90. William O. Shanahan, *Prussian Military Reforms, 1786–1813*, p. 25.

91. Whitehall, 28 February 1715/16, W.O. 71/14, p. 88.

92. *Rules and Articles* (1718), p. 38.

93. Simes, *Regulator*, pp. 166–167.

94. Cuthbertson, *System*, pp. 146–147.

95. Simes, *Regulator*, p. 167.

96. W.O. 71/17, pp. 60, 113; W.O. 71/34, pp. 182, 183.

97. W.O. 71/14, pp. 62–63, 139, 141, 171, 172, 189; W.O. 71/34, pp. 230, 266.

98. W.O. 71/14, p. 80; W.O. 71/34, pp. 6, 42–43, 152, 186.

99. W.O. 71/15, p. 107; W.O. 71/73, p. 9.

100. For Enlightenment reforms, see John Gagliardo, *Enlightened Despotism*, pp. 51–54; the reference to the abandonment of *peine forte et dure* is found in Wiener, *Civilians under Military Justice*, p. 110 n. 145.

101. Radzinowicz, *History of English Criminal Law*, p. 151.

102. The statistics cited in Tables 10–12 and accompanying text are based on an analysis of a sample of 2,061 criminal actions brought before general courts from 1666 until 1782. Due to the difficulty of organizing the material into precise categories, only those offenses considered capi-

tal throughout the entire period are included—murder, sexual offenses, plunder, desertion, treason, and mutiny. Because the purpose of the analysis is to observe broad shifts over a long span of time, the data have been grouped into three periods: 1666–1718; 1719–1753; 1754–1782. The sample was taken from W.O. 71/14–19, W.O. 71/34–38, W.O. 71/65–67, W.O. 71/73, W.O. 71/75, W.O. 71/77, W.O. 71/80–95, and W.O. 89/1–2. For obvious reasons citation of each individual case is impractical.

103. Art. 6, p. 4, Art. 9, p. 6, Art. 28, p. 22, Art. 35, p. 27, Art. 41, p. 31, *Rules and Articles* (1718).

104. Art. 5, p. 3, Art. 39, p. 28, Art. 40, p. 29, *Rules and Articles* (1722).

105. Specifically the rules now read "or such other punishment as the court shall think fit," Art. 3, p. 7, Art. 13, p. 39, Art. 14, p. 40, Art. 18, 19, p. 41, Art. 21, p. 42, *Rules and Articles* (1753).

106. Art. 8, pp. 18–19, *Rules and Articles for the Better Government of All His Majesty's Forces* (1789).

107. W.O. 71/15, pp. 285–287; W.O. 71/17, p. 154; W.O. 71/18, pp. 86, 168; W.O. 71/19, p. 45; W.O. 71/36, pp. 300–305, 318, 320–321; W.O. 71/37, pp. 43, 103, 127, 173; W.O. 71/38, p. 254; W.O. 71/65, p. 213.

108. Art. 1, Sect. 23, pp. 75–76, *Rules and Articles for the Better Government of All His Majesty's Forces* (1786).

109. Articles of War published by King Richard I, in his expedition to the Holy Land, A.D. 1189, W.O. 93/6.

110. Articles of War by King Richard II transcribed from a manuscript in the Harleyan Library, W.O. 93/6.

111. Articles of War for the Government of Her Majesty's Forces Serving in the Low Countries under the command of the Earl of Leicester, Anno. 1586 Eliz. I, W.O. 93/6.

112. Robert Devereaux, 3d Earl of Essex, *Camp Discipline, or The Soldier's Duty: In Certain Articles and Ordinances of Warre . . .* , p. 5.

113. Art. 1, p. 2, *Military Orders and Articles Established by His Majesty, for the Better Ordering and Government of His Majesty's Army* (1642). The rules of war of 1718 removed blasphemy from the cognizance of military courts and provided instead that offenders be handed over to a civil magistrate "to be punished according to law"; *Rules and Articles* (1718), p. 3.

114. W.O. 71/82, p. 67; W.O. 71/92, pp. 271–272.

115. W.O. 71/95, pp. 210–212, 212–214, 214–215.

116. O'Connell, "Nature of British Military Law," p. 148.

117. T. C. Hansard, *Parliamentary Debates*, 3d ser., 156: 1175.

118. Ibid., p. 1180.

119. Doehla, "Journal," p. 245.

120. Hamilton, *Duties of a Regimental Surgeon*, 1: 45.

121. 57 George III, c. 75.

122. 7 & 8 George IV, c. 28, s. 8; 7 & 8 George IV, c. 29; 9 George IV, c. 31; 5 & 6 Vict., c. 51.

123. Hansard, *Parliamentary Debates*, 3d ser., 156: 1183.

124. Richard L. Blanco, "Attempts to Abolish Branding and Flog-

ging in the Army of Victorian England before 1881," *Journal of the Society for Army Historical Research*, 46 (1968): 140 n. 17.

125. Maurer Maurer, "Military Justice under General Washington," *Military Affairs*, 28 (Spring 1964): 11−12; Stuart L. Bernath, "George Washington and the Genesis of American Military Discipline," *Mid-America*, 49 (April 1967): 89, 97.

126. Examples of cases of soldiers sentenced to be whipped by an entire regiment are numerous before 1740; see W.O. 71/14, pp. 55, 62−63, 64, 125, 150, 151, 187−188, 264, 268, 269, 290; W.O. 71/15, pp. 67, 71−72, 73−74, 75, 79−81, 105−106, 108−109, 109−110, 114, 132−133, 150−151, 151−152; W.O. 71/16, pp. 7, 12, 22, 23, 26, 29, 37; W.O. 71/34, pp. 6, 43, 146, 152, 163, 173, 186, 314, 325, 336, 346, 356, 367, 370, 373, 381, 382, 409, 414; W.O. 71/37, pp. 6, 13.

127. W.O. 71/34, p. 414.

128. Ibid., p. 163.

129. Ibid., p. 173.

130. Ibid., pp. 373, 375.

131. My search of the records uncovered no penalties after 1740 as extreme as those cited above, and only seven cases in which the penalty given was over 1,000 lashes; one private received 1,200 lashes, W.O. 71/65, pp. 122−124; three received 1,500, W.O. 71/69, pp. 156−157, W.O. 71/71, p. 177, W.O. 71/75, pp. 242−245; and three were given 2,000, although in one of these the sentence was remitted to 1,000, see W.O. 71/65, p. 326; W.O. 71/38, pp. 116−117, W.O. 71/65, pp. 329−330.

132. Hamilton, *Duties of a Regimental Surgeon*, 2: 23, 65.

133. Wiener, *Civilians under Military Justice*, p. 107.

134. Simes, *Military Course*, pp. 172−173.

135. Simes, *Military Guide*, pp. 2−3.

136. Adye, *Treatise on Courts-Martial*, p. 136.

137. Cuthbertson, *System*, pp. 153−154.

138. E. L. Woodward, *The Age of Reform, 1815−1870*, p. 260.

139. Blanco, "Attempts to Abolish Branding and Flogging," p. 145.

5. TRAINING AND CAMPAIGNING

1. Richard Kane, *A System of Camp Discipline, Military Honours, Garrison Duty, and Other Regulations for the Land Forces*, pp. 1−4; Kemble, "Journals," p. 69.

2. W.O. 36/1, p. 139.

3. Details on the daily activities of the soldier can be found in regimental orderly books, some of which have been cited earlier, including Ainslie Orderly Book, L.C.; Buckeridge Order Book (37th Regiment); "General Orders by Major General the Honourable William Howe"; and Orderly Book for King's American Regiment, Clements Library. Among unpublished sources not previously cited are Frederick Baum, Burgoyne's Orders at Montreal and Crown Point, L.C.; Orderly Books, Capt. Beamsley Glasier, 2d Battalion, 60th Regiment, British Army at Niagara, 1771−1773, L.C.; Orderly Book for the 10th Regiment of Foot, Boston,

1775, Item 105, Clements Library; Capt. Hatfield's Orderly Book, kept at Boston, 1776, L.C.; Carleton's Order Book, 1782–1783, Mackenzie Papers.

4. Smith, *Universal Military Dictionary*, p. 118; Bland, *Treatise of Military Discipline*, pp. 185–188, 206–210, 227, 232–237, describes and discusses guard duties in detail.

5. Orders for the Provost Martial, 30 June 1775, Mackenzie Papers.

6. Paret, *Yorck*, pp. 13–46, gives a detailed discussion of Prussian tactics. Although European battalions were deployed in three ranks, from the 1750s on British infantry drew up in two ranks. See also Peter Paret, "Colonial Experience and European Military Reform at the End of the Eighteenth Century," *Bulletin of the Institute of Historical Research*, 37 (May 1964): 52, n. 7. See also Robert S. Quimby, *The Background of Napoleonic Warfare*, especially pp. 14–16; Quimby challenges the notion that eighteenth-century generals were reluctant to engage in battle, preferring instead the less dangerous method of maneuvering.

7. Quimby, *Background*, pp. 54–55.

8. It was considered "beneath the dignity" of an officer to instruct soldiers in the "minute parts of discipline"; Dalrymple, *Military Essay*, p. 54. In fact many officers knew little or nothing at all about military science. During the Revolution, Lieutenant Colonel Stephen Kemble complained that some officers on the Nicaraguan expedition had never seen prior service and were totally ignorant of the duties rank entailed; Kemble, "Journals," p. 276. When the army in Boston was desperately in need of cartographers to map the countryside, few could be found among the officers. Some of the assistant engineers did not know the different parts of a fortification; Mackenzie, *Diary*, 1: 31; 2: 466, 521, 540, 551. See also Schaukirk, "Occupation of New York City," p. 24.

9. For an interesting discussion of the distinctive values of the officer corps, see Arthur N. Gilbert, "Law and Honour among Eighteenth-Century British Army Officers," *The Historical Journal*, 19, No. 1 (1976): 75–87.

10. Robson, "Purchase and Promotion," pp. 57–72.

11. Huntington, *The Soldier and the State*, pp. 24–25, 30–36.

12. Robin Higham, ed., *A Guide to the Sources of British Military History*, pp. 126–128.

13. Sullivan, "The Common British Soldier," p. 224.

14. McDonald, "Letter-Book," p. 208.

15. John Adams, *The Adams Papers: Diary and Autobiography of John Adams*, ed. L. H. Butterfield, 3: 289–290. See also Pausch, *Journal*, pp. 107–109.

16. Anburey, *Travels*, 1: 191.

17. *Carl von Clausewitz: On War*, ed. Michael Howard and Peter Paret, p. 319.

18. Pausch, *Journal*, p. 100; although Pausch thought the exercise healthy, he noted that it "came the harder on my men as they had never been drilled in it before."

19. Mackenzie, *Diary*, 1: 6, 13.

20. Edward Harvey, *The Manual Exercise, as ordered by His Majesty in*

1764, and Cavan, *A New System*, pp. 66, 70–80, 90, 94–95, both describe the exercises in detail.

21. 3 May 1772, Orderly Books, Capt. Beamsley Glasier, gives instructions for saluting. Simes, *Military Guide*, p. 165, and Cavan, *A New System*, p. 29, emphasize the importance of subordination.

22. Dalrymple, *Military Essay*, pp. 48, 54.

23. Pausch, *Journal*, pp. 107–109, says the German mercenaries laughed at the British performing the quick step.

24. Hughes, *Journal*, p. 6.

25. Anburey, *Travels*, 1: 205.

26. Digby, *British Invasion*, p. 153.

27. Harvey, *Manual Exercise*, p. 34.

28. Rogers, *Weapons of the British Soldier*, pp. 85, 90–93.

29. Cavan, *A New System*, p. 23, said that it was not unusual for half the muskets in a company to be out of commission because the face of the hammer was insufficiently hardened to produce fire when it made contact with the flint. Rogers, *Weapons of the British Soldier*, p. 94, estimates accuracy at only up to 80 or 100 yards, depending on the bore.

30. Rogers, *Weapons of the British Soldier*, pp. 110–114. See also David Patten, "Ferguson and His Rifle," *History Today*, 28, No. 7 (1978): 446–454.

31. Cavan, *A New System*, pp. 67–115, describes the firearms exercise in detail.

32. N. H. Gibbs, "Armed Forces and the Art of War," in *The New Cambridge Modern History*, ed. C. W. Crawley (1965), 9: 67.

33. Anburey, *Travels*, 1: 333.

34. Paret, *Yorck*, p. 15.

35. Paret, "Colonial Experience," pp. 52–53.

36. W.O. 36/1, pp. 12, 56, 59, 105; Stevens, ed., *Howe's Orderly Book*, pp. 201, 204; Krafft, "Journal," p. 164; Mackenzie, *Diary*, 1: 4, 144; Hughes, *Journal*, p. 111.

37. "Orders by Maj.-Gen. Daniel Jones," in New-York Historical Society, *Collections*, 16 (1883): 606, 607, 608, 610, 611, 613, 614, 615, 616, 619, 621, 623.

38. Cavan, *A New System*, pp. 21, 90.

39. Mackenzie, *Diary*, 1: 45.

40. Anburey, *Travels*, 1: 213.

41. Kemble, "Journals," p. 80.

42. British accounts of the massacre disagree as to the number of casualties; Robertson, *Diaries*, p. 149, estimates 400–500 killed and wounded. André, *Journal*, p. 50, puts the number of dead at 200, with 71 prisoners of war. Lt. Henry Stirke, "A British Officer's Revolutionary War Journal, 1776–1778," ed. S. Sydney Bradford, *Maryland Historical Magazine*, 56, No. 2 (1961): 172, estimates near 300 dead; Bradford's own estimate is 150 casualties.

43. Anthony Allaire, *Diary of Lieut. Anthony Allaire*, p. 31; Lamb, *Journal*, p. 307.

44. Wickwire and Wickwire, *Cornwallis*, pp. 63–65, 214, 298–300.

45. Cavan, *A New System*, pp. 15, 18, 20–21, 24–25.

46. Anburey, *Travels*, 1: 160.

47. Ibid., p. 379. See also "The Soldiers Load and Equipment on the March, 1808," in T. H. McGuffie, ed., *Rank and File: The Common Soldier at Peace and War, 1642–1914*, pp. 43–44.

48. Digby, *British Invasion*, p. 139.

49. Ibid., p. 117; George F. G. Stanley, ed., *For Want of a Horse; Being a Journal of the Campaigns against the Americans in 1776 and 1777*, p. 96.

50. Anburey, *Travels*, 1: 303.

51. Ibid., pp. 144, 277; Digby, *British Invasion*, p. 118.

52. Anburey, *Travels*, 2: 8–9.

53. Lamb, *Journal*, pp. 159–160; Stanley, ed., *For Want of a Horse*, p. 148; Anburey, *Travels*, 1: 413–415.

54. Anburey, *Travels*, 1: 431.

55. Ibid., p. 422. The dead were, moreover, often superficially interred on or near the field of battle, which contributed to health problems as well as to the mental agitation of the troops. During the Long Island campaigns of 1776, General Howe expressed fear that a "pestilential infection" would result from improper burial practices; "General Orders by Major General William Howe," p. 416. Reports from Hubbardton after Burgoyne's troops seized it in a bloody confrontation in July 1777 revealed that wolves came down from the hills in large numbers to tear the bodies from their shallow graves; Digby, *British Invasion*, p. 246.

56. Stanley, ed., *For Want of a Horse*, pp. 160, 163, 166; Lamb, *Journal*, p. 165.

57. Anburey, *Travels*, 1: 453.

58. Digby, *British Invasion*, p. 300.

59. Stanley, ed., *For Want of a Horse*, p. 164; Digby, *British Invasion*, p. 301; Charles Stedman, *History of the Origin, Progress and Termination of the American War*, 1: 343.

60. Stanley, ed., *For Want of a Horse*, p. 166; Digby, *British Invasion*, p. 304.

61. Riedesel, *Letters and Journals*, p. 126.

62. Anburey, *Travels*, 1: 8–9; Stanley, ed., *For Want of a Horse*, p. 166.

63. Digby, *British Invasion*, p. 305.

64. Digby, *British Invasion*, p. 307.

65. Stedman, *History of the American War*, 2: 210.

66. Cornwallis to Germain, 20 August 1780, C.O. 5/183.

67. Allaire, *Diary*, passim; the account of the battle of King's Mountain is on pages 30–31.

68. Stedman, *History of the American War*, 2: 224.

69. Wickwire and Wickwire, *Cornwallis*, p. 200; Stedman, *History of the American War*, 2: 215–218, 319 n.

70. Graham, "English Officer's Account," p. 248.

71. Stedman, *History of the American War*, 2: 316–318.

72. Wickwire and Wickwire, *Cornwallis*, pp. 251, 255; Banastre Tarleton, *A History of the Campaigns of 1780 and 1781 in the Southern Provinces of North America*, pp. 207–211.

73. Tarleton, *Campaigns*, pp. 214–215, 221; Stedman, *History of the American War*, 2: 319–320.

74. Stedman, *History of the American War*, 1: 322.
75. Tarleton, *Campaigns*, p. 217.
76. Graham, "English Officer's Account," p. 248.
77. Tarleton, *Campaigns*, pp. 222–225; Graham, "English Officer's Account," pp. 248–249.
78. Lamb, *Journal*, pp. 344–345.
79. Tarleton, *Campaigns*, pp. 226, 228–229, 231; Lamb, *Journal*, p. 346; Graham, "English Officer's Account," p. 249.
80. Lamb, *Journal*, p. 348; Stedman, *History of the American War*, 2: 332, 335.
81. Tarleton, *Campaigns*, p. 234.
82. Ibid., p. 269.
83. Lamb, *Journal*, p. 381.
84. Tarleton, *Campaigns*, p. 270; Lamb, *Journal*, p. 357; Stedman, *History of the American War*, 2: 346.
85. For details see Wickwire and Wickwire, *Cornwallis*, pp. 274–310.
86. Stedman, *History of the American War*, 2: 346.
87. Ibid., p. 348; see also Cornwallis to Germain, 17 March 1781, C.O. 5/184.
88. Cornwallis to Germain, 10 April 1781, Cornwallis to Germain, 18 April 1781, C.O. 5/184.
89. Edward Barrington De Fonblanque, *Political and Military Episodes in the Latter Half of the Eighteenth Century Derived from the Life and Correspondence of the Right Honourable John Burgoyne*, pp. 17–18.
90. Ibid., p. 65.

6. BONDS AND BANNERS

1. John Keegan, *The Face of Battle*, pp. 113–114, 181–182, 241.
2. Popp, "Journal," p. 246.
3. Baurmeister, *Revolution in America*, pp. 41, 314.
4. Ibid., p. 115.
5. Ibid., pp. 350, 363. For a discussion of the problems, legal, political, and military, associated with the question of spoils, see R. Arthur Bowler, "Sir Henry Clinton and Army Profiteering: A Neglected Aspect of the Clinton-Cornwallis Controversy," *William and Mary Quarterly*, 3d ser., 31 (January 1974): 111–122.
6. Descriptions of the raids can be found in Moore, ed., *Diary*, 2: 366–368; Graham, "English Officer's Account," pp. 247–248; Simcoe, *Military Journal*, p. 194; Tarleton, *Campaigns*, pp. 335–340. The estimate as to the monetary value of the goods is taken from Mackenzie, *Diary*, 2: 522.
7. Tarleton, *Campaigns*, pp. 344, 349, 358; Baurmeister, *Revolution in America*, pp. 411, 442.
8. Ibid., pp. 284, 422.
9. Clinton to Germain, 18 July 1781, B.H.P.
10. Welborn Ellis to the Lords of the Treasury, 2 October 1782, B.H.P.
11. Keegan, *Face of Battle*, p. 114.

12. Simes, *Military Course*, p. 229.
13. Hanway, *Soldier's Faithful Friend*, p. 86.
14. Ibid., pp. 81–82, 83.
15. Ibid., p. vii.
16. *Articles and Rules for the Better Government of His Majesty's Forces by Land during this present War* (1673), p. 2; *Rules and Articles* (1718), p. 3; *Rules and Articles* (1722), p. 2; *Rules and Articles* (1753), p. 4; *Rules and Articles* (1783), p. 4; *Rules and Articles* (1789), p. 4; *Rules and Articles for the Better Government of All His Majesty's Forces* (1790), pp. 4–5.
17. *Rules and Articles for the Better Government of His Majesty's Horse and Foot-Guards and All Other His Forces in Great-Britain and Ireland, Dominions beyond the Seas, and Foreign Parts* (1777), pp. 15–16.
18. Clode, *Military Forces*, 2: 367.
19. Cuthbertson, *System*, pp. 156–157.
20. Corvisier, *L'Armée française*, 2: 865.
21. Clode, *Military Forces*, 2: 267; Simes, *Military Course*, p. 230.
22. A board of general officers met in 1783 to hear the claim of a Mr. Panton, chaplain of the Prince of Wales's Regiment; the board concluded "that the appointment of, and paying a deputy out of the chaplain's pay is justified by the custom of the army," Proceedings of a Board of General Officers, 30 March 1783, B.H.P. See also Benjamin Moore to Carleton, 30 July 1783, B.H.P.
23. Gage to Barrington, 21 February 1776 in Clarence Edwin Carter, ed., *The Correspondence of General Thomas Gage and the Secretaries of State, 1763–1775*, 2: 338–339.
24. Memorial of Rev. Bromhead to Charles Jenkinson, B.H.P.; Schaukirk, "Occupation of New York City," p. 24.
25. Hanway, *Soldier's Faithful Friend*, p. 97.
26. After the Battle of Sheensborough a thanksgiving service was held; see Stanley, ed., *For Want of a Horse*, p. 119; also Digby, *British Invasion*, pp. 222, 225; Barker, *British in Boston*, pp. 6, 12.
27. Hanway, *Soldier's Faithful Friend*, p. 93.
28. Serle, *American Journal*, pp. 56–57.
29. Rawdon to the 10th Earl of Huntingdon, 5 August 1776, and Rawdon to the 10th Earl of Huntingdon, 23 September 1776, in Historical Manuscripts Commission, *Manuscripts of Rawdon-Hastings*, 3: 179, 183.
30. See Tables 2–9; see also Fann, "Infantryman's Age," pp. 165–170, which shows the same tendency in the Prussian army.
31. Gilbert, "Law and Honour," pp. 75–87.
32. Robertson, *Diaries*, pp. 151, 163.
33. McDonald, "Letter-Book," pp. 337, 340.
34. Hughes, *Journal*, pp. 1, 3, 45, 53, 115, 123; the father Hughes died of a "violent fever" at Chambly, 4 October 1780.
35. For examples of officers begging commissions for relatives, see John Campbell to Secretary of War, 1 November 1777, Joseph Goreham to Howe, 3 January 1778, A. Prevost to Clinton, 11 February 1780, Memorial of Esther Troup, Lord Adam Gordon to Carleton, 22 July 1782, Prevost to Carleton, 5 August 1782, Major William Anstruther to Carleton, 3 October 1782, General John Leland to Carleton, 25 Novem-

ber 1782 and 6 February 1783, and Brig. Gen. Monfort Browne to M. Morgann, 27 March 1783, B.H.P.

36. Hamilton, *Thoughts*, p. 19.

37. W. O. 71/83, p. 163.

38. Memorial of Serjeant Charles Atkinson, 5 August 1782, B.H.P.

39. W.O. 71/83, pp. 11, 81.

40. W.O. 71/82, p. 434; W.O. 71/92, pp. 35–37.

41. Cuthbertson, *System*, pp. 21–22.

42. Ibid., pp. 80–81.

43. Ibid., p. 40.

44. Gilbert, "Law and Honour," p. 75.

45. Simes, *Military Course*, p. 240.

46. McDonald, "Letter-Book," pp. 15, 417.

47. Smith, *Universal Military Dictionary*, p. 33.

48. Simes, *Military Course*, p. 210.

49. Samuel Bever, *The Cadet: A Military Treatise*, p. 84.

50. Simes, *Regulator*, p. 61.

51. Farquhar, *The Recruiting Officer*, p. 36.

52. Major R. Money Barnes, *A History of the Regiments and Uniforms of the British Army*, p. 73.

53. Ibid., p. 20.

54. Sergeant Lamb, for example, notes that at the battle of Camden haziness in the air prevented the smoke from rising, making it very difficult for the opposing armies to see the effects of their fire; Lamb, *Journal*, pp. 303–304.

55. Ibid., p. 305.

56. Quoted in ibid., pp. 224–226.

57. Hanway, *Soldier's Faithful Friend*, p. 33.

58. Mackenzie, *Diary*, 1: 156.

59. Barnes, *History of Regiments*, p. 61.

60. Simes, *Military Course*, pp. 218, 240.

61. Perkin, *Origins of Modern English Society*, pp. 17–38.

62. James Hayes, "Scottish Officers in the British Army," *Scottish Historical Review*, 37 (April 1958): 23–27. A recent study of the British army elite covering the period 1870–1959 reveals that nearly 90 percent of all officers were from the propertied and professional strata. Between one-half and one-third were members of aristocratic or gentry families. Barely 3 percent of senior officers came from the lower middle classes. See C. B. Otley, "Militarism and the Social Affiliations of the British Army Elite," in Jacques Van Doorn, ed., *Armed Forces and Society*, pp. 84–108.

63. See Morris Janowitz, *The Professional Soldier: A Social and Political Portrait*, pp. 60–61, for a discussion of the ascriptive military establishment.

64. Bowman, *Morale*, pp. 29–32.

65. Stanislav Andreski, *Military Organization and Society*, pp. 34, 83, 87, discusses the influence of the method of equipping and remunerating the troops on establishing the authority of the officer corps.

66. See Smith, *Universal Military Dictionary*, pp. 12, 240.

67. Report of the Director of Clothing for the Year 1882–83, W.O. 33/55.
68. Janowitz, *Professional Soldier*, pp. 215–217; Gilbert, "Law and Honour," pp. 75–87.
69. Lamb, *Journal*, p. 179, and Anburey, *Travels*, 1: 423, both record the story.
70. Bever, *The Cadet*, p. 153.
71. Lamb, *Journal*, p. 36; Tarleton, *Campaigns*, p. 276.
72. Cornwallis to Germain, 17 March 1781, B.H.P.
73. Rawdon to Clinton, 23 March 1781, B.H.P.
74. Fortescue, *History of the British Army*, 3: 159–160, 241, 363, 386; Tarleton, *Campaigns*, pp. 138, 310–311; Kemble, "Journals," pp. 86, 135, 137, 154; Baurmeister, *Revolution in America*, p. 187; Return of Killed, Wounded and Missing at the Battle of Camden, S.C., 16 August 1780, B.H.P.; Lt. Col. Stuart and Capt. Goodrich of the Guards, Lt. Robinson of the 23d, and Lt. O'Hara of the Artillery were killed; Cornwallis to Rawdon, 17 March 1781, B.H.P.; Fortescue, *History of the British Army*, 3: 159–160, 241, 363, 386.
75. Keegan, *Face of Battle*, pp. 182, 324.
76. See Elias Boudinot, Commissary General of Prisoners, Report, 13 November 1777, Howe to the Commissioners, 5 March 1778, and W. Phillips to Clinton, 12 July 1780, B.H.P.
77. Officers were gentlemen primarily because of their social backgrounds and because they were preoccupied with the rules of chivalry; the common soldier, disqualified by occupation, manners, and behavior, could make no claims to gentility; see Janowitz, *Professional Soldier*, p. 217.
78. Gilbert, "Law and Honour," pp. 85–86.
79. Lamb, *Journal*, pp. 224–227.
80. Simes, *Regulator*, p. 144.
81. Rawdon to 10th Earl of Huntingdon, 17 May 1776, Historical Manuscripts Commission, *Manuscripts of Rawdon-Hastings*, 3: 172.
82. Serle, *American Journal*, pp. 31, 64, 79.
83. Murray, *Letters*, p. 33.
84. Earl Percy to Rev. Dr. Percy, 1 September 1776, in *Memoranda of Lieutenant Colonel Eld, of the Cold-Stream Guards*, p. 19.
85. Lamb, *Journal*, pp. 87, 110.
86. John Burgoyne, *A State of the Expedition from Canada . . .* , p. xxxiii.
87. Cornwallis to Germain, 17 March 1781, B.H.P. For further documentation of the quality of the performance of British soldiers, see Appendix.
88. Jesse Lemisch, "Jack Tar in the Streets: Merchant Seamen in the Politics of Revolutionary America," *William and Mary Quarterly*, 3d ser., 25 (July 1968): 371–407.
89. An address to the mercenary troops prepared at the direction of Congress appears in Butterfield, "Psychological Warfare," pp. 234–235.
90. Address of Henry Humphrey to "my dear brother soldiers," n.d., B.H.P.

91. Alexander Leslie to Clinton, 12 March 1782, B.H.P.
92. Evelyn, *Memoir*, p. 52; Willard, ed., *Letters*, pp. 36–37, 51–52, 60–61; Doehla, "Journal," pp. 240, 269–271; and Anburey, *Travels*, 2: 309; all deal with German desertions.
93. Depositions before a board of three officers . . . ; Extract from the Instructions of the Inspector General of the Treasury and Secretary at War, Philadelphia, 11 July 1782, to James Reed, B.H.P.
94. Lt. Carl Reinking to Carleton, 12 October 1782, and Lossberg to Carleton, 19 June 1783, B.H.P.
95. Carleton to Maj. Gen. Benjamin Lincoln, 28 June 1783, and Report of Maj. Charles Baurmeister, respecting the German prisoners of war detained in the American states contrary to their inclinations, 18 July 1783, B.H.P.
96. Anburey, *Travels*, 2: 440; Sergeant Lamb, in his account of his own escape, claims that he reported his intention to escape to his superior officer; Lamb, *Journal*, p. 389.
97. Order Book of the 43d Regiment, 28 January, 29 January, and 31 January 1781, B.H.P.
98. W.O. 36/1, p. 28.
99. Ibid., p. 88.
100. Timothy Pickering to the President of the Continental Congress, 12 October 1779, Papers of the Continental Congress, National Archives, Washington, D.C.
101. To President James Bowdoin, 17 March 1778, in *The Writings of George Washington from the Original Manuscript Sources, 1745–1799*, ed. John C. Fitzpatrick, 11: 98–99; To President James Bowdoin, 31 March 1778, in ibid., 11: 180; To Major William Heath, 29 April 1778, in ibid., 11: 320–321.
102. To Governor James Johnson, 8 April 1779, in ibid., 4: 349; To President Jeremiah Powell, 19 May 1778, in ibid., 11: 424.
103. Washington to Heath, 29 April 1778, in ibid., 11: 320–321.
104. M. Lewis to P. Stephen, 3 December 1781, W.O. 4/604.
105. Mortality rates, even in years of peace, remained extremely high at posts abroad until well into the nineteenth century: 28 per thousand at Bermuda, 71 in the Windward Islands, 121 at Jamaica. At Sierra Leone the figures reached 75–80 percent; see Woodward, *Age of Reform*, p. 257.
106. Lamb, *Journal*, p. 111.

CONCLUSION

1. For a discussion of the impact of the military regimen on group personality, see G. Dearborn Spindler, "American Character as Revealed by the Military," *Psychiatry*, 11, No. 3 (August 1948): 275–281.
2. By contrast, American soldiers in World War II, accustomed to more democratic civilian habits, resented the army status system even though they recognized the need for it. See Samuel A. Stouffer et al., *The American Soldier: Adjustment during Army Life*, 1: 71–72.

3. Cavan, *A New System*, p. 29.

4. Ibid., pp. 29–30.

5. Ibid., p. 32.

6. For a discussion of the symbolic meaning and social significance of uniforms, see Donald J. Marcuse, "The 'Army' Incident: The Psychology of Uniforms and Their Abolition on an Adolescent Ward," *Psychiatry*, 30, No. 4 (November 1967): 350–375.

7. Gilbert, "Law and Honour," pp. 85–86.

8. The cases can be found in W.O. 71/85 and W.O. 71/91.

9. Depending upon the nature of the crime, officers convicted of a violation of the rules of war were usually given a public reprimand, were reduced in rank, or were dismissed from the service; see throughout, . Court Martial Records, W.O. 71.

10. William Fawcitt to Lord Barrington, 6 November 1776, Allowed Officers at Boston, 1769, Questions of Lt. Col. Clerk, and Clinton to Maj. Gen. Campbell, 21 October 1780, B.H.P.; Lamb, *Journal*, pp. 222–223.

11. "Manuscript of Colonel Stephen Jarvis," *Journal of American History*, 1, No. 3 (1907): 731.

12. Spindler, "American Character," p. 276.

13. See for example, Meyer H. Maskin and Leon L. Altman, "Military Psychodynamics: Psychological Factors in the Transition from Civilian to Soldier," *Psychiatry*, 6, No. 3 (August 1943): 267.

14. Hugh Mullan, "The Regular Service Myth," *American Journal of Sociology*, 53, No. 4 (January 1948): 278.

15. Maskin and Altman, "Military Psychodynamics," pp. 264–265; Malcolm R. McCallum, "The Study of the Delinquent in the Army," *American Journal of Sociology*, 51 (March 1946): 481.

16. Frederick Elkin, "The Soldier's Language," *American Journal of Sociology*, 51 (March 1946): 418; Maskin and Altman, "Military Psychodynamics," p. 266.

17. Mullan, "Regular Service Myth," p. 277.

APPENDIX

1. For brief political biographies of the M.P.'s, see Sir Lewis Namier and John Brooke, *The House of Commons, 1754–1790*. For an analysis of party politics, see Sir Lewis Namier, *Structure of Politics at the Accession of George III*, and idem, *England in the Age of the American Revolution*.

2. Cobbett, ed., *Parliamentary History*, 19: 485–495.

3. Ibid., p. 363.

4. Ibid., pp. 533–538.

5. Ibid., p. 1195.

6. Ibid., pp. 1200–1202.

7. Ibid., p. 1373; 20: 74.

8. Ibid., 20: 780–801.

9. Ibid., pp. 746, 747–748.

10. Ibid., p. 770.

11. Ibid., 19: 529.

12. Ibid., 20: 818.
13. De Fonblanque, *Political and Military Episodes*, p. 410.
14. Cobbett, ed., *Parliamentary History*, 22: 985.
15. Ibid., pp. 1028–1048.
16. Ibid., p. 991.
17. Ibid., p. 994.
18. Ibid., p. 997.
19. Ibid., pp. 993, 1114–1150.
20. Ibid., pp. 1170–1200.
21. Sir Henry Clinton, *The American Rebellion: Sir Henry Clinton's Narrative of His Campaigns, 1775–1782*, ed. William B. Willcox, pp. 299–329.
22. Ibid., p. 261.
23. Ibid., p. 267.
24. Ibid., p. 242.
25. Charles C. Cornwallis, *An Answer to that Part of the Narrative of Lt. General Sir Henry Clinton, K.B., Which Relates to the Conduct of Lt. General Earl Cornwallis during the Campaign in North America in the Year 1781*, pp. xi, xv, xvi. B. F. Stevens, *The Campaign in Virginia . . .* , (London, 1888), vol. 1, contains the six pamphlets by Clinton and Cornwallis and also their correspondence between 17 May 1780 and 31 May 1781.
26. Cornwallis, *An Answer*, p. 11.
27. Ibid., p. 81.
28. Ibid., pp. 206, 207, 211, 212.
29. Tarleton, *Campaigns*, pp. 377, 382, 384, 379.
30. The best short analysis of the British strategy is William B. Willcox, "The British Road to Yorktown: A Study in Divided Command," *American Historical Review*, 52 (October 1946): 1–35.

Bibliography

PRIMARY SOURCES: UNPUBLISHED

Public Record Office, London: Official Records

Adm. 96/153. Admiralty Office. Marine Correspondence, 1772–1780.
Adm. 97/86–87. Admiralty Office. Medical Departments. In Letters, 1766–1775, 1776–1779.
A.O. 3/55. Audit Office. Accounts, Various, 1776–1784.
A.O. 3/126–128. Audit Office. Miscellaneous Accounts of Governors and others in America, Nova Scotia, New Brunswick, etc., 1711–1819.
C.O. 5/7–8. Colonial Office. America & West Indies. Original Documents, 1755–1779.
C.O. 5/88. Colonial Office. Petitions, 1768–1781.
C.O. 5/114–117. Colonial Office. Petitions, 1768–1781.
C.O. 5/138–144. Colonial Office, Correspondence of Secretary of State for the Colonies with other Secretaries, 1771–1781.
C.O. 5/145–153. Colonial Office. Correspondence of Secretaries of State for the Colonies with the Treasury and Custom House, 1771–1781.
C.O. 5/154–158. Colonial Office. Promiscuous and Private Letters, 1771–1781.
C.O. 5/182–184. Colonial Office. Promiscuous Military Correspondence, 1779–1784.
C.O. 5/519–526. Colonial Office. Manuscript Journals of the Proceedings of the Board of Police, Charleston, 1780–1782.
C.O. 5/1573. Colonial Office. Letters to the Secretary of State, 1774–1777. Virginia Entry Book.
H.O. 28/1–3. Home Office. Letters from the Admiralty, 1782–1783.
H.O. 32/1. Home Office. Letters to the Secretary of State, 1782–1789.
H.O. 42/1–3. Home Office. Original Correspondence, 1782.
H.O. 50/452. Home Office. Return of Anspachers for America.
S.P. 41/27. State Papers. Letters from the Secretary at War, the Officers of the Ordnance and others to the Secretaries of State and other papers relating to Military Affairs, 1702–1782.
T 1/510–595. Treasury. Miscellaneous Papers, 1774–1783.
T 29/1–54. Treasury Board Minute Books, 1667–1783.
T 29/628. Treasury Minutes, Relating to the American War, 1771–1777.
T 38/812–814. Treasury Accounts of the German Auxiliary Troops, 1776–1784.
T 64/102–103. Commissary General in Canada to Treasury.
T 64/114. Commissary General in America to Treasury, 1778–1779.
T 64/200. Treasury–Navy Board Correspondence, 1779–1780.

W.O. 1/10. War Office. In Letters, 1776–1780.
W.O. 1/51. War Office. Letters and Papers from the West Indies, 1777–1788.
W.O. 1/683. War Office. Letters from Lord George Germain, Secretary of State for the Colonies, to Secretary Barrington, concerning American Affairs, 1776–1781.
W.O. 1/890. War Office. Statistics, 1776–1783.
W.O. 1/972–1020. War Office. Miscellaneous Letters of Secretary of War, 1756–1783.
W.O. 4/273–275. War Office. American Letter-Books, 1775–1784.
W.O. 4/604. War Office. Letter-Book for Deserters, 1781–1783.
W.O. 4/965–967. War Office. Press Act, 1778–1781.
W.O. 4/1044. War Office. Miscellaneous, 1763–1767.
W.O. 7/96. War Office. Medical Department, 1781–1789.
W.O. 24/771–772. War Office. Establishments.
W.O. 24/825–827. War Office. Establishments.
W.O. 25/435. War Office. Records of the 58th Regiment of Foot, 1756–ca. 1800.
W.O. 25/1145. War Office. Embarkation Returns, 1758–1797.
W.O. 26/28. War Office. Miscellany Books, 1620–1817.
W.O. 27/33. War Office. Inspection Returns, 1775–1776.
W.O. 27/34. War Office. Inspection Returns, 1775.
W.O. 27/42. War Office. Inspection Returns, 1779.
W.O. 28/2–10. War Office. Head Quarters Records, America, 1775–1783.
W.O. 33/51. War Office. Reports, 1882–1883.
W.O. 33/55. War Office. Reports and Miscellaneous Papers.
W.O. 34/188. War Office. Amherst Papers, 1778–1782.
W.O. 36/1–4. War Office. American Rebellion. Entry Books, 1773–1799.
W.O. 71/14–19. War Office. Courts Martial. Proceedings, 1710–1746.
W.O. 71/33. War Office. Courts Martial. Proceedings, 1794–1796.
W.O. 71/34–38. War Office. General Courts Martial. Home and Foreign Stations, 1715–1745.
W.O. 71/65–77. War Office. General Courts Martial. Marching Regiments, 1756–1758.
W.O. 71/80–95. War Office. General Courts Martial. Marching Regiments, 1774–1781.
W.O. 72/1–8. War Office. Courts Martial. Letters and Miscellaneous Documents, 1696–1780.
W.O. 81/1–2. War Office. Letter Books, 1715–1739.
W.O. 89/1–2. War Office. General Courts Martial, 1666–1698.
W.O. 93/6. War Office. Miscellaneous Records.
W.O. 116/1–7. War Office. Returns, Out-Pensions Records, Royal Hospital, Chelsea. Admission Books, 1715–1782.

Public Record Office, London: Other Collections

P.R.O. 30/11. Cornwallis, Charles (1738–1805), second Earl Cornwallis and first Marquis Cornwallis, Papers, 1614–1854.
P.R.O. 30/55. Carleton Papers.

Scottish Record Office, Edinburgh

G.D. 1/46. Inglis Papers.

G.D. 13–94. Campbell of Balliveolan Muniments.

G.D. 21. Cunningham of Thortoun Papers, 1746–1782, 1876–1883. Notebooks containing the Journal of Lt. John Peebles of the 42d or Royal Highland Regiment during the War of Independence.

G.D. 24. Abercarrny Collection, Sec. 1, 458. Letters of Thomas Sterling relating to campaigns in America, 1760–1787.

G.D. 26, Sec. 9, Nos. 512–523. Leven and Melville Muniments. Papers of General Alexander Leslie and Captain William Leslie.

G.D. 153, H48c. Gilchrist of Opisdale Muniments. Letters of Capt. John Ross of Auchnacloich with the 71st Highlanders.

G.D. 174. MacLaine of Lochbuie Muniments. Papers of Captain Murdock MacLaine of the 84th or Royal Highland Emigrants, 1775–1784 (No. 34). Pay and Roll book of the grenadier company, 71st Highlanders, 1782–1783 (No. 57).

G.D. 248, Nos. 52/3. Seafield Papers. Letters relating to recruiting in Strathspey for regiments for America, 1776.

British Museum, London

Add. Mss. 21,657. General and Regimental Orders, 1759–1764.

Add. Mss. 21,658. Miscellaneous Papers, 1757–1765.

Add. Mss. 21,661–21,892. Haldimand Papers.

Add. Mss. 23,651. Rainsford Papers.

Add. Mss. 32,413. Diary of the War of Independence by Lt. William Digby, 1776–1777.

Add. Mss. 32,893, f. 62. Papers by Lord Barrington relating to recruiting, 1759.

Add. Mss. 38,340–38,375. Various Papers Relating to the Army in North America, 1768–1783.

Add. Mss. 38,378. An account of men lost and disabled in His Majesty's Land Service in North America and the West Indies from 1 November 1774.

Add. Mss. 39,190. MacKenzie Papers.

Add. Mss. 42,071, ff. 195–230. Letters and Papers relating to raising of the 78th Regiment of Foot or Seaforth's Highlanders.

Add. Mss. 42,449–42,450. Order Books of the 43d Regiment at Yorktown, 1781.

Add. Mss. 43,395, f. 321. Florence Nightingale. Army Sanitary Reform under the Late Lord Sidney Herbert. 1862.

Add. Mss. 46,840. Miscellaneous Papers. Diary of the American Siege of Quebec, by John Danford.

Libraries and Archives

Alderman Library, University of Virginia, Charlottesville. Cornwallis, Charles, 1738–1805. Papers, 1614–1854. Microfilm of Cornwallis Papers, P.R.O. 30/11.

Bodleian Library, Oxford. Ms. Top. Oxon, d. 224. Records of Campaigns of the 52d (Oxfordshire) Light Infantry, 1755–1822, in America, 1774–1779.
Clements, William L., Library, Ann Arbor, Michigan. Clinton, Sir Henry, 1731?–1795. Papers, 1750–1812.
———. Gage, Thomas, 1721–1787. Papers, 1754–1783.
———. Germain, George Sackville, 1st Viscount Sackville, 1716–1785. Papers, 1683–1785.
———. Hooke, George Philip. Journal, 1779–1780.
———. Howe, Lt. Gen. Sir William. Orderly Books.
———. Knox, William, 1732–1810. Papers, 1757–1809.
———. Mackenzie, Frederick. Papers, 1755–1783.
———. Moncrief, James. Letter Book, 1780–1782.
———. Orderly Book for the 10th Regiment of Foot, Boston, 1775, Item 105.
———. Orderly Book for King's American Regiment, 1776–1777, Item 106..
———. Original Manuscript Journal of a Hessian Soldier who served in Revolutionary War, 1776–1784.
———. Simcoe, John Graves, 1752–1806. Papers, 1774–1824.
———. Sumner, Jethro. Papers.
———. Vaughan, Sir John, 1738?–1795. Papers, 1779–1781.
———. Wray, George. Papers, 1770–1793.
Colonial Williamsburg, Inc., Williamsburg, Virginia. British Headquarters Papers, America. Microfilm of Carleton Papers, P.R.O. 30/55.
Fordham University Library, New York City. Register of British Deserters, Munn Collection.
Howard-Tilton Library, Tulane University, New Orleans. British Headquarters (Sir Guy Carleton) Papers. Microfilm of Carleton Papers, P.R.O. 30/55.
Library Company of Philadelphia. Theatre Broadsides.
Library of Congress, Washington, D.C. Ainslie, Thomas. Orderly Book, 1775–1781. George Chalmers Collection. Peter Force Papers: Ser. 8A, No. 58.
———. America, British Colonies. Two Folio Volumes of Documents Relating to the Equipment of the British Forces in America, 1728–1792.
———. Army in Ireland and North America. Papers, 1751–1771. Peter Force Papers: Ser. 8D.
———. Baum, Frederick. Burgoyne's Orders at Montreal and Crown Point.
———. Colebrooke, Colebrooke, Nesbitt and Franks. Collection of Business Records, 1756–1789.
———. Cornwallis, Lord. Orderly Books, British General and Brigade Orders, Virginia and Yorktown, 23 May–22 October 1781.
———. French, Christopher. Journal of Christopher French, a British Army Officer, 1756–1764, 1776–1778.
———. Glasier, Capt. Beamsley, 2d Battalion, 60th Regiment, British Army at Niagara. Orderly Books, 1771–1773.
———. Hatfield, Capt. Orderly Book, kept at Boston, 1776.

———. Home, Capt. Walter. Officer's Memorandum Book. George Chalmers Collection. Peter Force Papers.

———. ———. Walter Home's Military Journal, 1770–1772.

———. Orderly Books. Regimental Order Book, British Army, Siege of Savannah, 2 July–2 October 1779.

———. Wyvill, Major Richard Augustus, of the British Army. Journals and Diaries.

National Archives, Washington, D.C. Papers of the Continental Congress, 1774–1789.

———. Return of a British Brigade of Foot Guards, March 1776–December 1779. Preliminary Inventory No. 144 (Revised), Entry 23.

National Army Museum, London. Order Book of the 37th Regiment kept by Charles Allen Buckeridge.

———. 6912/14, Nos. 31–50. Order Books, Letter Books, Journals, Letters, and Other Documents of Lt. Gen. Sir Eyre Coote, relating to the American War of Independence, 1776–1782.

National Library of Scotland, Edinburgh. Mss. 3422. Manuscripts relating to the 73d Regiment of Foot.

———. Mss. 3942–3988. Robertson-MacDonald Papers, 1765–1805.

New-York Historical Society. Theatre Royal Account Book.

Rhodes House Library, Oxford. Mss. Can. r. 2. Diary of the Siege of Quebec, 1775–1776, kept by an English soldier.

University of Edinburgh Library. La. II. 506. Laing Manuscripts, 1635–1832.

PRIMARY SOURCES: NEWSPAPERS

New York Gazette and Weekly Mercury, 1777–1781.
Pennsylvania Ledger, 1777–1798.
Royal Gazette, 1778–1781.
Royal Georgia Gazette, 1781.
Virginia Gazette, 1775–1781.

PRIMARY SOURCES: BOOKS AND ARTICLES

An Abridgement of the English Military Discipline: Printed by Special Command for the Use of His Majesty's Forces. London, 1686.

Adams, John. *The Adams Papers: Diary and Autobiography of John Adams.* Edited by L. H. Butterfield. 4 vols. Cambridge, Mass., 1962.

Advice to the Officers of the British Army: With the Addition of Some Hints to the Drummer and Private Soldier. 6th ed. London, 1783.

Adye, Stephen Payne. *A Treatise on Courts-Martial, with an Essay on Military Punishment and Rewards.* New York, 1769; 2d ed., Philadelphia, 1779.

Allaire, Anthony. *Diary of Lieut. Anthony Allaire.* New York, 1968.

Anburey, Thomas. *Travels through the Interior Parts of America, by an Officer.* 2 vols. London, 1789.

André, John. *Major André's Journal: Operations of the British Army under*

Lieutenant Generals Sir William Howe and Sir Henry Clinton. Tarrytown, N.Y., 1930.

Articles and Rules for the Better Government of His Majesty's Forces by Land during this present War. London, 1673.

Authentic Copies of Letters between Sir Henry Clinton, K.B., and the Commissioners for Auditing the Public Accounts. London, 1793.

Bamford, William. "Bamford's Diary: The Revolutionary Diary of a British Officer." *Maryland Historical Magazine,* 27 (December 1932): 240–259; 28 (March 1933): 9–26.

Barker, John. *The British in Boston.* Cambridge, 1924.

————. "A British Officer in Boston in 1775." *Magazine of History,* 18 (January 1914): 1–15.

Baurmeister, Carl Leopold. *The Revolution in America: Confidential Letters and Journals, 1776–1784, of Adjutant General Major Baurmeister of the Hessian Forces.* Translated by Bernhard A. Uhlendorf. New Brunswick, N.J., 1957.

Bever, Samuel. *The Cadet: A Military Treatise.* 2d ed. London, 1772.

Bland, Humphrey. *A Treatise of Military Discipline . . .* 2d ed. London, 1727.

Bostwick, Elisha. "A Connecticut Soldier under Washington: Elisha Bostwick's Memoirs of the First Years of the Revolution." Edited by William S. Powell. *William and Mary Quarterly,* 3d ser., 6 (January 1949): 94–107.

Brocklesby, Richard. *Oeconomical and Medical Observations from the Year 1758 to 1763.* London, 1764.

Burgoyne, John. *Orderly Book of Lt. Gen. John Burgoyne.* Edited by E. B. O'Callaghan. Albany, 1860.

————. *A State of the Expedition from Canada as laid before the House of Commons by Lt. Gen. Burgoyne . . .* London, 1780.

————. *The Substance of General Burgoyne's Speeches, on Mr. Vyner's Motions, on the 26th of May; and upon Mr. Hartley's Motion on the 28th of May.* London, 1778.

"Camp Life in 1776: The Siege of Boston." *Historical Magazine,* 8 (1864): 326–332.

Carter, Clarence E., ed. *The Correspondence of General Thomas Gage and the Secretaries of State, 1763–1775.* 2 vols. New Haven, 1931.

Cavan, Richard Lambart, 6th Earl of. *A New System of Military Discipline Founded upon Principle.* Philadelphia, 1776.

Clausewitz, Karl von. *Karl von Clausewitz: On War.* Edited and translated by Michael Howard and Peter Paret. Princeton, 1976.

Clinton, Henry. *The American Rebellion: Sir Henry Clinton's Narrative of His Campaigns, 1775–1782.* Edited by William B. Willcox. New Haven, 1954.

————. *Narrative of Lt. Gen. Sir Henry Clinton, Relative to His Conduct during Part of His Command of the King's Troops in North America.* London, 1783.

Cobbett, William, ed. *The Parliamentary History of England from the Earliest Period to the Year 1803.* 36 vols. London, 1806–1820.

Collins, V. L., ed. *A Brief Narrative of the Ravages of the British and Hessians at Princeton in 1776–1777.* Princeton, 1906.

Cornwallis, Charles C. *An Answer to that Part of the Narrative of Lt. General Sir Henry Clinton, K.B., Which Relates to the Conduct of Lt. General Earl Cornwallis during the Campaign in North America in the Year 1781.* London, 1783.

Cuthbertson, Bennett. *A System for the Compleat Interior Management and Oeconomy of a Battalion of Infantry.* N.p., 1776.

Dalrymple, Campbell. *A Military Essay: Containing Reflections on the Raising, Arming, Cloathing and Discipline of the British Infantry and Cavalry.* London, 1761.

The Detail and Conduct of the American War under Generals Gage, Howe, Burgoyne and Vice Admiral Lord Howe: With a very full and correct state of the whole of the evidence as given before a committee of the House of Commons . . . 3d ed. London, 1780.

Devereaux, Robert.. *Camp Discipline or the Soldier's Duty: In Certain Articles and Ordinances of Warre, commanded to be observed in the Armie.* London, 1642.

"Diary of a Voyage from Stade in Hanover to Quebec in America of the 2d Division of Ducal Brunswick Mercenaries." *Quarterly Journal of the New York State Historical Association,* 8 (October 1927): 323–351.

Digby, William. *The British Invasion from the North: The Campaigns of Generals Carleton and Burgoyne, with the Journal of Lt. William Digby.* Albany, 1887.

Doehla, Johann Conrad. "The Doehla Journal." Translated by Robert J. Tilden. *William and Mary Quarterly,* 2d ser., 22 (July 1942): 229–274.

Emmerich, Andrew. *The Partisan in War; or the use of a corps of light troops to an army.* London, 1789.

Evelyn, W. Glanville. *Memoir and Letters of Captain W. Glanville Evelyn, of the 4th Regiment, from North America, 1774–1776.* Oxford, 1879.

Farquhar, George. *The Recruiting Officer.* Edited by Michael Shugrue. Lincoln, 1965.

Georgia Historical Society. *Collections,* 3 (1873). "Letters from Gov. Sir James Wright . . . to the Secretaries of State for America" (pp. 180–375).

———. *Collections,* 5 (1901). "Account of the Siege of Savannah, from a British Source" (pp. 129–139).

———. *Collections,* 10 (1952). "Proceedings and Minutes of the Governor and Council of Georgia, 1774–1775, 1779–1780" (pp. 1–129).

Gibbs, R. W., ed. *Documentary History of the American Revolution.* 3 vols. Columbia, S.C., 1853.

Graham, Samuel. "An English Officer's Account of His Services in America, 1779–1781: Memoirs of Lt.-General Samuel Graham." *Historical Magazine,* 9 (August–September 1865): 241–249, 267–274, 301–308.

Hadden, Lt. James M. *Journal and Orderly Books: A Journal Kept in Canada and upon Burgoyne's Campaign.* Albany, 1884.

Hamilton, Robert. *The Duties of a Regimental Surgeon Considered.* 2 vols. London, 1787.

———. *Thoughts Submitted to the Consideration of the Officers in the Army . . .* Lincoln, England, 1783.

Hansard, T. C. *Parliamentary Debates.* 3d ser. 365 vols. 1830–1891.

Hanway, Jonas. *The Soldier's Faithful Friend: Being Moral and Religious Advice to Soldiers.* London, 1776.

Harvey, Edward. *The Manual Exercise, as Ordered by His Majesty in 1764, Together with plans and explanations of the methods generally practis'd at reviews and field-days.* New York, 1780.

Hinde, Captain (Royal Regiment of Foresters). *The Discipline of the Light Horse.* London, 1778.

Historical Manuscripts Commission. *The Manuscripts of Mrs. Stopford-Sackville,* London, 1910.

———. *Report on the Manuscripts of Reginald Rawdon-Hastings.* London, 1934.

Howe, William. *General Sir William Howe's Orderly Book at Charleston, Boston and Halifax, June 17, 1775, to 26 May 1776; to which is added the official abridgement of General Howe's correspondence with the English government during the siege of Boston.* Edited by Benjamin Franklin Stevens. London, 1890; reissued, Port Washington, N.Y., 1970.

———. *The Narrative of Lieutenant General William Howe, in a Committee of the House of Commons, on the 29th of April, 1779 . . .* London, 1780.

Hughes, Thomas. *A Journal by Thomas Hughes, 1778–1789.* Cambridge, 1947.

Hulton, Anne. *Letters of a Loyalist Lady.* Cambridge, Mass., 1927.

Jarvis, Stephen. "Manuscript of Colonel Stephen Jarvis." *Journal of American History,* 1, No. 3 (1907): 441–464, 727–740.

Jenny (or Jeney), M. de. *The Partisan; or the Art of Making War in Detachments with plans proper to facilitate . . . the Several Dispositions and Movements Necessary . . . to Accomplish their Marches, Ambuscades, Attacks, and Retreats with Success.* London, 1760.

Johnson, John. *Orderly Book of Sir John Johnson during the Oriskany Campaign, 1776–1777.* Annotation by William L. Stone. Albany, 1882.

Jones, Daniel. *See* New-York Historical Society.

Jones, John. *The Surgical Works of the Late John Jones, M.D.* New York, 1775.

———. *Treatment of Wounds and Fractures, with an Appendix on Camp and Military Hospitals, Principally Designed for the Young Military and Naval Surgeons in North America.* New York, 1970. (Reproduction of the 1776 edition.)

Jones, Thomas. *History of New York during the Revolutionary War.* 2 vols. New York, 1879.

Kane, Richard. *A System of Camp Discipline, Military Honours, Garrison Duty, and Other Regulations for the Land Forces.* London, 1757.

Kemble, Stephen. *See* New-York Historical Society.

Krafft, John Charles Philip von. *See* New-York Historical Society.

Lamb, Roger. *An Original and Authentic Journal of Occurrences during the Late American War.* Dublin, 1809.

Lambart, Richard. *See* Cavan, Richard Lambert, 6th Earl of.

Lind, James. *A Treatise of the Scurvy, in Three Parts.* London, 1757.

Lochée, Lewis. *An Essay on Military Education.* London, 1773.

McDonald, Alexander. *See* New-York Historical Society.

McGuffie, T. H., ed. *Rank and File: The Common Soldier at Peace and War, 1642–1914.* London, 1964.

Mackenzie, Frederick. *A British Fusilier in Revolutionary Boston: Being the Diary of Lieutenant Frederick Mackenzie, Adjutant of the Royal Welch Fusiliers, January 5–April 30, 1775; With a Letter Describing His Voyage to America.* Edited by Allen French. Cambridge, Mass., 1926.

———. *Diary of Frederick Mackenzie, Giving a Daily Narrative of His Military Service as an Officer of the Regiment of Royal Welch Fusiliers during the Years 1775–1781.* Edited by A. French. 2 vols. Cambridge, 1930.

Marshall, William. *The Rural Economy of the Midland Counties, Including the Management of Livestock in Leicestershire and Its Environs.* 2 vols. London, 1790; 2d ed., 1796.

———. *The Rural Economy of the West of England.* London, 1793.

Memoranda of Lieutenant-Colonel Eld, of the Cold-Stream Guards, during His Service in America, 1779–1780; Original Letters of Hugh, Earl Percy and Afterwards Duke of Northumberland, between 17 April 1774 and 11 July 1778. Boston, 1892.

Military Orders and Articles Established by His Majesty, for the Better Ordering and Government of His Majesty's Army; Also Two Proclamations, one against Plundering and Robbery, the other against Selling or Buying of Armes and Horse. Oxford, 1642.

Monro, Donald, M.D. *An Account of the Diseases which were most Frequent in the British Military Hospitals in Germany, from January 1761 to the Return of the Troops to England in March 1763.* London, 1764.

Montresor Journals. See New-York Historical Society.

Moore, Frank, ed. *Diary of the American Revolution: From Newspapers and Original Documents.* 2 vols. New York, 1860.

Morton, Robert. "The Diary of Robert Morton." *Pennsylvania Magazine of History and Biography*, 1, No. 1 (1877): 1–39.

M'Roberts, Patrick. "Patrick M'Roberts' Tour through Parts of the North Provinces of America, 1774–1775." Edited by Carl Bridenbaugh. *Pennsylvania Magazine of History and Biography*, 59, No. 2 (1935): 134–180.

Murray, James. *Letters from America: Being the Letters of a Scots Officer, Sir James Murray, to His Home during the War of American Independence.* Edited by Eric Robson. Manchester, 1951.

A Narrative of the Excursion and Ravages of the King's Troops under the command of General Gage on the 19th of April 1775; Together with the Depositions Taken by Order of Congress to support the truth of it. Worcester, 1775.

Newsome, A. R., ed. "A British Orderly Book, 1780–1781." *North Carolina Historical Review*, 9 (January 1932): 57–58, 163–186, 273–298, 366–392.

New-York Historical Society. *Collections*, 8 (1875). "Official Letters of Major General James Pattison" (pp. 1–430).

———. *Collections*, 12 (1879). *Revolutionary Papers*, vol. 2. "Commissary Rainsford's Journal of Transactions, Etc., 1776–1778" (pp. 213–543).

———. *Collections*, 13 (1880). *Revolutionary and Miscellaneous Papers*, vol. 3. "Journal of the Most Remarkable Occurrences in Quebec, 1775–1776" (pp. 173–236).

———. *Collections*, 14 (1881). *The Montresor Journals*, ed. G. D. Scull.

———. *Collections*, 15 (1882). "Journal of Lieutenant John Charles Philip von Krafft, of the Regiment von Bose, 1776–1784," edited and translated by T. H. Edsall (pp. 1–202); "Letter-Book of Captain Alexander McDonald, of the Royal Highland Emigrants, 1775– 1779" (pp. 203–498).

———. *Collections*, 16 (1883). *The Kemble Papers*, vol. 1 (1773–1789). "Journals of Lieut.-Col. Stephen Kemble" (pp. 1–247); "Order Books of Lieut.-Col. Stephen Kemble" (pp. 249–626, including "General Orders by Major General The Honourable William Howe," pp. 249–586; "Gen. Sir Henry Clinton's Orders," pp. 586–603; "Orders by Maj.-Gen. Daniel Jones," pp. 604–626).

———. *Collections*, 17 (1884). *The Kemble Papers*, vol. 2 (1780–1781). "Kemble's Journals" (pp. 1–65); "Kemble's Orders" (pp. 66–163); "Documents and Correspondence" (pp. 164–431).

———. *Collections*, 49 (1916). *Proceedings of a Board of General Officers of the British Army at New York, 1781.*

Orderly Book of the Three Battalions of Loyalists Commanded by Brigadier General Oliver De Lancey. New York, 1917.

Palmer, William P., et al., eds. *Calendar of Virginia State Papers and Other Manuscripts . . . Preserved . . . at Richmond (1652–1869).* 11 vols. Richmond, 1875–1893.

Pattison, James. *See* New-York Historical Society.

Pausch, Georg. *Journal of Captain G. Pausch, Chief of the Hanau Artillery during the Burgoyne Campaign.* Translated by William L. Stone. Albany, 1856.

Pettengill, Ray W., ed. and trans. *Letters from America, 1776–1779: Being Letters of Brunswick, Hessian and Waldeck Officers with the British Armies during the Revolution.* Boston, 1924.

Popp, Stephan. "Popp's Journal, 1777–1783." Edited by Joseph G. Rosengarten. *Pennsylvania Magazine of History and Biography*, 26, Nos. 1–2 (1902): 25–41, 245–254.

Pringle, Sir John. *Observations on the Diseases of the Army.* 7th ed. rev., 1775. (1st ed., 1757.)

Rainsford, Commissary. *See* New-York Historical Society.

Resseguie, Timothy. "Journal of Timothy Resseguie, a British Soldier during the War of the Revolution." *Journal of American History*, 4 (January–March 1910): 127–131.

Riedesel, Frederika Charlotte Luise, Baroness von. *Letters and Journals Relating to the War of the American Revolution, and the Capture of the German Troops at Saratoga.* Translated by William L. Stone. Albany, 1867.

Robertson, Archibald. *Archibald Robertson, Lieutenant General, Royal Engineers: His Diaries and Sketches in America, 1762–1780.* Edited by Harry Miller Lydenberg. New York, 1930.

Rules and Articles for the Better Government of His Majesty's Land-Forces in Pay during This Present Rebellion. London, 1685.

Rules and Articles for the Better Government of Our Horse and Foot-Guards and All Other Our Land-Forces in Our Kingdoms of Great-Britain and Ireland, Dominions Beyond the Seas. London, 1718.

Rules and Articles for the Better Government of Our Horse and Foot-Guards and

All Other Our Land-Forces in Our Kingdoms of Great-Britain and Ireland, and Dominions beyond the Seas. London, 1722.

Rules and Articles for the Better Government of His Majesty's Horse and Foot-Guards, and All Other His Majesty's Forces in Great-Britain and Ireland, Dominions beyond the Seas and Foreign Parts. London, 1753.

Rules and Articles for the Better Government of His Majesty's Horse and Foot-Guards and All Other His Forces in Great-Britain and Ireland, Dominions beyond the Seas, and Foreign Parts, from the 24th of March, 1777. London, 1777.

Rules and Articles for the Better Government of All His Majesty's Forces, from the 24th Day of March, 1786. London, 1786.

Rules and Articles for the Better Government of All His Majesty's Forces, from the 24th Day of March, 1789. London, 1789.

Rules and Articles for the Better Government of All His Majesty's Forces, from the 24th Day of March, 1790. London, 1790.

Rush, Benjamin. *Directions for Preserving the Health of Soldiers Recommended to the Consideration of the Officers of the Army of the United States by Dr. Benjamin Rush.* Philadelphia, 1778.

Schaukirk, Ewald Gustav. "Occupation of New York City by the British." *Pennsylvania Magazine of History and Biography*, 10, No. 1 (1886): 418–445.

Schoepff, Johann David. *The Climate and Diseases of America during the Revolution.* Translated by James Read Chadwick. Boston, 1875.

Serle, Ambrose. *The American Journal of Ambrose Serle, Secretary to Lord Howe, 1776–1778.* Edited by Edward H. Tatum. San Marino, Calif., 1940.

Seume, J. G. "Memoirs of a Hessian Conscript: J. G. Seume's Reluctant Voyage to America." Translated by Margaret Woeffel. *William and Mary Quarterly*, 3d ser., 5 (October 1948): 553–570.

Simcoe, John Graves. *Simcoe's Military Journal: A History of the Operations of a Partisan Corps, called the Queen's Rangers . . . , during the War of the American Revolution.* New York, 1844; reprint, 1968.

Simes, Thomas. *A Military Course for the Government and Conduct of a Battalion . . .* London, 1777.

———. *The Military Guide for Young Officers.* 2 vols. London, 1776.

———. *The Military Medley: Containing the Most Necessary Rules and Directions for Attaining a Competent Knowledge of the Art.* 2d ed. London, 1768.

———. *The Regulator, or Instructions to Form the Officer and Complete the Soldier . . .* London, 1780.

Smith, Adam. *An Inquiry into the Nature and Causes of the Wealth of Nations.* Edited by James E. Thorold Rogers. 2 vols. 2d ed. Oxford, 1880. (1st ed., 1776.)

Smith, George. *An Universal Military Dictionary.* London, 1779.

Stanley, George F. G., ed. *For Want of a Horse: Being a Journal of the Campaigns against the Americans in 1776 and 1777 Conducted from Canada, by an Officer Who Served with Lt. Gen. Burgoyne.* Sackville, N.B., 1961.

The Statutes (1235–1948). 3d rev. ed. 32 vols. 1950.

Stedman, Charles. *The History of the Origin, Progress and Termination of the American War.* 2 vols. London, 1794.

Sterne, Laurence. *Letters of the Late Rev. Mr. Laurence Sterne to which are Prefix'd Memoirs of His Life and Family*. 3 vols. London, 1775.

Stirke, Lt. Henry. "A British Officer's Revolutionary War Journal, 1776–1778." Edited by S. Sydney Bradford. *Maryland Historical Magazine*, 56, No. 2 (1961).

Sullivan, Thomas. "The Battle of Princeton." *Pennsylvania Magazine of History and Biography*, 32, No. 1 (1908): 54–57.

———. "Before and after the Battle of Brandywine." *Pennsylvania Magazine of History and Biography*, 31, No. 4 (1907): 406–418.

———. "The Common British Soldier—From the Journal of Thomas Sullivan, 49th Regiment of Foot." Edited by S. Sydney Bradford. *Maryland Historical Magazine*, 62 (September 1967): 219–253.

———. "From Brandywine to Philadelphia." *Pennsylvania Magazine of History and Biography*, 34, No. 2 (1910): 229–232.

———. "Some Account of Vice Admiral Howe's Voyage from Elk River, Maryland, to Billingsport, New Jersey." *Pennsylvania Magazine of History and Biography*, 34, No. 2 (1910): 241–242.

Swietan, Gerhard Freiherr van. *The Diseases Incident to Armies, with the Method of Cure, Translated from the Original of Baron Van Swietan, Physician to their Imperial Majesties; To which are added: The Nature and Treatment of Gun-Shot Wounds, by John Ranby, Esq., Surgeon General to the British Army*. Philadelphia, 1775.

Tarleton, Banastre. *A History of the Campaigns of 1780 and 1781 in the Southern Provinces of North America*. London, 1787.

Tucker, St. George. "St. George Tucker's Journal of the Siege of Yorktown, 1781." Edited by Edward M. Riley. *William and Mary Quarterly*, 3d ser., 5 (July 1948): 375–395.

Uhlendorf, B. A., ed. and trans. *The Siege of Charleston, with an Account of the Province of South Carolina: Diaries and Letters of Hessian Officers from the von Jungkenn Papers in the William L. Clements Library*. Ann Arbor, 1938.

Washington, George. *The Writings of George Washington from the Original Manuscript Sources, 1745–1799*. Edited by John C. Fitzpatrick. 39 vols. Washington, D.C., 1931–1944.

Willard, Margaret Wheeler, ed. *Letters on the American Revolution, 1774–1776*. Boston, 1925.

SECONDARY SOURCES

Alden, John. *General Gage in America*. Baton Rouge, 1948.

Andreski, Stanislav. *Military Organization and Society*. Berkeley and Los Angeles, 1968.

Applegate, Howard L. "The Medical Administrators of the American Revolutionary Army." *Military Affairs*, 25 (Spring 1961): 1–10.

Ashton, T. S. *Economic Fluctuations in England, 1700–1800*. Oxford, 1959.

———. *An Economic History of England: The Eighteenth Century*. London, 1955.

Baker, Norman. *Government and Contractors: The British Treasury and War Supplies, 1775–1783*. London, 1971.

Barnes, R. Money Major. *A History of the Regiments and Uniforms of the British Army*. London, 1962.

Berkner, Lutz. "The Use and Misuse of Census Data for the Historical Analysis of Family Structure." *Journal of Interdisciplinary History*, 5, No. 4 (Spring 1975): 721–738.

Bernath, Stuart. "George Washington and the Genesis of American Military Discipline." *Mid-America*, 49 (April 1967): 83–100.

Blanco, Richard L. "Attempts to Abolish Branding and Flogging in the Army of Victorian England before 1881." *Journal of the Society for Army Historical Research*, 46 (1968): 137–145.

———. "Henry Marshall (1775–1851) and the Health of the British Army." *Medical History*, 14, No. 3 (July 1970): 260–276.

———. "The Prestige of British Army Surgeons." *Societas: A Review of Social History*, 2 (Autumn 1972): 333–351.

Blanton, Wyndham. *Medicine in Virginia in the Eighteenth Century*. Richmond, 1931.

Blumenthal, Walter Hart. *Women Camp Followers of the American Revolution*. Philadelphia, 1952.

Bowler, R. Arthur. *Logistics and the Failure of the British Army in America, 1775–1783*. Princeton, 1975.

———. "Sir Henry Clinton and Army Profiteering: A Neglected Aspect of the Clinton-Cornwallis Controversy." *William and Mary Quarterly*, 3d ser., 31 (January 1974): 111–122.

Bowman, Allen. *The Morale of the American Revolutionary Army*. Port Washington, N.Y., 1943.

Briggs, Asa. *The Age of Improvement, 1783–1867*. New York, 1959.

Brownlee, John. "The Health of London in the Eighteenth Century." Royal Society of Medicine, *Proceedings*, 18, Pt. 2 (1925): 73–85.

Buer, M. C. *Health, Wealth and Population in the Early Days of the Industrial Revolution*. London, 1926.

Butterfield, Lyman H. "Psychological Warfare in 1776: The Jefferson-Franklin Plan to Cause Hessian Desertions." American Philosophical Society, *Proceedings*, 94, No. 3 (June 1950): 233–241.

Bythell, Duncan. "The Hand-loom Weavers in the English Cotton Industry during the Industrial Revolution: Some Problems." *Economic History Review*, 17 (December 1964): 339–353.

Cantlie, Sir Neil. *A History of the Army Medical Department*. 2 vols. Edinburgh and London, 1974.

Carman, W. Y. *British Military Uniforms*. New York, 1957.

Cash, Arthur. *Laurence Sterne: The Early and Middle Years*. London, 1975.

Chambers, J. D., and G. E. Mingay. *The Agricultural Revolution, 1750–1880*. London, 1966.

Churchill, Winston. *Marlborough: His Life and Times*. 4 vols. New York, 1933–1938.

Clark, Sir George. *War and Society in the Seventeenth Century*. Cambridge, 1958.

Clode, Charles M. *Military Forces of the Crown*. 2 vols. London, 1869.

Corvisier, André. *L'Armée française de la fin du XVII' siècle au ministère de Choiseul: Le Soldat.* 2 vols. Paris, 1964.

Craig, Alexander G. *The Politics of the Prussian Army, 1640–1945.* Oxford, 1955.

Crow, Jeffrey J. "Slave Rebelliousness and Social Conflict in North Carolina, 1775–1802." *William and Mary Quarterly,* 3d ser., 37 (January 1980): 79–102.

———, and Larry E. Tise, eds. *The Southern Experience in the American Revolution.* Chapel Hill: University of North Carolina Press, 1978.

Curtis, Edward E. *The Organization of the British Army in the American Revolution.* New Haven, 1926.

———. "The Recruiting of the British Army in the American Revolution." American Historical Association, *Annual Report,* 1 (1922): 311–322.

Darling, Anthony D. *Red Coat and Brown Bess.* Ottawa, 1970.

Davis, David B. *The Problem of Slavery in Western Culture.* Ithaca, N.Y., 1966.

Deane, Phyllis. *The First Industrial Revolution.* Cambridge, 1967.

De Fonblanque, Edward Barrington. *Political and Military Episodes in the Latter Half of the Eighteenth Century Derived from the Life and Correspondence of the Right Honourable John Burgoyne.* London, 1876.

Dorn, Walter L. "The Prussian Bureaucracy in the Eighteenth Century." *Political Science Quarterly,* 46 (September 1931): 403–423; 47 (March 1932): 75–94, 259–273.

Duffy, John. *Epidemics in Colonial America.* Baton Rouge, 1953.

———. "The Passage to the Colonies." *Mississippi Valley Historical Review,* 38 (June 1951–March 1952): 21–38.

Earle, Edward M., ed. *Makers of Modern Strategy.* Princeton, 1941.

Elkin, Frederick. "The Soldier's Language." *American Journal of Sociology,* 51 (March 1946): 414–422.

Fann, Willard R. "On the Infantryman's Age in Eighteenth Century Prussia." *Military Affairs,* 41, No. 4 (December 1977): 165–170.

Forrest, Sir George. *Life of Lord Clive.* 2 vols. London, 1918.

Fortescue, John W. *A History of the British Army.* 13 vols. New York, 1899–1930; London, 1910–1935.

Frey, Sylvia R. "The British and the Black: A New Perspective." *The Historian,* 39 (February 1976): 117–131.

———. "Courts and Cats: British Military Justice in the Eighteenth Century." *Military Affairs,* 43, No. 7 (1979): 5–11.

Fuller, J. F. C. *British Light Infantry in the Eighteenth Century.* London, 1925.

Gagliardo, John. *Enlightened Despotism.* New York, 1967.

Gee, Olive. "The British War Office in the Later Years of the American War of Independence." *Journal of Modern History,* 26 (June 1954): 123–136.

George, Dorothy. *London Life in the Eighteenth Century.* New York, 1925.

Gibson, James. "The Role of Disease in the 70,000 Casualties in the American Revolutionary Army." College of Physicians of Philadelphia, *Transactions and Studies,* 4th ser., 17 (December 1949): 121–127.

Gilbert, Arthur N. "An Analysis of Some Eighteenth Century Army Recruiting Records." *Journal of the Society for Army Historical Research*, 54 (Spring 1976): 38–47.

———. "Army Impressment during the War of the Spanish Succession." *The Historian*, 36 (August 1976): 689–708.

———. "Law and Honour among Eighteenth-Century British Army Officers." *The Historical Journal*, 19, No. 1 (1976): 75–87.

———. "The Regimental Courts Martial in the Eighteenth Century British Army." *Albion*, 8, No. 1 (Spring 1976): 50–66.

Gradish, Stephen F. "The German Mercenaries in North America during the American Revolution: A Case Study." *Canadian Journal of History*, 4 (March 1969): 23–46.

Griffenhagen, George B. *Drug Supplies in the American Revolution*. Washington, D.C., 1961.

Habakkuk, H. J. H. "English Population in the Eighteenth Century." *Economic History Review*, 2d ser., 6, No. 2 (1953): 117–133.

Hajnal, J. "European Marriage Patterns in Perspective." In *Population in History*, edited by D. V. Glass and D. E. C. Eversley, pp. 101–143. London, 1965.

Hammond, J. L., and Barbara Hammond. *The Skilled Laborer, 1760–1832*. London, 1927.

Hayes, James. "Scottish Officers in the British Army." *Scottish Historical Review*, 37 (April 1958): 23–33.

———. "The Social and Professional Backgrounds of the Officers of the British Army, 1714–1763." M.A. thesis, University of London, 1956.

Higham, Robin, ed. *A Guide to the Sources of British Military History*. London, 1972.

Hobsbawm, Eric J. *The Age of Revolution*. New York, 1962.

Huizinga, Johan. *Homo Ludens: A Study of the Play Element in Culture*. Boston, 1950.

Huntington, Samuel P. *The Soldier and the State: The Theory and Politics of Civil-Military Relations*. Cambridge, 1959.

Janowitz, Morris. *The Professional Soldier: A Social and Political Portrait*. Glencoe, Ill., 1960.

Keegan, John. *The Face of Battle*. New York, 1976.

Kennett, Lee. *The French Armies in the Seven Years' War: A Study in Military Organization and Administration*. Durham, N.C., 1967.

King, Lester S. *The Medical World of the Eighteenth Century*. Chicago, 1958; Huntington, N.Y., 1971.

Laslett, Peter, ed. *Household and Family in Past Time*. Cambridge, 1972.

Latham, R. J. W. *British Military Bayonets from 1700 to 1945*. London, 1967.

Lemisch, Jesse. "Jack Tar in the Streets: Merchant Seamen in the Politics of Revolutionary America." *William and Mary Quarterly*, 3d ser., 25 (July 1968): 371–407.

Lockridge, Kenneth. *Literacy in Colonial New England*. New York, 1974.

Lowell, Edward J. *The Hessian and Other German Auxiliaries of Great Britain in the Revolutionary War*. New York, 1884.

Lynd, Staughton. "After Carl Becker: The Mechanics of New York City Politics, 1774–1801." *Labor History*, 5 (1964): 215–224.

McCallum, Malcolm R. "The Study of the Delinquent in the Army." *American Journal of Sociology*, 51 (March 1946): 481.

McKeown, Thomas, and R. G. Brown. "Medical Evidence Related to English Population Changes in the Eighteenth Century." *Population Studies*, 9 (July 1955): 119–141.

Marcuse, Donald J. "The 'Army' Incident: The Psychology of Uniforms and Their Abolition on an Adolescent Ward." *Psychiatry*, 30, No. 4 (November 1967): 350–375.

Maskin, Meyer H., and Leon L. Altman. "Military Psychodynamics: Psychological Factors in the Transition from Civilian to Soldier." *Psychiatry*, 6, No. 3 (August 1943): 263–269.

Mathias, Peter. "The Social Structure in the Eighteenth Century: A Calculation by Joseph Massie." *Economic History Review*, 2d ser., 10 (1957–1958): 30–45.

Maurer, Maurer. "Military Justice under General Washington." *Military Affairs*, 28 (Spring 1964): 8–16.

Minchinton, W. E., ed. *Essays in Agrarian History*. 2 vols. Newton Abbot, England, 1968.

Montgomery, David. "The Working Classes of the Pre-Industrial American City, 1780–1830." *Labor History*, 9, No. 1 (1968): 3–22.

Mullan, Hugh. "The Regular Service Myth." *American Journal of Sociology*, 53, No. 4 (January 1948): 276–281.

Namier, Sir Lewis. *England in the Age of the American Revolution*. 2d ed. London, 1961.

———. *The Structure of Politics at the Accession of George III*. 2d ed. New York, 1957.

———, and John Brooke. *The House of Commons, 1754–1790*. 3 vols. London, 1964.

O'Connell, D. P. "The Nature of British Military Law." *Military Law Review*, No. 19 (January 1963): 141–155.

Paret, Peter, "Colonial Experience and European Military Reform at the End of the Eighteenth Century." *Bulletin of the Institute of Historical Research*, 37 (May 1964): 47–59.

———. *Yorck and the Era of Prussian Reform, 1807–1815*. Princeton, 1966.

Pargellis, Stanley. *Lord Loudoun in North America*. New Haven, 1968.

Patten, David. "Ferguson and His Rifle." *History Today*, 28, No. 7 (1978): 446–454.

Perkin, Harold. *The Origins of Modern English Society, 1780–1880*. London, 1969.

Peterkin, A., and William Johnston, eds. *Commissioned Officers in the Medical Services of the British Army, 1660–1960*. London, 1968.

Pollard, Sidney. "Factory Discipline in the Industrial Revolution." *Economic History Review*, 16 (December 1963): 254–271.

Preston, Richard A., and Sydney F. Wise. *Men in Arms*. 2d rev. ed. New York, 1970.

Quarles, Benjamin. "Lord Dunmore as Liberator." *William and Mary Quarterly*, 3d ser., 15 (October 1958): 494–507.

———. *The Negro and the American Revolution*. Chapel Hill, 1967.

Quimby, Robert S. *The Background of Napoleonic Warfare: The Theory of Military Tactics in Eighteenth Century France*. New York: Columbia University Press, 1957.

Radzinowicz, Leon. *A History of English Criminal Law and Its Administration from 1750: The Movement for Reform, 1750–1833.* New York, 1948.
Rankin, Hugh F. *The North Carolina Continentals.* Chapel Hill, 1971.
———. *The Theater in Colonial America.* Chapel Hill, 1960.
Redlich, Fritz. *The German Military Enterpriser and His Work Force: A Study in European Economic and Social History.* 2 vols. Wiesbaden, 1964–1965.
Robson, Eric. "The Armed Forces and the Art of War." In *The New Cambridge Modern History*, vol. 7, *The Old Regime, 1713–1763*, edited by J. O. Lindsay. Cambridge, 1957.
———. "Purchase and Promotion in the British Army in the Eighteenth Century." *History*, 36 (February 1951): 57–72.
Rogers, H. C. B. *The Mounted Troops of the British Army, 1066–1945.* London, 1959.
———. *Weapons of the British Soldier.* London, 1960.
Ropp, Theodore. *War in the Modern World.* Durham, N.C., 1959.
Sanderson, Michael. "Literary and Social Mobility in the Industrial Revolution in England." *Past and Present*, 56 (August 1972): 75–103.
Scouller, R. E. *The Armies of Queen Anne.* Oxford, 1966.
Shanahan, William O. *Prussian Military Reforms, 1786–1813.* New York, 1945.
Shryock, Richard H. *Medicine and Society in America: 1660–1860.* Ithaca, N.Y., 1960.
Shy, John. *Toward Lexington: The Role of the British Army in the Coming of the American Revolution.* Princeton, 1965.
Spindler, G. Dearborn. "American Character as Revealed by the Military." *Psychiatry*, 11, No. 3 (August 1948): 275–281.
Squibb, G. D. *The High Court of Chivalry: A Study of Civil Law in England.* Oxford, 1959.
Stearns, Peter N. *European Society in Upheaval: Social History since 1800.* London, 1967.
Stouffer, Samuel A., et al. *The American Soldier: Adjustment during Army Life.* 2 vols. Princeton, N.J.: Princeton University Press, 1949.
Stryker, William S. *The Battles of Trenton and Princeton.* Boston and New York, 1898.
Thompson, E. P. *The Making of the English Working Class.* New York, 1963.
Thursfield, Hugh. "Smallpox in the American War of Independence." *Annals of Medical History*, 3d ser., 2 (July 1940): 312–318.
Van Doorn, Jacques, ed. *Armed Forces and Society.* The Hague, 1968.
Walton, Clifford. *History of the British Standing Army, A.D. 1660–1700.* London, 1894.
Watson, Steven. *The Reign of George III, 1760–1818.* London, 1960.
Waugh, William T. *James Wolfe, Man and Soldier.* London, 1928.
Western, J. R. *The English Militia in the Eighteenth Century: The Study of a Political Issue, 1660–1802.* London, 1965.
Whitworth, Rex. *Field Marshal Lord Ligonier: A Study of the British Army 1702–1770.* Oxford, 1958.
Wickwire, Franklin, and Mary Wickwire. *Cornwallis: The American Adventure.* Boston, 1970.

Wiener, Frederick Bernays. *Civilians under Military Justice: The British Practice since 1689 Especially in North America.* Chicago and London, 1967.

Willcox, William B. "The British Road to Yorktown: A Study in Divided Command." *American Historical Review,* 52 (October 1946): 1–35.

Williams, Dale. "The English Bread Riots of 1766." M.A. thesis, Tulane University, 1972.

Woodward, E. L. *The Age of Reform, 1815–1870.* Oxford, 1938.

Index

131; shortage of supplies for, 32, 146

Wildman, William, Lord Barrington, 5

Williams, Thomas Charles, 114

Wives: donations to, 58; of officers, 20; services of, 20; support of, 57

Women. *See* Camp followers; Prostitutes; Wives

Wooden horse, 83, 89

Wounded: at Bunker Hill, 44, 46–47; care of, 44; at Guilford Court House, 45, 110; at Saratoga, 45; at Ticonderoga, 44

Milton Keynes UK
Ingram Content Group UK Ltd.
UKHW010335180724
445696UK00001B/64